ADVANCE PRAISE FOR *OTTAWOLOGY*

"I can see *Ottawology* being THE BOOK on Ottawa for the next generation."

—**Peter Hodgins,** School of Canadian Studies, Carleton University

"An exceptionally vibrant narrative that brings to life Ottawa's places, memories, historical events. Packed with micro-stories valuing the banal, on a fascinating range of topics, such as trees, work, and markets, Davidson's attention to detail, wealth of insight, and breadth of knowledge make the ordinary exceptional, evoking a child's awe of new discovery. With a depth of perspective attuned to how colonialism, race, gender, and class shape Ottawa's places, *Ottawalogy* is a must read for urbanists, urban geographers, urban historians, urban sociologists, and especially any Ottawalogist — budding or seasoned."

—**Roger Picton,** School of the Environment, Trent University

"*Ottawology* is a roadmap to Ottawa as it's really lived — a city shaped by its people, places, and everyday connections, and by the forces and decisions that shape its future. From river paths to bus stops, nightclubs to neighbourhood parks, Tonya K. Davidson charts the routes that link Ottawa's history, culture, and daily life, while challenging assumptions and uncovering overlooked truths. It's a guide to discovering what you didn't know about Ottawa — and seeing what you thought you knew in a completely new light."

—**Joanne Chianello,** former *Ottawa Citizen* and CBC Ottawa City Hall journalist

"Ottawa is an iconic place in the mythical landscape of Canadian nationalism. This new book sheds new light on these icons, myths, and locales. Part urban studies, part tourism studies, part labour studies, this book provides a social and cultural geography of Canada's capital city, uncovering the making of this place and all of its meanings. Capital cities captivate public views in unique ways, and this book charts new directions in how to study these unique sites. Anyone interested in urban studies, cultural geography, and tourism studies should want to read this book."

—**Kevin Walby,** Department of Criminal Justice, University of Winnipeg

"In *Ottawology*, Tonya K. Davidson guides the reader through the rich history of Ottawa, extending beyond its role as Canada's capital. This sociological exploration is filled with unexpected insights and discoveries. It challenges us to comprehend the land we recognize as a colonial settler site, situated on unceded Anishinabe Algonquin territory, and reveals how it came to be established at the confluence of the Ottawa and Rideau Rivers. The narrative weaves together the social dynamics of work (represented by the civil service), home (in the Ottawa Valley and housing), and 'third places' (like transit, libraries, parks, and green spaces) that have influenced the city's geography, its residents, and their neighborhoods.

From its origins as an early union town, with the Parliament Hill stonecutters at the forefront of workers' rights, to the community hub of Dundonald Park in Centretown and the surprising early achievements of the Ottawa Transportation Commission (now OC Transit), each page offers fresh insights that will invite readers to revisit the book time and again. Davidson crafted this work 'in its entirety, while waiting for the #7 Carleton.' It's rare to find gratitude in long transit waits, but this is certainly one of those occasions!"

—**Catherine McKenney,** MPP for Ottawa Centre

OTTAWOLOGY

TONYA K. DAVIDSON

Fernwood Publishing
Halifax & Winnipeg

Copyright © 2025 Tonya K. Davidson

All rights reserved. No part of this book may be reproduced or transmitted in any form by any means without permission in writing from the publisher, except by a reviewer, who may quote brief passages in a review. The publisher expressly prohibits the use of this work in connection with the development of any software program, including, without limitation, training a machine learning or generative artificial intelligence (AI) system.

Development Editor: Fiona Jeffries
Copyediting: Jenn Harris
Cover Design: Zainab's Echo
Text Design: Brenda Conroy
Printed and bound in the UK

Published by Fernwood Publishing
2970 Oxford Street, Halifax, Nova Scotia, B3L 2W4
Halifax and Winnipeg
www.fernwoodpublishing.ca

Fernwood Publishing Company Limited gratefully acknowledges the financial support of the Government of Canada through the Canada Book Fund and the Canada Council for the Arts. We acknowledge the Province of Manitoba for support through the Manitoba Publishers Marketing Assistance Program and the Book Publishing Tax Credit. We acknowledge the Nova Scotia Department of Communities, Culture and Heritage for support through the Publishers Assistance Fund.

Library and Archives Canada Cataloguing in Publication
Title: Ottawology / Tonya K. Davidson.
Names: Davidson, Tonya K., 1979- author
Description: Includes bibliographical references and index.
Identifiers: Canadiana 20250252384 | ISBN 9781773637600 (softcover)
Subjects: LCSH: Ottawa (Ont.)—Social life and customs—21st century. | LCSH: Ottawa (Ont.)—Social conditions—21st century.
Classification: LCC FC3096.3 .D38 2025 | DDC 971.3/84—dc23

CONTENTS

Acknowledgements / vii

Introduction: Advance-Ottawa-En Avant / 1

Chapter 1: Settler Colonial Capital / 11

Chapter 2: Trees / 27

Chapter 3: Libraries / 38

Chapter 4: Work / 49

Chapter 5: The Civil Service / 60

Chapter 6: Getting Housed / 75

Chapter 7: Suburbia / 101

Chapter 8: Transit / 120

Chapter 9: Security / 136

Chapter 10: Markets and Malls / 155

Chapter 11: Goodnight Ottawa / 169

References / 192

Index / 215

ACKNOWLEDGEMENTS

This book is the result of years of teaching sociology of Ottawa courses at Carleton University. I owe special thanks to the students in 2019–2020 and 2021–2022's pandemic-impacted first-year seminars. In part because it was the only in-person class for all of us since the pandemic had begun, the 2021–2022 class was a special experience. We went on a lot of field trips, had a lot of fun, and insights from that class are in this book. Conversations with students in a 2023 sociology of third places class and an urban sociology class in 2024 helped me work through some of the material in this book. The students in various Lifelong Learning classes on Ottawa have enriched my understanding of Ottawa immensely by sharing their broad-ranging memories. Tyrez Hawco, Sydney Phillips, Seemah Mullaly, Catherine Macdonald, and Chanel Fortin were excellent research assistants at various stages of this project.

I owe much gratitude to the following friends and colleagues who read and commented on sections of this book: Bonar Buffam, Mike Bulthuis, Sarah E.K. Smith, Alanna MacDougall, David Hugill, Julie Tomiak, Mike Steinhauer, Kim Farris-Manning, Sarah Gelbard, Neil Abraham, Dan Rück, Stuart MacKay, David Dean, Hollis Moore, Nomi Lazar, Aaron Doyle, and Forrest Pass. I am so grateful to have friends and colleagues with such a breadth of expertise. I thank the blind reviewers for their excellent suggestions. The friends I made in 1998 at Carleton University when I first fell in love with Ottawa have been reliably available in our group chat to fact check some of my late 1990s memories. My pub trivia team, curling team, documentary club, Earth Path wilderness class, and my piano teacher, Marg Stubington, have expanded the breadth of my understanding of sociable, natural, and musical Ottawa, very useful for this book and for life. My family — my parents Tom and Kathe, and Stephanie, Georg, Lou, and Max — and my friends Tamara Legris, Mireille McLaughlin, Katie Bonier, Naomi K. Lewis, Carolina Cambre, Ondine Park, Sarah Rotz, Kevin Cardoza, Anne Dance, and Rebecca Dolgoy have been the most enthusiastic supporters of all of my projects including this one, and I am very grateful. I am also deeply appreciative of the generations of community members that have created and enlivened Ottawa's many community associations, the Ottawa Historical Society, Heritage Ottawa, the many activist groups discussed in this book, and local journalists who have reported on the richness of Ottawa.

Fiona Jeffries at Fernwood Press is an inspiring editor. Without her enthusiasm and commitment, this book would be twice as fat and also comfortably cocooning on my desktop forever. The entire team at Fernwood Publishing has been delightful to work with. Special thanks to Jenn Harris, copyeditor extraordinaire, and Tim Pearson for his indexing.

Finally, I thank and also dedicate this book to all the kids that have let me share in a little slice of their Ottawa childhoods. This book is for Hugh, Abby, Henry, Fiona, Hazel, Rosa, Isla, Teddy, Samara, and Nora.

Introduction

ADVANCE-OTTAWA-EN AVANT

Newscasters and pundits make big claims about what's going on in Ottawa, and by that they mean what federal politicians are up to. People conjure images of the Parliament building perched on the hill by the Ottawa River, or maybe the art deco Supreme Court of Canada, or a glistening Rideau Canal full of jolly skaters when they think of Ottawa. Yet Ottawa's role as Canada's capital is far from the whole story of this city.

Just a few kilometres from Parliament Hill, two acres of green space, known since 1906 as Dundonald Park, offers a counterpoint to the government buildings; Dundonald Park is distinctly for the people of Ottawa. In the late 1800s, this block of land on Somerset Street was an informal dump and a common grazing land for neighbourhood cows and horses. Locals pushed for the creation of a park and by 1903 urban planner Frederick Todd included a park here in his plan for the city. Pathways, a ring of trees, and a fountain were installed in 1905. The city named the new park after the Earl of Dundonald, a British commander of the Canadian Militia who had been dismissed for "political agitation against the Government of Canada." The Ottawa Improvement Commission (OIC), and the Liberal government refused to use the name of a dismissed, insubordinate military leader. Yet it became officially known as Dundonald Park in 1911 when Borden's Conservatives came to power (Smythe 2022).

Ever since, Dundonald Park has been taken for granted, widely used, and, like its namesake, maligned; in 1905, the initial landscaping was deemed "disappointing" (Smythe 2022). In recent decades, its location across from the Beer Store has led some to call it "Beer Store park." Non-locals often only see the park as a site of deviance and social disorder. There is constant police surveillance here. In 2022, an elderly woman doing tai chi with an ornamental sword was arrested (Raymond 2022). Yet for locals, Dundonald Park offers so much. There is a playground, along with benches, chess tables, planters, and trees. Sociologist Susan Kerr engaged in participant observation in the park and described it as a "living room" for many in the neighbourhood, especially those living in the crowded rooming houses nearby, noting that many people met up with social workers, parole officers, and had supervised visits with their kids in this park (Kerr 2004, 82). It has been the starting and ending point for protest marches, the location of countless picnics, impromptu concerts by brass bands and folk singers, and activities of the Centretown Community Association. Many people cut through the park's diagonal path on their daily travels and experience the flowers and shade of the trees, if only for a few minutes. As a counterpoint to Parliament Hill, Dundonald Park hints at the depth and breadth of experiences of Ottawa as a city of over a million people — and also a city of trees, beer, playgrounds, cops, live music, and protests.

Geographer David Gordon refers to discord between two Ottawas — Ottawa on Parliament Hill, the ring of "crown jewels" circling the Ottawa River and other national institutions — and Ottawa the messy, sprawling amalgamated city-suburban-rural complex, as the "town" versus "crown" tension (Gordon 2015). A story of this tension is on opulent display at the National Gallery of Canada (NGC). On the ground floor of Moshe Safdie's 1988 glass-domed gallery, flanked on one side by the "garden court" and on the other by the "water court," in the centre of a wing dedicated to Indigenous and Canadian art, is the Rideau Chapel. The sounds of choral singers draw visitors to the space; a 2001 audio installation by artist Janet Cardiff, *Forty-part Motet*, has been playing here since 2018. Forty speakers positioned around the chapel project the deconstructed voices of a forty-person choir singing a sixteenth-century choral piece. Visitors can walk to each speaker to listen to each individual voice.

The chapel is in a room specially designed to permanently house the interiors of an 1888 chapel that was originally at Rideau and Waller Streets, an addition to the Convent of Our Lady of the Sacred Heart. In 1972, the Sisters of Charity sold their property and the convent was slated for demolition. Local groups organized, and while they could not save the chapel, they saved its interiors, with a promise from the NGC that the interiors would find a home in their not-yet-built art gallery. The interiors' most striking feature is the cream, gold, and blue fan vaulted ceiling. Modestly made out of wood, largely reflecting the limited means of the convent (Noppen 1988), the nevertheless awe-inspiring ceiling works in concert with the voices of the auditory installation to create an enthralling experience. People have been known to weep in this space, to lie down and spend minutes in silence on the few benches. It is a precious public space in which to be still in a busy city. It is sacred but, repurposed in a postmodern cathedral to art, it is de-sacralized. The Rideau Chapel expresses an adroit negotiation between the needs of the town (the citizens committed to saving their local church) and the crown (those responsible for designing and safeguarding art in the national art gallery).

Nineteenth-century French sociologist Émile Durkheim spent much of his career parsing distinctions between the sacred and the profane; the sacred are those things, ideas, and moments set apart from the everyday, which is the profane (Durkheim 2001). The Rideau Chapel is, in a way, a counterpoint to the everydayness (the profane) of Dundonald Park. Durkheim further identifies that one of the effects of religion is the generation of what he called "collective effervescence" (Durkheim 2001, 226) — that spirit beyond oneself that many identify as a god spirit, but Durkheim identifies as the spirit of the social collective. In the Rideau Chapel, we are moved by an overwhelming feeling of belonging to something bigger than ourselves; the social invoked there is beyond the town and crown to an even larger encompassing humanity. As we are surrounded by the singers of the *Forty-part Motet*, the collective effervescence is what elicits tears to flow. The piece is a powerful metaphor for society, reflecting what can be accomplished together (the choral music) and the potential for locating the individual within a larger collective (the individual voices). That it brings people to tears is telling. Yet a spirit of collective effervescence is also inspired in the protests and impromptu concerts at the very everyday Dundonald Park. The "Ottawa" at the heart of this book is the social collective, a historic collective that built and destroyed the spaces Ottawa now occupies, as well as the current unfolding (fraught, complex, inspiring) social collective forging new spaces and new societies.

"NOT A HANDSOME CITY": OTTAWA AND URBAN SOCIOLOGY

Ottawology is the systematic, interdisciplinary study of Ottawa the town. In this book I draw on history, urban geography, and especially on sociological studies of Ottawa. Sociology is, briefly, the study of the stuff between people, the "socius." There's a lot of stuff there: interpersonal relationships, language, social institutions, nations, wars, media, schools, religions. Sociologists begin by taking some aspect of the social (a hockey game, a church service, breakfast at a diner) that is taken for granted as natural, and they ask questions about it, answering those questions through the use of sociological research methods (qualitative interviewing, gathering and analyzing statistics, participant observation), and generating, applying, or testing sociological theories.

Sociologists are motivated by what C. Wright Mills called the "sociological imagination." For Mills, key to having a sociological imagination is the ability to see the relationship between private troubles and public issues (Mills 1959). To give you a very consistent personal trouble faced by many in Ottawa: the bus is late, or hasn't arrived, so an individual is inconvenienced. Yet when so many Ottawans can't rely on public transit to get to school or work, this is a public issue, a crisis in fact. Student attendance suffers, employers are distraught as employees are constantly late, leisure spots are impacted when people worry about how to get home late at night. This book understands many private troubles sociologically as public issues: getting housed, pay equity in the civil service, facing police violence, anti-Black and anti-Asian racism in the immigration system, the shuttering of beloved dive bars, the felling of neighbourhood-cooling trees.

Sociologist Peter Berger suggested that the starting point of sociological inquiries is to look at what is taken-for-granted as "familiar" and ask questions, making this familiarity "strange" (Berger 1963). The starting point for a sociological inquiry of Ottawa is to problematize its existence, troubling the taken-for-granted-ness of a settler colonial city on unceded Algonquin Anishinaabe land at the confluence of the Ottawa and Rideau Rivers. This troubling is the focus of Chapter 1.

Urban sociology begins with cities as its object of study. Urban sociologists ask questions like: how do cities offer opportunities for ecologically sustainable living? How do strangers interact when living so closely together? What makes cities more or less functional? And who are they made functional for? In the mid-nineteenth century, when Bytown was being renamed Ottawa, horses were pulling streetcars on a new transit system and lumber barons were fixated on extracting resources from the region's rich forests, sociologists including Durkheim, Georg Simmel, and Friedrich Engels were all asking questions about urban life in the rapidly urbanizing contexts in Western Europe, where they lived. Durkheim asked: how is it that cities with populations of such diverse people (in Durkheimian terms, a high degree of "dynamic density"), doing different jobs and living in close proximity, manage to function? This is a pertinent question for thinking about Bytown's early history as a community that was created with a population of multiple ethnicities, languages, and religions from the outset. In the 1840s, Engels asked of industrial Manchester: why and how does industrial capitalism create cities of great inequality, where the rich trot off to healthy rural villas and the poor factory workers live in squalor with tuberculosis, cholera, and smallpox epidemics? Like Manchester, Ottawa was also stricken with infectious diseases (typhoid, smallpox, tuberculosis) that disproportionately impacted the poor. In Berlin, Georg Simmel asked if living in a city, with its multiple stimuli and highly rational forms of interpersonal interactions, gave rise to a specific type of urban personality. This line of thinking informs the discussions here of interactions on public transit and on streets. All of these modes of engaging in urban sociology inform the Ottawology in this book; however, the urban sociology and urban planning being developed closer to home — in Chicago, a settler colonial city on the land of the Ojibwe, Odawa, and Potawatomi nations — has more intimate ties and similarities to the urban condition of Ottawa.

Sociologist and founder of American social work Jane Addams established Hull House in Chicago in 1889 based on the settlement homes she'd visited in England. The settlement houses were created as a response to the social problems immigrants faced in growing, industrial cities. Hull House was home to twenty-five full-time residents, and was visited by approximately two thousand people weekly who would participate in the house's kindergarten, coffeehouse, laundry facilities, and art and drama classes and visit the house's museum and art gallery. The community residents (largely immigrant and working-class women) researched the living conditions in Chicago and published their findings in the *Hull House Maps and Papers*. The establishment of Hull House's "Working People's Social Science Club" in 1890 pre-dated the creation of the Department of Sociology at the University of Chicago (Spain 2011). The result of the research of the Hull House residents was tremendous: "Nearly every piece of significant housing reform legislation during the Progressive Era was based on research conducted by settlement house residents" (Spain 2011, 57). Earlier, German philosopher, and the inspiration of an entire school of sociological thought, Karl Marx, wrote, "philosophers have only interpreted the world, in various ways; the point, however, is to change it" — a pull quote so significant it's on Marx's grave. Back in the United States, W.E.B. Du Bois, a Black sociologist known for his comprehensive ethnography of the lives of Black people in Philadelphia, was integral to the creation of the National Association for the Advancement of Colored People (NAACP) in 1909. Many Ottawa-based sociologists, like those who created the Criminalization and Punishment Education Project (CPEP) and those studying and working with tenants facing evictions, work in the same vein as these thinkers, studying the social world with an orientation toward improving social conditions.

Addams had an influence on William Lyon Mackenzie King, undoubtedly the most influential Canadian sociologist. That's right, sociologist. Canada's longest-serving prime minister studied sociology at the University of Chicago and interned at Hull House after meeting Addams in 1895. Mackenzie King's sociology background and his interactions with Addams influenced his work as the first employee of Canada's Ministry of Labour and his commitment to labour reform (including banning the use of phosphorous in match factories, greatly impacting women working in Hull match factories). Towards the end of Mackenzie King's life, he mused in his diary about what Addams would have thought of his life's work (Gordon 2002b). Mackenzie King didn't, however, reflect on the disjuncture between his socially minded approach to labour reform and urban design and his anti-Semitic policies and internment of Japanese Canadians during World War II.

Chicago became a hub for urban sociology in part because the great fire of Chicago in 1871 positioned the city — being rapidly rebuilt in the context of immigration, urbanization, and industrialization — as a laboratory of urban living; the sociologists at Hull House and the University of Chicago seized the opportunity to engage in empirical, mapping, and ethnographic studies of the growing city. Ottawa also experienced devastating fires in this era, but it was not yet an object of sustained sociological study. For much of the nineteenth century, Ottawa was a great fire risk, built of wooden houses, full of the "natural tinderboxes provided by lumber stockyards," and with limited firefighting infrastructure. In late April 1900, twelve thousand people found themselves homeless after a fire, beginning in Hull, jumped along the wooden bridge at Victoria Island to Ottawa, eventually destroying 40 percent of Hull and 15 percent of urban Ottawa, from the Ottawa River to Dow's Lake, and from east of Hintonburg to the Rideau Canal (Walsh 2001, 165). In the aftermath of the fire, some made direct references to Chicago, like this newspaper editorial: "The great fire at Chicago may almost be said to have been a blessing in disguise, by converting a wooden city into one of stone and steel, and it would not be unreasonable to expect a similar change in Ottawa" (in Walsh 2001, 170). Indeed, the fire happened just a few years after politicians were considering that something should be done about Ottawa's ... ahem ... ugliness. As a MP in 1884, Wilfrid Laurier famously told an audience in Montreal: "I would not wish to say anything disparaging of the capital, but it is hard to say anything good of it. Ottawa is not a handsome city and does not appear destined to become one either." He offered a more optimistic estimation of Ottawa as the leader of the Opposition in 1893: "It shall be my pleasure and that of my colleagues, I am sure, to make the city of Ottawa as attractive as possibly could be; to make it the centre of the intellectual development of this country and above all the Washington of the North" (Woods 1980, 190). In 1899, prompted by the wife of the governor general, Lady Aberdeen, then–prime minister Laurier established the OIC, the precursor to the National Capital Commission (Gordon 2002a). While it did not immediately become a hotbed of urban sociology like Chicago,

Ottawa emerged from the 1900 fire as a city onto which broad-sweeping urban plans were inscribed. In 1903, the OIC hired landscape architect Frederick Todd, an apprentice of famed American landscape architect Frederick Law Olmstead, to create the first urban plan for Ottawa. Key recommendations of the Todd report were the building of a boulevard between Rideau Hall and Parliament, the beginning of conservation in the Gatineau Park region (National Capital Commission 1998), and, of course, Dundonald Park.

In the ashes of the great fires the late nineteenth and early twentieth century, new buildings — skyscrapers — shot right up into the clouds in Chicago and other American cities. Ottawa had but one Chicago-style skyscraper, the Daly Building, at Sussex Drive and Wellington Street. Designed by Moses Chamberlain Edey, the 1904 Daly Building included Chicago-style skyscraper features: "steel joists and cast iron pillars, masonry cladding (Gloucester limestone), distinctive three-part 'Chicago windows' with large fixed centre panels, and ornamental cornice" (Jones 2017). It was demolished in 1991 and replaced with a Claridge condominium building in 2005. Ottawa's embrace of skyscrapers was slowed by planning dictates stipulating that the height of downtown buildings could not exceed 150 feet, to not eclipse the 322-foot-high Peace Tower, a policy not challenged until 1965 when local developer Robert Campeau successfully persuaded the city to approve his plan to build 225-foot-high office buildings at Lyon and Albert Streets (Gordon 2015, 238). Ottawa was influenced by Chicago-style architecture nonetheless. Ottawa architect Francis C. Sullivan worked for Chicago architect Frank Lloyd Wright from 1911 to 1916 (Duhamel 1961), and Wright's influence can be noted in some of Sullivan's prairie-style houses in Centretown, including a prominent and distinguished yellow house at 429–431 Bay Street (the Powers House) to which Sullivan added "broad overhangs, steep rooflines and banding with stucco" in his 1915 renovations to the 1887 building, which "reflect Chicago roots" (Waldron, Coffman, and Kalman 2017, 66). The house Sullivan built for himself at 346 Somerset Street East similarly reflects Wright's signature prairie style (Waldron, Coffman, and Kalman 2017). The Ottawology in this book focuses not on the style of homes but on the tenure of their ownership. From the nineteenth century until the mid-twentieth century, renting a home was not seen as subordinate to home-ownership, and many carefully designed neighbourhoods like Manor Park, Lindenlea, and Carlington, with single-detached homes, were built for renters. Of more urgent Ottawological concern today is the upselling of un-ecologically sustainable and socially anemic condos and suburban homes, as well as the deplorable condition in some rooming houses, public housing, and bunkhouses.

Mackenzie King was incredibly influential in the twentieth-century transformation of Ottawa. As a civil servant in the 1890s, Mackenzie King was exposed to the Garden City movement from Governor General Earl Grey. In Mackenzie King's 1918 *Industry and Humanity*, he spends a lot of the book detailing the impact that planning — with access to green space and clean, affordable, well-designed housing — has on a population. As prime minister in the postwar period, Mackenzie King guaranteed that planning and publicly built housing were key parts of the federal government's social policies (Gordon 2002b). Acting on his belief in the potential of a carefully planned city, Mackenzie King hired French urban planner Jacques Gréber to create a comprehensive plan for Ottawa. Gréber's 1950 plan included expropriating the lands of LeBreton Flats — plans that privileged aesthetics and national infrastructure over the homes of working-class people and were at odds with the sociology of Addams and other urban planning tenets, which had so moved Mackenzie King earlier in his career. Gréber's plan also included moving the downtown train station, decentralizing government office buildings, creating the Greenbelt, and developing Gatineau Park. Gréber's fingerprints are visible throughout this book in the discussions of creating the Queensway, relocating the train station, suburbanization, the pedestrianized Sparks Street mall, and the placement of the Supreme Court. While early on disparaged as not being "handsome" and not embraced as a laboratory of urban living, Ottawa emerged in similar conditions to Chicago — influenced by burgeoning urban planning strategies, the unfolding history of architecture, and the increasing and novel "dynamic density" of residents differing in religion, class, and ethnicity—all in the context of settler colonial urbanism on unceded Indigenous lands.

THE PROMISE OF SOCIOLOGY; THE PROMISE OF OTTAWA SOCIETY

Mills suggests that engaging a sociological imagination is both "terrifying" and "magnificent" (Mills 1959, 5). Understanding that public issues (historic homophobia in the civil service, the violent policing of sex workers and of Black people, the buses that never show up, the many blights and climate-change derechos impacting the city's tree canopy) exist, and that they exist quite outside of individual actions — they are structural, systemic, large — can be, indeed, terrifying. We are born into social structures — a nationality, a religion, a language, existing structures of social class, gender, race, ability — which inform our socialization, worldviews, aspirations, social ties, and life opportunities. Here is the promise of sociology and society: we are also born with what sociologists refer to as agency — capacities to make decisions within the contexts of our lives, to conform, resist, negotiate (Giddens 1984). Social change is the result of generations of people making decisions that honour both their own desires and what society demands. Ottawa society is shaped by people organizing to create new social forms and opportunities for human flourishing and to resist oppressive structures — to live up to the city's motto: "Advance-Ottawa-En Avant."

The chapters in this book broadly address three forms of social interaction: at work (work, the civil service), at home (settling the Ottawa Valley, getting housed, suburbia), and in the many interstices of a dynamic, functional city (security, libraries, markets and malls, transit, trees, nighttime spaces). One of the threads that emerged throughout the writing of this book were the many ways in which individuals and collectives worked together toward realizing the city's motto in big and small ways: saving trees, unionizing workers, challenging evictions, resisting different forms of violence.

Many of the opportunities for collective well-being, for both social progress and for maintaining the rich, functional society that already exists, happen at what sociologist Ray Oldenburg called "third places." Third places are not one's primary home (first place), or place of work or education (second place), but those other places in society that allow for the creation of community and contribute to individual and community well-being. These are places demarcated for play (even if that play is referred to as sport or hanging out). Third places are marked with a feeling of hominess, levity, the levelling of social hierarchies, and friends "by the set." They are places that don't require appointments — when you arrive someone will be there to talk to or share in some activity. For Oldenburg, third places have individual and societal benefits. They are places of individual uplift and well-being, and societally, they are places where social divisions (age-based, occupational, political), can potentially be transgressed (Oldenburg 1999). Casual places for broad sociability, like what's found at Dundonald Park and the city's many average pubs, are underappreciated for the heavy lifting of society building and maintenance that they enable. They are at the heart of the promise of Ottawa. Beyond the scope of this book are Ottawa schools, hotels, health care, and infrastructure for play (pools, arenas, rivers, curling clubs, and playgrounds), all of which deserve comprehensive sociological engagement as sites that have also been mired in the morass of structures of oppression and places where individuals and groups have worked to push Ottawa ahead.

SACRED AND PROFANE ... SPIDERS

This book does not purport that Ottawa is especially distinct — it's not more distinct than how all cities are distinct. Only one city sits at the crux of the Red and Assiniboine rivers (Winnipeg), was the nation's only fortified city (Quebec City), boasts its own style of donair (Halifax). Every city is a distinct snowflake, so of course, as Canada's capital, at the junction of the Ottawa and Rideau Rivers, Ottawa is special. Yet, while it is easy to be dazzled by the architecture and experiences that are designed to invoke a collective and spiritual feeling of the sacred (the neo-Gothic Parliament buildings! Waterfalls!) that are distinct to Ottawa, it is also possible and important to notice the profane: the chess games played by neighbours in Dundonald Park, the interactions between customers and cashiers at an Overbrook butcher shop, evenings at the Bytowne Cinema, phenomena that might have similar counterparts in other cities. This offering of Ottawology should hopefully whet readers' appetites for thinking about this city and nation's capital with a sociological imagination, curiosity and enthusiasm, and perhaps inspire readers to pursue inquiries into those parts of Ottawa not discussed.

In the summer of 2017, a giant spider and a giant dragon puppet brought by France-based puppet company La Machine invaded the city. The puppets battled in the ByWard Market and at LeBreton Flats, and crowds swelled to 750,000 people to watch. Outside of the NGC, the thirteen-metre-wide spider climbed down the spire of the Notre Dame Basilica, gathering courage, I am sure, from the presence of its comrade, the giant Louise Bourgeois spider sculpture, *Maman*, before fighting the giant puppet dragon. A small orchestra of musicians buried inside the puppets provided the soundtrack for the epic battle. While some interpreted the spectacle as sacrilegious, the archbishop of the basilica defended the show, tweeting: "Our Lady who in Revelation defeats Dragon (& fulfills Genesis promise of crushing serpent) reigns again undisturbed." He added that the Catholic Church was happy to be a part of the street theatre spectacle, hoping it would contribute to a good relationship between the church and the community (Miller 2017). This whole mise-en-scène — giant imported puppets, a church, the national art gallery, a tweeting archbishop, thousands of locals and tourists, spiders, the Parliament buildings in the background — is a bit of a metaphor for the richness of Ottawa explored in this book. Whimsy exceeds bureaucratic order, locals show up, the capital city complex is decentred, and the profanity of spiders and the scaredness of spires collaborate to produce an ephemeral, and promising, moment for Ottawa society.

Chapter 1

SETTLER COLONIAL CAPITAL

THE CITY OF OTTAWA BEGINS MANY OF ITS EVENTS with this land acknowledgement:

> Ottawa is built on un-ceded Anishinabe Algonquin territory.
> The peoples of the Anishinabe Algonquin Nation have lived on this territory for millennia. Their culture and presence have nurtured and continue to nurture this land.
> The City of Ottawa honours the peoples and land of the Anishinabe Algonquin Nation.
> The City of Ottawa honours all First Nations, Inuit and Métis peoples and their valuable past and present contributions to this land. (City of Ottawa, Community and Social 2024)

What does it mean for Ottawans to say and listen to this statement? To think about Ottawa sociologically, to trouble the taken-for-granted existence of this city requires asking why and how Ottawa was established here, at the confluence of Ottawa and Rideau rivers, south of the Canadian Shield, on the vast clay plains left by the receded prehistoric Champlain Sea, the territory of the Anishinaabe Algonquin people. The editors of the book Settler City Limits define settler colonial cities as: "sites where settlers have come to constitute a sizeable demographic majority independent of ties with any metropolitan sponsor and assert a sovereignty distinct from that of the metropolitan core" (Dorries et al. 2019, 9). In other words, unlike in other colonial cities where a colonial minority ruled a colonized majority, in settler colonial cities, the population of settlers overwhelm and create a city in a colonized land.

The first step in the colonization of this land was imagining that it was, in fact, uninhabited and available for European settlement, that it was *terra nullius*. Patrick Wolfe describes settler colonialism as "a structure not an event" (Wolfe 2006, 388). Settler colonialism has, for hundreds of years, systematically structured land dispossession, displacement, starvation campaigns, and systemic forms of colonial violence, including overpolicing of Indigenous people, underpolicing of crimes against Indigenous people, and inequities in education, health care, and housing, all rooted in a "logic of elimination" that "strives for the dissolution of native societies" (Wolfe 2006, 388). Yet the structure of settler colonialism and *terra nullius* logic was challenged from the beginning in the region that became Ottawa, through Anishinaabe Algonquin resistance — "movements and embodied practices focused on addressing and fighting against settler colonial and state violence" (Dorries et al. 2019, 7). The Anishinaabeg (plural form of Anishinaabe) refers to a number of Indigenous groups, including Ojibwe, Odawa, Potawatomi, Mississaugas, Nipissing, and Algonquin. This chapter begins by detailing forms of Algonquin resistance, and Algonquin, Métis, Inuit, and other Indigenous resurgence that take place in Ottawa, expressing individual and collectively organized agency in the face of the structure of settler colonialism. In Ottawa, these acts of resistance and resurgence challenge the overwhelming spatialization of the capital city of Canada as *terra nullius* onto which dreams of a white settler nation could be effortlessly manifested.

The second move in creating a settler colonial city was to facilitate the settlement of the land by European and American settlers, who were often invited and given provisions and land by colonial government agents. Relationships between settlers were marked by deep and persistent class, religious, and linguistic rifts in the nineteenth century. In the twentieth century, different contexts for immigration (a shifting federal immigration system, different push factors around the world), shaped the growth of the city, which continues to be marked by divisions, hostility, and many forms of racism that inform policing, housing development, schooling, and work today. Yet Ottawa has also been shaped by communities that have worked together to welcome refugees from Southeast Asia and Syria and resisted the anti-Black racism influencing many of the experiences of Somali and other African refugees. The second half of this chapter details this history and the interplays between structural forces and individual agency that have informed the unfolding of Ottawa as a multicultural city.

THE LAND OF THE ANISHINAABE ALGONQUIN NATION

Key to processes of settler colonialism is the coveting and exploitation of land. Because everyone has the same basic human needs — namely, good land and access to water — while all of Canada is on Indigenous land, cities in Canada were frequently developed at the specific sites of Indigenous habitations. In what would become Ottawa, the first settler buildings were constructed on the banks of the Ottawa River at what is now known as LeBreton Flats, by Chaudière Falls, a symbolically and politically significant site for the Algonquin people. The site that became Ottawa was always a site of inter-nation Indigenous meeting and exchange; in fact, "adawe" — the origin of the name Ottawa — is the Algonquin word for "trade" (Tomiak 2016).

The 148,000-square-kilometre watersheds of the Ottawa River, called the Kiji Sibi or Kiji Zibi by Algonquin people, have been occupied by Algonquin people since time immemorial. To acknowledge that Ottawa is on "unceded" Algonquin land means that no agreement has been ratified between any level of colonial government and the Anishinaabe Algonquin people to cede their rights to the land; the vast territory that includes the city of Ottawa was never surrendered. From earliest contact onwards, Algonquin people have stopped settler incursions, petitioned various governments, and resisted their land dispossession in numerous ways.

From 1924 to 1996, a monument to an unnamed Indigenous guide crouched at the base of a grander monument to French explorer Samuel de Champlain that had been unveiled at Kìwekì (then Nepean) Point in 1915. This monument — with a triumphant, named white colonizer, standing above an unnamed, underdressed Indigenous figure — contributed to the spatialization of a dominant settler colonial narrative that concealed deep histories of Algonquin resistance. In 1613, Champlain met Chief Tessouat, leader of the Kichesipirini Algonquins of Morrison's and Allumette Islands at Tessouat's home, hoping to establish a friendly relationship and advance west along the river into Huron and Wendat territory. Tessouat refused to allow Champlain passage, arguing that the Nipissing, who lived further along the river, were too dangerous (Graham 2021). Upon the completion of renovations beginning in 2020, both Champlain and the Indigenous guide were returned to Kìwekì Point in 2025. Now Champlain is pedestal-less and the Indigenous man, now named Kichi Zibi Innini, is on his own, closer to the point's summit. Furthermore, a monument to Chief Tessouat was unveiled at the Canadian Museum of History in 2017. Of course, Algonquin of this region have a much longer history than its history of engagements with settlers. William Commanda (1913–2011), the Great Chief of the Algonquin, descendent of nineteenth-century Chief Pakinawatik, was the holder of many wampum belts. Wampum belts are made from shell-beads and have been used by the Algonquin to tell stories, record history, and, post-contact, make agreements with other nations. Commanda was the holder of the Seven Fires Prophecy Belt, a belt that dates back to the fifteenth century (Thumbadoo 2018).

The Royal Proclamation of 1763 transferred large swaths of North America from the French to the British. Under the British, people could not buy land directly from Indigenous peoples, Indigenous people could only sell their land to the British Crown. This set the stage for the ensuing land grabs in the region by churches, English, French, Scottish, and American speculators buying land from the Crown, and acquiring land after squatting. In 1772, Algonquin people unsuccessfully petitioned to remove settlers and recognize their land title (Tomiak 2016). The 1791 Constitutional Act made the Ottawa River the border between Upper and Lower Canada (what would become Ontario and Quebec), dividing the Algonquin nation. Beginning in 1793, the British hastened their aggressive logging and exploitation of other natural resources on Algonquin land. Two Algonquin families asked Philemon Wright — the American who, along with five families, arrived and settled on the north side of the Ottawa River in 1800 — to stop his land clearing because it was driving back their game. Yet, in his journal, Philemon Wright concludes that the Algonquin people he'd encountered had relinquished "all claim to the land, in compensation for which they receive annual grants from the Government, which shall be withheld if they molest settlers" (Wright Carr-Harris 1903, 11, in Smith 2011, 82). In 1802, the Algonquin unsuccessfully petitioned to the Upper Canada government to stop Philemon Wright from illegally clearing their land (Lawrence 2012).

Chief Pierre-Louis Constant Pinesi (1786–1834), the Great Chief of the Algonquin by 1830, fought in the War of 1812 on the side of the British. When Pinesi later requested that his own land be secured for hunting and fishing for his people, he was ignored (Jenkins 2020). Meanwhile, French, Scottish, and English War of 1812 veterans flooded the region and became some of the most lauded "founders" of the city. War of 1812 veteran François Dupuis built a log cabin in the region that became Orléans in the 1830s. This cabin is now a part of the Cumberland Heritage Village Museum. In thanks for his service in 1812, Scottish immigrant Archibald Petrie was given eight hundred acres, including the land that quickly bore his name, Petrie Island (SFOPHO 2023). Louis-Théodore Besserer was a lieutenant with the second military battalion of Quebec City during the War of 1812. He purchased an estate in Bytown in 1828 that would become the neighbourhood of Sandy Hill, with a street bearing his name (Gravel 1976). English and Scottish War of 1812 veterans were given land based on their rank; privates were given a hundred acres, sergeants two hundred, lieutenants four hundred, and captains eight hundred. An exhibit in the Goulbourn Museum in Stittsville in the summer of 2023 titled "Supplied for Survival" displayed objects (such as a broadaxe and adze) that government agents gave settlers to help them survive in the region. Ottawa Valley's earliest roads, stores, and hotels were all developed to service the settling British, French, and other War of 1812 Loyalist veterans, all while dispossessing the Algonquin of their land.

From 1827 to 1832, Irish, French, and British labourers, led by British Colonel John By and a crew of engineers, built the Rideau Canal, a project of settler colonial military might. This project transformed the Pasapkwediwanong Sibi (known as the Rideau River) into a navigational system to facilitate the national security of British North America. The entrance to the canal shifted Bytown's downtown from LeBreton Flats to the ByWard Market neighbourhood. The canal also transformed settlers' orientation to the region from extractive colonialism to settler colonialism and military colonialism. Bytown grew as a settler colonial city.

From 1842 onward, Algonquin people petitioned for lands on Bob's Lake, 130 kilometres southwest of Ottawa (Tomiak 2016). In 1851, as the lumber industry thrived, the Canadian government began forcing Indigenous peoples to live on reserves. In 1853, a reserve established near Maniwaki, Quebec, became the Kitigan Zibi reserve (Bulmer 2017). The government created a reserve on Golden Lake — a lake on the Bonnechere River, 150 kilometers west of Ottawa — in 1873. This is the home of the Pikwakanagan First Nation and it is the only federally recognized Algonquin reserve in Ontario. The Indian Act of 1876 transferred power to the Department of Indian Affairs to control almost all the affairs of First Nations peoples (not Inuit or Métis) in Canada.

The beginning of the era of the Indian Act was also the era of Confederation. In Ottawa uncritical celebrations of Confederation abound. The author of the Indian Act, Sir John A. Macdonald, has been memorialized through a Parliament Hill statue, a named parkway (until its renaming in 2023), and as the name of the city's airport. Macdonald's French counterpart, Georges-Étienne Cartier, is also commemorated through the city's airport, a street name, and a statue; the conciliatory narrative of Canada as the coming together of English and French societies is well represented here.

While Ottawa, and most of the country, was aglow during Canada's Centennial in 1967, Chief Commanda hosted the first meeting of what he called the "Circle of All Nations" in Eganville, Ontario. He began hosting annual Circle of All Nations gatherings at his Kitigan Zibi home beginning in 1969 (Thumbadoo 2018, 11). Thousands of people from around the world came to these gatherings to participate in inter-national dialogue "unified by his fundamental and unshakeable conviction that as children of Mother Earth, we belong together and with nature, irrespective of individual colour, creed or culture" (*Circle of All Nations* n.d.). In 1997 the Circle of All Nations appropriated an abandoned mill on Victoria Island (Eade 1997) and Commanda embarked on a long process of persuading the city and federal governments to return Victoria Island and Chaudière Falls (a region Algonquin people refer to as Asinabka) to its sacred purposes. Commanda's plan included freeing Chaudière Falls, creating a park and historical interpretive centre, and building a "peace building meeting site" and an "Asinabka National Indigenous Centre" (Thumbadoo n.d.). Heather Dorries and colleagues (2019, 7) define Indigenous resurgence as "movements and embodied practices focused on rebuilding nation-specific Indigenous ways of being and actualizing self-determination." Commanda's plan has not been realized, although a former rail bridge near the site repurposed for pedestrians and cyclists opened in 2022 as William Commanda Bridge.

On December 11, 2012, in response to the Harper government's recent passage of Bill C-45, which challenged certain Indigenous land and other rights, Chief Theresa Spence of Attawapiskat, a Treaty 9 community on the west coast of James Bay, began what would become a six-week hunger strike on Victoria Island, demanding a meeting with Prime Minister Harper to discuss, among other things, the untenable housing conditions in her community. Spence occupied the sacred Algonquin site in a moment of pan-Indigenous resistance. Ottawa, as both the land of the Algonquin Anishinaabe and the capital of a settler colonial nation, is often the site of pan-Indigenous forms of resistance. In 2017, when the city was awash in nationalist pomp for Canada's 150th celebration, the Bawating Water Protectors erected a teepee on Parliament Hill as a reminder that Indigenous communities were still without running water and experiencing inequitable access to education and state-led colonial violence (Ballingall 2017). In the summer of 2022, a spontaneous memorial of shoes, stuffies, and flowers grew at the Centennial Flame in the wake of news stories about the presence of unmarked graves of over two hundred children at a residential school in Kamloops, British Columbia. Protests, vigils, and political actions for Indigenous rights frequently occupy Parliament Hill and the Canadian Tribute to Human Rights on Elgin Street.

Resurgence, like the type enacted by Chief Commanda, exists throughout the city, much of it concentrated in the eastern neighbourhood of Vanier, leading Michif woman Jamie Morse to dub the neighbourhood "a little Indigi-city" (Panico 2021). At the heart of this Indigi-city is the Wabano Centre for Aboriginal Health, which was designed by famed Blackfoot architect Douglas Cardinal and is highly reminiscent of his other national capital region project, the Canadian Museum of History in Gatineau. Ottawa has the largest population of Inuit outside of the Arctic. We can see Inuit resurgence here at Tungasuvvingat Inuit — a hub offering health care, child and youth services, and language and cultural programs — and, a bit west on Rideau Street at Nunavut Sivuniksavut College — a postsecondary institution dedicated to Inuit studies. An exhibit in the Sandy Hill Community Centre showcases the art of Inuit artist Annie Pootoogook, near to the park that now bears her name, and a *Qamutiik* (Inuit sled) monument, outside of what was formerly Southway Inn (now the Waterford Retirement Home) commemorates the role of the hotel in welcoming Inuit to Ottawa for decades. To honour "all First Nations, Inuit and Métis peoples and their valuable past and present contributions to this land," as the land acknowledgement proclaims, means to support these expressions (and others) of Indigenous resurgence.

BIOGRAPHY AND HISTORY: SETTLING THE OTTAWA VALLEY

C. Wright Mills argued that a robust sociological imagination sees the relationships between personal biographies and history, understanding that everybody is a child of history (Mills 1959). Broad-sweeping historical events including wars, a potato famine, economic contractions, and religious and ethnic persecution all created push factors that led to different waves of settlers and immigrants making themselves at home in Ottawa and the Ottawa Valley. The promise of free and plentiful land for immigrants was the dominant pull factor. The story of immigration is a story of social structures (immigration policies and schemes, structural land dispossession from Algonquin people) and agency (the initiative and labour of immigrants).

There were two significant waves of Irish immigration to Canada and the Ottawa Valley in the nineteenth century: the pre-famine immigration wave (1818–45) and famine-era immigration (1847–54). In the pre-famine wave, Irish immigration accounted for 60 percent of new arrivals to British North

America. As a result of this immigration, 54 percent of the population in counties on the Ontario side of the Ottawa River were Irish, representing the largest concentration of Irish in British North America (Trew 1999, 224). The colonial government facilitated pre-famine Irish immigration. Between 1818 and 1853, Richard Talbot sponsored groups of Irish immigrants from Tipperary County in a bid to secure his own access to land and status (Elliot 2004). An assisted emigration scheme was organized in 1823 by Peter Robinson, a member of the Upper Canada Legislature for York. Robinson believed that Catholics were more compliant than (and thus preferable to) Protestants, with fewer republican tendencies. Through this scheme, five hundred Irish immigrants, all under age forty-five, received the cost of travel, provisions, tools, and, upon arrival, rights to one hundred acres (Trew 1999, 226). Between 1823 and 1825, Lord Bathurst's assisted emigration scheme led to over two thousand immigrants from Cork, Ireland, arriving in the region (Vance 2012, 38). These immigrants would be commemorated with the 2008 building of the Corktown footbridge, which crosses the Rideau Canal at Somerset Street, where almost two hundred years earlier, the Cork immigrants worked on the Rideau Canal and lived in a shantytown known as Corktown (Elliot 1991). The potato famine of the 1840s led to a large wave of Irish immigration; in 1847, there was a 250 percent increase in Irish immigrants to British North America (Trew 1999, 226).

The Scots are well represented in Ottawa. At my neighbourhood pub, Deacon Brodie's (named after a famous Scottish deacon and criminal house robber), a plaque proudly details many of the celebrated and prosperous Scots who have had their names on streets in the neighbourhood: Elgin Street, after Scot Governor General Lord Elgin; Minto Park, after Scot Governor General Lord Minto; Macdonald Street, after John A. Macdonald; and MacLaren Street after James MacLaren. Lewis Street is named after an island in the Scottish Hebrides, Gilmour Street after the Gilmours of Glasgow. The neighbourhood includes the Church of Scotland with the Knox Presbyterian Church, and the Cameron Highlanders Museum in the Cartier Square Drill Hall.

The earliest Scottish settlements in the region were in Glengarry County east of Ottawa, between the St. Lawrence and Ottawa Rivers. Scottish Loyalists from the Clan Donald arrived in 1784 and were granted land after the American Revolution. After the War of 1812, Lord Bathurst instructed governors not to award land to Americans, suggesting instead giving passage and land to Scottish Highlanders, who were deemed more loyal to the Crown. The Highlanders had already earned a good reputation among the colonial governments because their Glengarry Light Infantry regiment had fought for British North America in the War of 1812. In 1815, Sir Francis Gore (lieutenant governor of Upper Canada) created townships along the Rideau River specifically for Scottish immigrants, serviced by new roads and three military depots in Perth, Lanark, and Richmond (Vance 2012). For these reasons, many Scots were pulled to Canada — while being pushed out of Scotland due to large-scale evictions of farmers from their land, known as the "Highland Clearances," between 1750 and 1860.

French Canadians settled throughout the towns of the Ottawa and St. Lawrence Valleys and the Outaouais beginning in the early nineteenth century. In 1674, there were two seigneuries established along the Ottawa River — the Petite Nation, and Pointe à L'Original — yet these remained unsettled until the nineteenth century (Gaffield 1997). As available land in the St. Lawrence Valley became taken and French Canadians migrated to New England, priests in Lower Canada started eyeing land in Upper Canada and embarking on "church-sponsored programmes of colonization," facilitating French-Canadian settlers' moves west by providing the "essential ingredients of French-Canadian culture, language, and religion" (Cartwright 1977, 3). In 1841, Bishop Bourget in Montreal recruited Oblate priests from France to promote Christianity and colonial values among Indigenous people in the Ottawa Valley and service a growing French community in Bytown (Cartwright 1977). The Oblates were established in France in 1816 to counter the revolutionary secularization that had been unleashed by the French Revolution, preach to the poor, and engage in missionary work (Britannica 2025). For the Catholic Church in Canada, that same anti-revolutionary spirit would be useful in Bytown, which was full of the revolutionary zeal of the Irish and underpopulated by the French.

The work of settling French Canadians in the region was led by Joseph-Bruno Guigues, who by 1846 had become a bishop with a jurisdiction including Prescott, Russell, Carleton, Lanark, and Renfrew counties. Guigues promoted the land of the Ottawa Valley to potential French-Canadian settlers as being similar to the land of the Eastern Townships. Parish priests worked like land agents, coordinating collective efforts to improve land drainage and instructing settlers on coordinating planting and harvesting alongside their time in lumbering work (Cartwright 1977). In Bytown, the Notre Dame Cathedral was built in 1848 on St. Patrick Street to serve the growing French-Catholic community. Across the street is Rochon House, inhabited by sculptor Flavien Rochon from 1853 to

1897, which has been preserved by the National Capital Commission as an embodiment of a workingman's house (Centre de recherche en civilisation canadienne-française 2017a). By 1901, 52.5 percent of Bytown's population was French (Centre de recherche en civilisation canadienne-française 2017b), and, as this book details, that density would impact religious, political, social, and cultural life in the city.

The English that settled in the Ottawa Valley arrived as prospectors, appointed government officials, canal engineers, wannabe aristocrats, and predominantly as War of 1812 veterans. They also arrived as poor, parentless children. From 1869 until the 1940s over 100,000 poor English children were brought to Canada without their parents. Imagined and treated as orphans, many of them were not — they were just visibly poor and scooped up by British authorities from the streets of London as a part of a program called the "Child Migrant Scheme." The children as young as two were sent to Canada; some parents were notified of their children's whereabouts after they were at sea. While parents were told the children would grow up in the clean air wonderland of Canada and the welcoming embrace of Canadian adoptive parents, instead they often lived in squalid conditions, including group homes. Ottawa's New Orpington Lodge for British Home Children opened on Richmond Street in Hintonburg in 1895. An inspector's report condemned the home for its cheap camp beds, lack of ventilation, and skimpy blankets and pillows. In response, the home was renovated and renamed St. George's Home in 1904, and it was run by the Sisters of Charity of St. Paul until its closure in 1935 (Home Children Canada 2025).

Nineteenth-century settlement was not smooth; while Algonquin people were being systematically pushed off their land, the new arrivals brought with them religious, linguistic, and ethnic biases from their homelands. By the nineteenth century, the Outaouais was run by an American — Philemon Wright; a Scot — Archibald McMillan, who had sponsored an emigration scheme from Scotland to Montreal in 1802 and established settlements in Templeton, Lochaber, and Grenville beginning in 1806; and a French Canadian — Joseph Papineau, who had purchased the Petite Nation seigneury in 1801 (Gaffield 1997). Contact between Wright, McMillan, and Papineau and their American, Scottish, and French communities was sparse, and the communities were distinct, geographically and in form. The Petite Nation was structured along the seigneurial tradition — long strips of land with river footage — while Hull took the form of a New England village, and the British townships "followed the grid pattern preferred by British authorities" (Gaffield 1997, 147). In Bytown, linguistic, religious, and class differences were also spatialized — the more well-heeled Protestant British settled on the upper lands south of Parliament Hill, known as Uppertown, while the Catholic French and Irish labourers, joined soon by Eastern European Jewish and Italian immigrants, settled in the lower, swampy lands of the ByWard Market, Lowertown.

In 1849, Governor General Lord Elgin signed the contentious Rebellion Losses Bill, which granted government compensation to both the rebels and the Loyalists who participated in the Rebellions of 1837. This bill angered Loyalists so much that they set the Parliament buildings (then in Montreal) on fire and pelted Elgin's carriage with eggs as he travelled through Montreal in April 1849. A few months later, on September 17, 1849, Lowertowners were meeting in the market to plan the festivities for an upcoming visit of Lord Elgin. They had set up a platform, and speeches were underway when fifteen hundred Loyalists (still not fans of Elgin) from Uppertown and neighbouring townships descended on the meeting (Mika and Mika 1982, 206). A riot ensued; people on both sides started throwing sticks and stones, there were a few gun shots, and one man, David Borthwith, was shot and killed. This event became known as "Stoney Monday." It occurred outside the Shouldice Hotel, a building which became the bar "Stoney Mondays" in the 1990s. Tensions were driven by class, politics, religion, and language, and these tensions would become codified in societies, lie dormant, and erupt throughout the city's history.

Many contemporary sociologists have critiqued Durkheim for his rigid separation of religious and political worlds. Sociologist Bonar Buffam details how a universal division of the sacred and profane, church and society, does not exist. His research on Canadian Sikh Gurdwaras shows that these are places of sacred rituals *and* places of prosaic, everyday service to society and political organizing (Buffam 2020). In Ottawa, churches were built to create opportunities for praising God and warding off the Devil, as in the medieval design of the asymmetrical towers of the 1891 Saint Francois d'Assise Church in Hintonburg (Leaning 2003), but churches were also places for socializing and for political mobilization, including the organizing of "secret" fraternal societies that provided opportunities for nurturing social capital and mobility for men.

The Orange Order — named for seventeenth-century King William of Orange — established halls throughout the region. Orangeism is a fraternal, oath-based Protestant order that had incredible social and political salience in nineteenth-century Ontario and was notably anti-Catholic. An Orange Lodge was built in the 1850s in Bell's Corners (Elliott 1991, 54), and there are still Orange Lodge Halls in Richmond and Hintonburg. The town of Orangeville (now a neighbourhood known as the Glebe Annex, between Bell and Booth Streets) was named for its residents' extensive membership in the Orange Order before being renamed Mount Sherwood in 1873 (Stefko 2023). After the municipal election in 1856, sleigh-loads of Protestants, rejoicing in winning the majority of council, stopped off at a Catholic-owned tavern, trashed the house, and beat up customers. Denie Tierney Jr. was murdered; his death was deemed "caused by persons unknown" (Elliott 1991, 70). Tierney's murder became a rallying cry for those angry about anti-Catholic discrimination.

However, the Orange Order was not the only secret society in town. Beginning in the 1850s, Bytown and then Ottawa was home to a number of Masonic Lodges: the Civil Service Lodge, Builders Lodge, Doric Lodge, Bytown Corinthian Lodge, and Dalhousie Lodge (Jenkyns 2010). Lumber industrialist E.B. Eddy was a freemason, and a Lodge was created in his name in the 1870s (Vincent-Domey 1994). The Independent Order of Odd Fellows — a fraternal society for tradesmen — and their female equivalent, the Rebekahs, established groups in Westboro in 1911 (Elliott 1991).

On Beechwood Avenue, St. Charles Church, a wooden Catholic church built in 1908, is now nestled in a condominium–courtyard–yoga studio plan by ModBox Developments. From 1908 until its decommissioning in 2013, the church nourished Franco-Ontarian religious and social life. It was here that Father Barrette and thirteen Francophone civil servants founded the secret fraternal Order of Jacques Cartier, also known as "La Patente." The order was established to respond to the overwhelming influence of the English and Protestant secret societies on the city and nation. The membership grew to over seventy thousand members across the country and was involved in issues like increasing French-English bilingualism on street signs and stamps and ensuring Francophones were promoted in the civil service (MacKinnon 2018). That this order was established in Eastview, a Francophone city that would later become the neighbourhood of Vanier, is not surprising.

People began settling in Janeville, a community built on land owned by Scottish settler Donald McArthur (and named for his wife Jane), east of the Rideau River in 1873. Janeville became a village with an English majority. The villages of Clarkstown and Clandeboye, both of which had Francophone majorities, grew north of Janeville in the 1880s. These towns were desirable for middle-class public servants, offering fresh air away from the bustle of Bytown, lower taxes, and fewer building restrictions. By 1887, two-thirds of the population of these towns was French. French establishments, schools, and churches — the Montfortains, the Notre Dame de Lourdes (1887) (which eventually built the St. Charles Church), the Pères Blanc/Missionnaires d'Afrique — nourished a Catholic, Francophone culture. The towns became incorporated as the city of Eastview in 1909, and by the time Eastview was renamed Vanier in 1969, after Canada's first French-Canadian governor general Georges-Philias Vanier (in office from 1959 to 1967), the city was the heart of Franco-Ontarian culture. The city's renaming occurred the same year as the passage of Canada's English-French Official Languages Act, a success that may have been, in fact, influenced by the activities of La Patente.

The nineteenth century also saw the beginning of immigration to Ottawa from Lebanon. Ottawa has the second largest population of Lebanese in Canada (after Montreal), and the highest concentration of Lebanese in Canada (Dib 2022). Lebanese-Canadian scholar Kamal Dib explained that the Lebanese who immigrated to the Ottawa Valley in the late nineteenth century initially worked as farmers and push-cart vendors. At that time the Lebanese and Syrians were all identified as "Turks" in Canadian records and were not recorded as Lebanese until after 1920. These early, largely Christian Lebanese immigrants established Ottawa's St. Elias Antiochian Orthodox Cathedral, Maronite Church, and Melkite Catholic Church. In the early twentieth century, Kfarmechki was a small town in Lebanon that, Dib joked, many in Ottawa presumed was the capital of Lebanon because so many from this town settled in Ottawa. In 1946, Diab and Jamily Boushey moved to Ottawa from Kfarmechki and established Boushey's Fruit Market, which served the community for seventy years (Deachman 2019). After it closed in 2016 the small plaza beside the former market was dedicated "Boushey's Square." Halim "Al" Saikali, a "pillar" of the Lebanese community also from Kfarmechki, opened Al's Steakhouse on Elgin Street as the neighbourhood's first fine dining restaurant in 1967, after learning how to cook as an employee of the Château Laurier as a new immigrant to the city in the early 1950s (Egan 2016).

In the nineteenth and early twentieth centuries, immigration policy affirmed early colonizers' visions of Canada as a white-settler society. The 1967 introduction of the "points system" of immigration — which assessed potential immigrants on education, economic contribution, and language rather than country of origin — changed the demographic makeup of the city. In Canada, multiculturalism has had four overlapping definitions. First, it refers to an old demographic reality — Canada's population has been ethnically and culturally diverse since the country's formation. Second, multiculturalism is an ideology — "normative descriptions about how Canadian society *ought* to be" — that suggests Canada should embrace cultural pluralism. Third, multiculturalism is "a process and a terrain of competition among and between minority groups for valuable economic and political resources" (Liodakis 2012, 258–9). Nikolaos Liodakis (2012) explains that the shift toward multiculturalism was not a natural or benign gift of the white majority. Ethnic groups, especially in relation to the Quebec sovereignty movement, fought for recognition, carving out this pluralist ideology. Finally, multiculturalism is a set of government initiatives and policies, most explicitly codified in the 1971 Multiculturalism Act. The twentieth and twenty-first centuries saw increasingly coordinated responses to refugee crises at the federal and municipal levels, reflecting a broader cultural adoption of multiculturalism.

During the Lebanese civil war (1975–1990), 75,000 largely Muslim Lebanese immigrants came to Canada, mostly from the war-impacted region of southern Lebanon. Because Lebanon was a French colony, many Lebanese speak French. In Ottawa, Lebanese-Canadians have higher rates of French-English bilingualism than other Canadians. Dib argues that it was Canada's openness as an immigrant-receiving country, and the French-English bilingualism in Ottawa, that made Ottawa an attractive place to settle.

In the aftermath of the Vietnam War, an acute and immense refugee crisis was unfolding in Southeast Asia. Malaysia, Singapore, and South Korea were facing arrivals of refugees in such numbers that by 1978 these countries often refused to admit them. After watching devastating news coverage of this crisis, Mayor Marion Dewar called a meeting for June 27, 1979, with a number of representatives of the Ottawa community. A federal representative confirmed that the Canadian government had recently increased the refugee target to eight thousand, and four thousand had already been selected for immigration. "Struck by the gap between the magnitude of the crisis as portrayed by the media and the official's comments, Dewar said, 'Fine. We'll take the other 4,000'" (Buckley 2008, 31). Project 4000 was born. The city approved a $25,000 budget for the project, and the *Ottawa Citizen* sponsored a family, advertised the project, and encouraged other organizations to similarly step up. Volunteer committees organized clothing, housing, education, health care, and settlement and adaptation for refugees, along with handling government relations and starting a newsletter (Buckley 2008, 34–36).

By July 1979 Joe Clark's government had raised refugee admissions to fifty thousand, and by the end of 1980, sixty thousand refugees had settled in Canada. Brian Buckley states that "the radically increased target of 50,000 was well beyond the expectations of even the most vocal activists" (Buckley 2008, 29). Slightly over 10 percent of the two million refugees from this crisis came to Canada. As Mike Lolloy, head of the government's "Refugee Task Force" concluded: "no question … Project 4000 in Ottawa and Operation Lifeline in Toronto were the most influential of the local initiatives responding to the 'Boat People' crisis" (Buckley 2008, 71). Project 4000 continues to be remembered and upheld as an exemplar of what the people of Ottawa are capable of; it was evoked as a strong and powerful precedent during the more recent immigration of Syrian refugees.

Vietnamese and Laotian refugees have made their mark on a strip of Somerset Street, known somewhat erroneously as Chinatown. The Hungarian revolution of 1956, ethnic cleansing by the Ugandan Amin government leading to the refugee crisis of Asian Ugandans in 1971, the Iranian revolution of 1979, droughts in Ethiopia, Eritrea, and Somalia during the 1980s, civil wars in Somalia, Sudan, and the Democratic Republic of Congo, the 2015 war in Syria, and the war in Ukraine (2022–) are likewise all global conflicts and phenomena that have shaped millions of individuals' personal biographies and contributed to the history, culture, experiences, and opportunities available in Canada. Meanwhile, Canadian groups have mobilized and pushed the federal government to adjust immigration policies, enabling new flourishing of cultural, ethnic, and racial difference in Canada and in Ottawa.

A NEW WAY FORWARD

In a book I co-edited on the monuments of Ottawa and Gatineau, we found that there are more monuments to white men named John than there are to Black Canadians, Asian Canadians, and named Indigenous people. From a cursory tourist perspective, it may thus appear that Ottawa and Canada have been created largely by British-descended white men. But this misconception is the result of a particular type of spatialized mythmaking. Confederation is lauded and the violence of the Indian Act, also orchestrated here, ignored. Yet Ottawans are increasingly realizing that they are living on Algonquin land. In 2015, Ottawa was the site of the conclusion of the work of the Truth and Reconciliation Commission, marked by a four-plus-kilometre walk from Gatineau, past Parliament, and ending at Ottawa's city hall. The TRC interviewed seven thousand residential school survivors in its nine years of work, and between seven and ten thousand people from across the country participated in the walk, understood to be, as one banner read, "A new way forward" ("Walk for Reconciliation Draws…" 2015).

Problematizing Ottawa — its white John-ness — requires denaturalizing Ottawa's whiteness. First, since the beginning of settlement, Ottawa has not been all white. Samuel de Champlain, celebrated as one of the first Europeans in the region, travelled with Mathieu de Costa, a Black Portuguese man celebrated for his facility with languages. When Wright arrived in the region, a Black man — London Oxford — was a member of his party. Oxford's two hundred acres at the mouth of the Gatineau River became the site of launching rafts during the early days of the lumber industry (Henderson 2023). Policies crafted in Ottawa largely prevented much Black immigration until the mid-twentieth century, while the Chinese head tax from 1885 to 1923 significantly curtailed Chinese arrivals, explaining Ottawa's small Chinatown. The city's early Lebanese immigrants were also imagined and welcomed as white immigrants, unlike the later waves of Lebanese. This is a whiteness largely uncritiqued; in fact, the designers of the Chinese head tax and anti-Black immigration policies are celebrated with statues and named streets and hotels.

Ottawa's landscape of religious and cultural practices — the Lebanese Orthodox churches, French and Irish Catholic churches, synagogues in Lowertown and Centretown, tensions among secret societies — have similarly reflected broader push-and-pull factors and function as important historical markers. History has shaped the structures and opportunities that underpin life in the city, but the city has also been full of actors — Bishop Guigues, John A. Macdonald, Marion Dewar, Father Barrette, Lord Bathurst, Richard Talbot — who have demonstrated that history is not merely something that unfolds, but it is a collective accomplishment, for better and worse.

Chapter 2

TREES

THERE'S A TREE AT THE ENTRANCE of the Dominion Arboretum in Ottawa — it's a huge Bebb's oak tree, and with its fat trunk and many low, strong and climbable branches it's the perfect welcome to the Arboretum's world of trees. After the murder of twenty-seven-year-old graduate student Ardeth Wood in 2003, the tree was named Ardeth's Tree. In fall 2017, the tree was severely damaged in a storm. However, arborists soon comforted saddened Ottawans by declaring that the tree still had many decades of life ahead. People invest feelings, histories, symbolism, hopes on to trees. Trees can represent paradise, spiritual growth, and individuals' personal qualities; they are metaphors for life. The leaf of the ever-giving sugar maple is one of Canada's most recognizable symbols, and the planting and naming of memorial trees, like Ardeth's Tree and the 152 commemorative trees that grace the grounds of Rideau Hall, hold profound personal and collective memories. Trees have been, in different times, imagined through an androcentric lens as hero, villain, and victim. Trees are treated as sacred — mythological, profound — and profane — a commodity to be harvested as efficiently and crudely as possible.

The thing about trees, though, is that we use them so often as metaphors that it's easy to lose sight of them outside of our own anthropocentric gaze. Trees have their own things going on quite unrelated to us. They have their own complex relationships to each other, to the birds and mammals that make them their home, and to their enemies — the destructive fungi and beetles that damage and suck life from them. Trees outlive us, they witness (maybe indifferently) our actions. For humans, trees make places livable. They do this through their capacity to get rooted, grow protective canopies and respirate, and stick around.

This chapter has three sections: trees for the empire, for the nation, and for the city.

TREES FOR THE EMPIRE

In 1605, when Champlain and his crew were canoeing the Ottawa River, stopping at Kìwekì Point to take in the view, they surveyed the magnificent forests replete with sugar maple, American beech, white elm, basswood, white birch, balsam fir, eastern hemlock, and many, many tall eastern white pine trees. And as he was waxing metaphoric about how the waterfalls east of Kìwekì Point looked like a curtain — "ah, c'est, c'est comme un rideau, n'est pas?," thus assigning "Rideau" as a place name for so much in the region for centuries to come — he was also saying, "Les arbres! Quels arbres magnifiques!" (probably). The lowlands that would become the ByWard Market were eastern white cedar swamps; there were beavers. Over four hundred years later, in the 2010s, a logging company gave a group of dendrochronologists some eastern white pine logs that had been preserved at the bottom of the Ottawa River for hundreds of years. The logs, some stamped with the B of the Booth Company, had sunk in transit from the depths of the woods to the shipyards of Britain sometime in the early nineteenth century (Dick et al. 2014). The interim — between "oh what trees" to recovering sunken, preserved logs — is the story of the role of trees in the development of Ottawa, and Ottawa's contributions to British industrialization, and extractive colonialism.

Starring in this story is the eastern white pine. It is the tallest tree in Eastern Canada, the official tree of Ontario, and, with its light wood, was one of the engines of the "extractive colonialism" (Anderson 2016) that marked nineteenth-century Eastern Ontario. Throughout the nineteenth century the Ottawa River was filled with rafts of wood, pulp, waste, and timber slides. In 1806, a few years after Philemon Wright and his family from Massachusetts settled "Wright's Town" (what would become Hull and then Gatineau), Napoleon Bonaparte created the Continental Blockade, which closed all European ports to British ships, ending Britain's access to the shipbuilding lumber it had customarily procured from the Baltic region. Now, with Britain at war and unable to locally acquire its needed materials, it called on its colonies. The tall, light white pine trees made perfect naval masts. It's possible to imagine that the masts of the H.M.S Erebus, one of the ships for Sir John Franklin's 1845 expedition in the Canadian Arctic, or the H.M.S. St. Lawrence, a British warship that occupied Lake Ontario during the War of 1812, were made from Ottawa-region lumber. Rapid British industrialization, railway booms, and tariffs that protected colonial imports all led to the mass export of lumber from the Ottawa Valley to England (Clifford and Castonguay 2022). England had immense need for wood: thirteen thousand miles of railways were built between 1830 and 1879, and the number of houses in Great Britain went from 1.4 million to 7.8 million in the nineteenth century. An estimate from 1854 is that a common London rowhouse needed between 100 to 120 cubic feet of timber (Clifford and

Castonguay 2022, 129–30). And as a "land without forest" (Clapham in Clifford and Castonguay 2022, 127), Great Britain needed to get its lumber from elsewhere. British industrialization was made possible, in part, because of the richness of the Laurentian forests.

The nature of the logging and the types of trees and lumber (from hewn lumber to sawn lumber) shifted over the century as the oldest trees were harvested, needs changed, and other sources of lumber opened up (the Baltic) and markets emerged (the United States). Throughout this industry, the majority of the Laurentian timber (76 percent) was white and red pine, and of that, 80 percent came from the Ottawa Valley (Clifford and Castonguay 2022, 134).

Industrious entrepreneurs like E.B. Eddy transformed waste wood into matches. A pulp and paper industry emerged. The lumberjacks developed their own shanty culture; folk heroes were born, dance styles developed, fiddle tunes provided the earworms of the day. The lumber barons, with their amassed wealth, invested in local and regional rail lines, entered politics, funded schools and hospitals, built themselves mansions, and continue to lend their names to streets in the national capital region (Bronson, Booth, Eddy, Gilmour). In the process, the forests were pillaged, both systematically, through the selling of Crown land rights, and through lawless pilfering. By 1871, Prime Minister John A. Macdonald lamented, "we are recklessly destroying the timber of Canada and there's scarcely a possibility of replacing it" (in Dean 2005, 46).

The timber trade was a seasonal industry. In September, crews of men with their horses, tools, and provisions would head out for months to live and work in the bush. Winter was the preferred season for logging because trees fell more easily when the sap wasn't running and the frozen ground facilitated moving around the bush. However, the removal of mature trees meant the removal of seed trees, and winter logging meant that cones would rot in snow rather than germinate; pine forests did not have a chance of regenerating (Clifford and Castonguay 2022).

Until 1912, lumberjacks relied on hand tools, timber axes, and crosscut saws. Oxen and horses were the means of transportation until the 1920s. In the bush, the workers built camps, cleared roads, and felled trees. By the spring, the logs were pulled by horses to the nearest stream to begin the "timber drive" down the Ottawa River. North of Ottawa the logs were cajoled by "log drivers" — men equipped with iron hooks and wearing caulk boots with metal studs on the soles for traction. Near Ottawa, loose timber was assembled into cribs in order to continue down the widest stretch of the Ottawa River to the St. Lawrence River and eventually across the ocean (Lee 2006, 80).

The 1979 National Film Board's *Log Driver's Waltz* celebrates log drivers for their adept footwork dancing on the logs in the rushing river. In this film and song, a young woman is encouraged by her parents to date doctors and lawyers from the city; however, "the log driver's waltz pleases girls completely," having learned on the white water how to "step lightly." The timber trade inspired a sort of lauded Ottawa Valley masculinity, a lumberjack that would endure as a compelling contrast to the dominance of the bureaucratic and office-restricted "Ottawa men." David Lee writes that understandings and representations of shantymen in the nineteenth century could be summed up as seeing the men as: "the bad, the pitiful, and the good" (Lee 2006, 157). Understanding shantymen as "bad" came from their springtime activities: gambling, drinking, fighting in towns after months of labouring six days a week and drinking only strong tea in the bush. The "pitiful" shantyman image was derived from witnessing these same activities; however, people began to see these workers as victims of predatory sharks and an elite bourgeoisie that was amassing great value off the dangerous and hard work of the shantymen. At the end of the nineteenth century the image of the shantymen shifted to become an image of admirable and rugged masculinity: "They were seen as athletes who could fell a tree in two or three swings of an axe and who could dance on logs as they rode down white-water rivers. They were still known as fighters, but more now as righteous defenders of the underdog" (Lee 2006, 159–60). In this context, Joseph Montferrand emerged as the great French-Canadian hero. Montferrand was Anglicized and popularized in the Stompin' Tom Conners song "Big Joe Mufferaw." Conners' lore crafts, "Now Joe had the portage from the Gattineau down / To see a little girl he had in Kempville town / He was back and forth so many times to see that gal / The path he wore became the Rideau Canal." The legendary figure has been appropriated by the Ottawa Redblacks football team for their mascot, "Big Joe." Canadian nationalism (reflected in folk heroes like Joseph Montferrand) is premised on a type of rugged masculinity that is both required and supported by the extractive colonial practices of the timber trade.

Over two hundred years of industrialization and urbanization along the river have disrupted its complex ecosystem. In a speech at Ottawa's Russell House Hotel in 1882, visiting playwright Oscar Wilde, after seeing the Ottawa River full of lumber and pulp said: "This is an outrage.... No one has a right to pollute the air and water, which are the common inheritance of all.... We should leave them to our children as we have received them" (Boswell 2016). For a century, the lumber industry used the river as its main transport system and dumping ground, leading to significant waste in the form of errant logs (those sunken B-stamped logs). The water-powered mills that drove the expanding sawn lumber industry in the 1850s were placed right over the river, so that sawdust pollution was very efficiently dumped into the water — by one estimate, 12,300,000 cubic feet of sawdust annually. Sawdust disrupted fish spawning sites so fish populations declined. Rotting sawdust on the bottom of the river released methane, so the river frequently exploded! (Gillis 1986, 90, 85) Lumber barons eventually agreed to regulations against dumping large waste. This agreement served them well as it made the river more navigable. But J.R. Booth staunchly resisted any regulations to prevent or limit sawdust dumping, arguing that waste incinerators increased their fire insurance rates and rebuilding mills would be an expensive death-knell to the industry. After thirty-five years of vacillating laws and regulations, Senator Francis Clemow's amendment to the Fisheries Act declared that no more exemptions to sawdust dumping laws were to be granted after May 1, 1895 (Gillis 1986).

The extractive colonialism that thinned the forests of century-old trees was eventually replaced by the planting and harvesting of pine plantations to support settlement. The Pine Grove, a red pine plantation begun in the 1950s, is the largest forest in Ottawa's Greenbelt. The Hunt Club Forest, before it was clear-cut in 2024, was part natural forest, part red pine plantation. Red pines have historically been the trees preferred by Hydro Ottawa for its poles.

While on the face of it the planting of trees seems good, this process of producing tree-based monocultures introduces its own issues, namely the loss of biodiversity. Between the 1950s and 1970s across North America, many sandhills and savannahs were destroyed when these spaces were transformed into pine plantations and agricultural land, a process that shrunk Ontario savannahs to 3 percent of their original size by the 1950s (Catling and Kostiuk 2010). The Constance Bay Sandhills in western Ottawa were "treeless and prairie-like in aspect, covered in low shrubs" (Porsild 1941 in Catling and Kostiuk 2010, 172) and viewed by people as somehow wasted land. Trees were planted to prevent wind erosion and to increase the land's productivity. Today, savannahs are one of the most at-risk ecosystems in North America.

The Ottawa Valley timber industry, including the extraction of white pines, strengthened the British Empire, led to the growth of Wright's Town and wealth in Bytown. Meanwhile, the red and white pines planted as replacements in plantations contributed to urban infrastructure for a growing Ottawa, at the expense of natural savannahs. The sunken logs offer a haunting reminder of the vast forests that have been lost.

TREES FOR THE NATION

Sugar maples, red maples, silver maples, Freeman maples, and Manitoba maples are plentiful in Ottawa. It would make sense, given the maple tree's role as a national symbol, and Ottawa's role as the national capital, that the maple tree would be the featured tree in this section. However, the hero of this story is a cold-tolerant, hearty, drought-resistant tree that was cultivated in Ottawa: the crabapple tree.

Between 1966 and 1967, the city planted crabapple trees across the city and distributed eighteen thousand crabapple saplings to Ottawa homeowners. A crabapple tree cultivar named the "Almey" was designated as Canada's centennial tree (Gillis 2017). However, tree historian Joanne Dean explains that "the abundant red crab apples became a messy nuisance underfoot on city sidewalks" (Gillis 2017). There are still crabapple trees everywhere in Ottawa: along the Rideau Canal, on the grounds of city hall, in a courtyard of the National Gallery. And, while the Almey did not take hold in Ottawa, Ottawans still take great delight in the healthy row of crabapple trees of different varieties that line Prince of Wales Drive, welcoming visitors to the Dominion Arboretum.

The Dominion Arboretum, first planted in 1889, was originally a sixty-four-acre livestock farm. While it was not high-quality land for growing crops, it was suitable for testing the viability of tree species (Anderson 2016, 41). William Saunders, a pharmacist and a self-educated entomologist from London, Ontario, was recruited by minister of agriculture John Carling to be the first director of Canada's national experimental farm system (Scott 2020). Saunders brought the Siberian crabapple tree to the arboretum from Russia in 1887 and began a breeding program with large eastern apple trees in 1894 (Hinchcliff and Popadiouk 2007). The arboretum was designed in concert with the experimental farms established across the country to test and study best agricultural practices. Trees were central to the development of agriculture in Western Canada because they could "influence local climate conditions," yield fuel, provide lumber for building, create windbreaks, provide fruit, and be transformed into potash fertilizer. Fruit trees were used as an "advertisement of the desirability of a district." Canadian fruit trees from the Dominion Arboretum were proudly on display at the World's Fair in Chicago in 1892, in part to dispel the perception of Canada as frozen wasteland (Anderson 2016, 42).

The row of crabapple trees on Prince of Wales Drive delights many with its short burst of springtime blooms. These trees can be accredited to Isabella

Preston. In 1920, Preston moved from Guelph to Ottawa to accept a position at the Central Experimental Farm. She was by then an accomplished breeder of lilies, lilacs, roses, columbines, and Siberian irises. When she accepted the job as a breeder at the farm, Preston broke a glass ceiling — before her, women there had only held secretarial roles. She was the first female plant hybridizer in Canada (Martin 2002). While working at the experimental farm, Preston developed many breeds of crabapple trees, which she named after Canadian lakes: Cowichan, Rousseau, Makamik, Arrow, Sissipuk, and Simcoe (Hinchcliff and Popadiouk 2007). While nearby Preston Street is named for a former alderman, I like to imagine that it is instead (or also) named for Isabella.

Trees not for but *of* the nation are on display elsewhere in the city. On the grounds of the National Gallery is a garden designed by Cornelia Hahn Oberlander in 1988, described in the museum's press release as "a landscape design that will recreate the Taiga, Canada's northern landscape immortalized by its famous Group of Seven painters." This garden includes plants from the Canadian North, including Siberian juniper and Arctic willow trees (National Gallery Archives 1987), as well as crabapple trees. The grounds of the Museum of Nature offer a more didactic presentation of three Canadian landscapes: the mammoth steppe, the Arctic tundra, prairie grasslands, and the boreal forest. In the grounds displaying the boreal forest, visitors are invited to walk among maple, birch, and black spruce trees.

TREES FOR THE CITY

From 1889 onward, eighty-six varieties of ash trees, including European, red, and white, have been planted in the Dominion Arboretum. Ash trees, as valuable resource trees (and also known as the hockey stick tree), are one of the most common native tree species in the Ottawa Valley. Ash trees were planted throughout the city after Dutch elm disease killed thousands of elms from 1948 to 1988. A mature ash can grow to be thirty metres tall, provide immense shade with its domed canopy, and is understood as a fairly robust city tree. The utility of ash trees pre-dates these urban uses by thousands of years, though — black ash bark has been and continues to be used in Indigenous peoples' basket-making in southern Ontario and the American midwest (Church 2016).

In 2002, the hearty ash tree fell victim to the invasive emerald ash borer. These beetles lay their eggs under tree bark, the larvae then tunnel their way out of the trees, chewing holes through the trees' cambium, eventually killing the trees. Between 2002 and 2017, fifty thousand ash trees were removed after being infested by the beetles. Today the black ash tree is an endangered species (White 2024). The city continues to run an ash tree replacement program. The ash tree is our hero and victim for this section on trees for the city.

As the trees closest to urbanites, street trees have an outsized impact as they "both reflect and influence how we think about the rest of the natural world" (Dean 2005, 46). During the early months of the pandemic, I saw trees anchoring swings and hammocks, providing shade for picnics, and being used as climbing play structures (very welcome during the months-long closure of playgrounds). I met friends at various favourite trees (hat tip to the big old willows on the west side of Pretoria Bridge). Trees are a taken-for-granted urban amenity, often most noted in times of crisis. During the devastating derecho of spring 2022, the significant tree loss in areas like McCarthy Woods left gaping holes in the landscape. In her study of peoples' relationships to trees in Ottawa, anthropologist Emma Bider detailed how threats to trees (the destruction of mature trees for a hospital parking lot, of a forest for an airport parking lot, climate and urban infrastructure perils facing downtown trees) were met with all sorts of protests and artistic responses. People wrote songs, poetry, and staged campaigns to express their deep attachment to these city trees. This is because trees make places both inhabitable and meaningful (Bider 2024). In conversation with me, Emma described that she routinely biked a certain route in south Ottawa. On one trip, following her same route, she discovered that seemingly overnight a trail of old yet diseased ash trees had been removed, rendering her homey route now foreign territory.

Early on, the city saw investment in street trees as aligning with its transformation into the nation's capital. The first tree-planting bylaw was passed in 1869, allowing street trees to be planted directly into the unpaved streets, and the city paid homeowners twenty-five cents for each properly planted tree on their property. A later bylaw asked property owners to fence trees to protect them from horses (Dean 2005). These bylaws led to a flourishing, albeit variable tree landscape. By 1884, the growing neighbourhood of New Edinburgh used its shade trees as a selling feature because "long avenues of uniform shade trees became associated with privilege and wealth." Metcalfe Street, home to lumber baron J.R. Booth, was also a decadently tree-lined street. In Frederick Todd's 1903 plan for the city, he designed Clemow Street in the Glebe to be wider than the neighbouring streets and to include a "uniform row of trees" (Dean 2005, 47–48).

Early twentieth-century adoption of asphalt and tar macadam led to the removal of street trees and, because paved streets compacted the soil and sent rainwater into storm sewers instead of tree roots, it threatened existing urban trees. Telephone lines, electric lights, and streetcars also endangered many trees. People began to see trees as hindrances rather than assets. By 1923, a new bylaw required homeowners to receive permission to plant trees on their properties. Trees could not interfere with the urban infrastructure, and people could not plant nut- and cone-bearing trees or Manitoba maple, sassafras, walnut, willow, or poplar trees (Dean 2005).

In 1965, the combination of building new sewage lines and the Macdonald-Cartier Bridge along with the emergence of the Dutch elm disease meant that the city cut down every elm tree on King Edward Avenue (Smythe 2011). While there were plans to replace the elms with maples, King Edward Avenue has never again been a linear tree-filled ramble. Monocultures — including those in urban forests — lead to greater devastation by tree blights. After Dutch elm disease, the city was struck by the emerald ash borer and is now preparing to address a potential arrival of oak wilt. Today street trees continue to be at odds with expanding urban infrastructure (as demonstrated with a new Ottawa hospital project leading to the destruction of hundreds of mature trees).

While lumber barons and the upper-middle class had greater access to street trees than working-class Ottawans in the nineteenth century, urban trees continue to be indexes of social class today. Using sensor and mapping technology to distinguish trees from other vegetation, a 2018 study showed tree canopy covering 31 percent of Ottawa and 45 percent of Gatineau, rates that exceeded other Canadian cities (Toronto's 2018 tree canopy coverage was 28.4 percent) (National Capital Commission 2019; City of Toronto 2021). Tree coverage also differs among city wards. The ward with the lowest tree coverage in this study was downtown Somerset at 22 percent, that with the highest was the inner suburban College ward with 48 percent. Smaller neighbourhoods within wards showed even larger differences. Constance Bay, a neighbourhood within West Carleton–March, had 80 percent canopy coverage (National Capital Commission 2019, 6), while the Orléans ward Industrial Park had coverage of just 10 percent. The study then analyzed the relationship between median income, population density, and tree canopy coverage; not surprisingly, neighbourhoods with lower median incomes had fewer trees, as did neighbourhoods with higher population densities.

The class-based distribution of street trees means that wealthier neighbourhoods are healthier neighbourhoods. Trees clean the air; a single mature tree can absorb forty-eight pounds of CO_2 in one year (US Forest Service 2021). The urban heat island effect refers to how dense urban areas, with less porous surfaces, heat-generating buildings, and traffic exhaust, are hotter than surrounding areas. The difference in temperature between large cities and their surrounding environments can be as large as 12°C (Oke 1987). Trees reduce the urban heat island effect through "intercepting solar radiation," affecting air movement, and capturing moisture (Bowler et al. 2010, 148). Well-treed neighbourhoods are cooler, allowing people to more easily withstand increasingly hot summers, go outside in the summer, and participate in their communities. Neighbourhoods with parks do even better. Dundonald Park in Centretown, along with its many other functions, offers a cooling respite for the neighbourhood in the summer heat. Trees, and other porous surfaces like gardens, meadows, porous parking lots, also protect waterways by reducing storm runoff, keeping rivers cleaner.

Today, the city is reluctant to plant ash trees because, due to the borer, they are unlikely to grow to maturity. The city ash trees continue to be a victim of the little beetles, but like all street trees, they are also heroic. They are often found together, planted as wind breaks, and thus offer opportune hammock-hanging opportunities, and even with their shortened lives, they do their part cooling their local climes, securing the soil, absorbing rainwater.

HEROES, VILLAINS, VICTIMS

Ottawa is a city built on trees. The first century of the city's industrial growth was premised on the extraction of pine and other trees from the surrounding forests. Depending on your orientation to industrialization and extractive colonialism, the eastern white pine is the hero of Ottawa — indeed, an image of a solitary white pine is central to the city's coat of arms — or victim. Noted by Algonquin communities early on, and then by Canadian lumber moguls and politicians, the plundering of the forests was unsustainable. Early twentieth-century pine plantations aligned with the extractive logic of nineteenth-century logging and have supplanted complex ecosystems with monocultures. The crabapple tree was developed and then celebrated as a heroic enabler of settler nationalism — or, for some averse to Canadian nationalism and/or rotting fruit underfoot, the villain. Street trees and those of the Dominion Arboretum are everyday heroes, cooling neighbourhoods, cleaning the air, preventing flooding, and providing spiritual and playful sustenance to children and adults. Yet from the androcentric perspective of urban expansion, trees have also been villainized: disrupting infrastructure, their roots cracking sidewalks, falling on power lines, and getting in the way of the need for more hospital parking.

We have attachments to trees — to certain willows by Pretoria Bridge, to ash trees on a bike route, or big oaks at the Dominion Arboretum — broadly, to forests, and abstractly, to the notion of trees and their right to thrive. We also have alienated relationships to the whiffs of trees and imagined fuzzy and nonspecific treescapes. In Ottawa there are fifteen streets named after apple trees, including Applewood Cres, Apple Lane, Apple Leaf Lane. There are twenty-one streets with variations of "maple" in their name: Maple Grove Road, Maple Forest Drive, Maplewood Avenue, Maple Stand Way. There are seventeen streets named after the disease-stricken elm tree, fourteen after the beetle-ravaged ash, and twenty-one streets named for the heroic pine tree. Trees are felled and replaced with generic plantations, but memories of treed landscapes and hopes for treed futures remain.

Chapter 3

LIBRARIES

It is impossible to be hyperbolic when describing the important community-building, socializing, "third place" quality of libraries. When other social institutions are overwhelmed, underfunded, and crumbling, libraries often pick up the slack. Libraries are free, providing warmth in cold winters and a cool space in hot summers; they offer worlds of intrigue, satisfy curiosity, and are safe spaces to hide away but in public. Through outreach programs, classes, and public lectures, they generate opportunities for much-needed human connection. In 2014, during the protests following the murder by police of Michael Brown in Ferguson, Missouri, protestors found refuge, Wi-Fi, water, and resources at the Ferguson Municipal Library, and in 2020, when protestors were setting the police station in Minneapolis on fire following the murder at the hands of police of George Floyd, someone tweeted a picture of chalk graffiti outside the Minneapolis library that read "I LOVE Libraries, FUCK 12" (12 being the police). Sociologist Eric Klinenberg notes, "You rarely see a police officer in a library" (2019, 45), which one could read as both a reflection and a precondition of a library's safety and openness.

Libraries are great sites of socialization. *Socialization* refers to the ongoing, lifelong processes of learning and adopting social norms, practices, and skills necessary to function in a given society. Socialization allows individuals to function within a society, and individuals' socialization collectively allows a society to function. We are socialized as children into basic individual biological and social functions like eating, walking, sleeping through the night, talking (this is called primary socialization), but we are also socialized throughout our lives into work roles, parenting, and how to be retired or a grandparent (secondary socialization). Sociologists describe the different groups invested in the socialization of members of society as *agents of socialization*. Libraries significantly socialize children into their role outside of being a child in a family. In libraries, children are not policed and told what to do, like in schools, and unlike in commercial spaces, children are welcomed in libraries. In libraries, children engage in secondary socialization, the process where children see themselves as members of a larger society outside of their families. For many children, a library card is their first piece of identification that they are responsible for. For my friend Kevin, his childhood memory of his town library is that it was the first place he was allowed to walk to (a one-kilometre journey) on his own. Libraries do not segregate based on age (excepting the children's library section) or gender. Teenagers shouldn't find themselves accused of loitering in a library and may in fact find respite from the demands of parents and peers. New parents are socialized into parenthood through books, parenting classes, and programming for small children. Libraries are some of the rare places where people voluntarily co-mingle with broad swaths of society and are, therefore, socialized into a productive, friendly civility. In this chapter I detail how, throughout the history of Ottawa's libraries, they have shifted from focusing on books to readers, to people, to spectacles. Consistent in the many forms libraries have taken is a promise of libraries as "emancipatory" spaces (Aptekar 2019), spaces of personal freedom, freedom from consumer society and from various formal and informal systems of surveillance. I conclude with three contemporary threats to the vitality of libraries.

FROM BOOKS TO SPECTACLES

The first modern library was the Biblioteca Malastiana in Casena, in northern Italy, opened in 1450 (Mickiewicz 2016). In the sixteenth century, monastic libraries were built across Europe exclusively for the religious elite. The first libraries in Canada were established by Jesuit colleges in the seventeenth century (Capillé 2018). In these earliest libraries, the focus was very much on the books that were treated as rare and venerated objects. Library design reflected this focus: "The very first reading rooms were domed spaces around which books lined the circular walls" (Mickiewicz 2016, 243). Sitting among awe-inspiring stacks, the readers read in spaces that were simultaneously public and intimate. Library scholar Brian Edwards explains that "the library was indeed once a space that looked 'inwards not outwards … one where the intellectual realm of society [was] captured within its walls'" (Edwards, 2009, 9, in Mickiewicz 2016, 244). Nowhere are books treated like precious gems more than in the Library of Parliament.

Immediately after the Act of Union of 1840, the Province of Canada began amassing a collection that was to be housed in the Library of Parliament. This proto-national library was kept in the country's first parliament buildings in Montreal, only to suffer substantial losses when the parliament buildings burned down in 1849. Only two hundred of the twelve thousand books were saved (Hilmer 2015). The Library of Parliament in the new capital city of Ottawa was completed in 1876, following the construction of the Centre Block between 1859 and 1865 (Young 1995, 100). Queen Victoria donated 47,000 books to the library, which arrived by barge in 1864. Pierette Landry describes the building, "Modelled in part on the Reading Room of the British Museum, it is crowned by a circular lantern with distinctive structural features — a ring of 16 flying buttresses, pinnacles, decorative windows and ornamental ironwork which highlight the Library's jewel-like attributes" (Landry 2001, 2). Upon entering the library, visitors immediately face a stunning white marble sculpture of Queen Victoria, and gazing upwards, find themselves encircled by three floors of books. With light streaming in through the windows, it makes sense why, in 2007, Canadians voted this library one of "The Seven Wonders of Canada" in a nationwide, online survey (Hilmer 2015).

The Library of Parliament is for parliamentarians, but in this same era the federal government created a national library and archives for Canadians. In its earliest days in 1872, the nation's archives were stored in three basement rooms in the West Block of the Parliament buildings. These archives were a collection of papers unsystematically assembled by the first Dominion archivist, Douglas Brymner, a clerk from the Department of Agriculture (Pass 2022). In 1906, the Dominion Archives became the domain of Canada's second Dominion archivist, Arthur Doughty, and were given a proper home at 330 Sussex Drive in a building designed by David Ewart as the National Archives, until 1967.

City libraries began in Bytown's hotels, the first social institutions established in the region. A reading room – the Bytown Athenaeum — was opened in the Royal British Hotel on George Street in 1838. The hotel subscribed to sixteen newspapers and four monthly periodicals (O'Regan 1994, 19). In 1847, a group of the city's elite, including Thomas McKay, poet and journalist William Lett, and Mayor John Scott, established the Bytown Mechanics' Institute. Mechanics' institutes were voluntary associations created by working-class men that focused on adult education and self-improvement, and they organized lending libraries in Ontario in the early 1800s (Capillé 2018). While established by the city's elite, by 1853 the Bytown Mechanics' Institute had recruited workers from an axe factory, a door and blind factory, sawmills, and textile mills as members. However, as Hirsch explains: "The original goal of helping the 'working man' to improve himself was good in theory at the time, but what really evolved was a social club where the lecture topics were of more interest to better educated middle and upper-class citizens" (Hirsch 1992, 5, 13).

By 1848 the institute had rented a room where, for a five-shilling annual fee, members could access over two hundred books to borrow. By 1855, this library had 899 books, 33 newspaper subscriptions, and a museum with 850 artifacts (including a complete set of false teeth). The institute — like institutes across the country — also encouraged governments to invest in public libraries. By 1858, the Ontario government was giving the institute an annual operating grant. In 1869 the institute merged with the Ottawa Natural History Society to create the Ottawa Literary and Scientific Society (Hirsch 1992, 4, 7, 9).

As they became publicly funded, libraries began to shift from a focus on books to a focus on readers. While books were historically only accessible through a librarian, in these new libraries, open stacks gave readers the freedom to browse. Architecturally, libraries began to adopt the "container/square" design model, and "reading rooms turned into foyer-like spaces and books were stored in galleries removed from the library's more public areas" (Mickiewicz 2016, 243).

In 1896, the Ottawa Council of Women persuaded local businessman George Perley to donate a building on Wellington Street to serve as the city's first public library. The city rejected this offer, citing a lack of funds for the project (Smythe 2012). That building became instead the Perley House for the Incurables in 1897. Instead, Ottawa's first public library was funded by American railroad billionaire and philanthropist Andrew Carnegie. According to lore, a local merchant in Carnegie's neighbourhood in Philadelphia lent children books. This had a profound impact on Carnegie's childhood as a Scottish working-class immigrant to the United States (Klinenberg 2019). As an adult, Carnegie funded 2,811 libraries around the world, including 125 in Canada. His aim was to create spaces where anyone could access books, classes, and an intellectual reprieve from daily life; he wanted libraries to be "palaces for the people" (Klinenberg 2019, 24).

In 1903, Carnegie's foundation gave $100,000 to Ottawa to build a library. As with all of the Carnegie libraries, the city was required to provide the site, an annual operating budget, and guarantee free public access (Smythe 2012). Carnegie wanted libraries to inspire not only through their contents, but through the spaces themselves; they thus featured vaulted ceilings and ornate designs (Klinenberg 2019, 218). The Ottawa Carnegie Library was no exception. The neoclassical library, designed by Edgar Lewis Horwood and sitting at the intersection of Metcalfe and Laurier Streets, included arched windows that allowed natural light to illuminate the reading rooms and open steel-reinforced stacks for visitors to browse (Smythe 2012). The library also featured an elaborate stained-glass window that paid tribute to global and local wordsmiths, including Charles Dickens, William Shakespeare, and local

Confederation-era poet Archibald Lampman. On the day of its opening in 1906, an event attended by Carnegie himself — the only Canadian library he personally opened — "the throngs were so heavy that they had to stay open several hours after the scheduled closing, by which time the books were in complete disarray and several items were missing" (Smythe 2012). A second Carnegie-funded library, the Rosemount Library, opened in 1918 in Hintonburg.

While Carnegie libraries embodied a new focus on readers, "the hundreds of public libraries founded through Andrew Carnegie's philanthropy in the early twentieth century stressed individual improvement over class solidarity, helping to reproduce an atomized and compliant workforce" (Aptekar 2019, 1204). The "palaces for the people" aligned with other means used by the elite to socialize the working class into what they deemed acceptable activities.

By the 1960s, there was a boom in new library construction and an embrace of brutalist architecture across the country. Brutalist architecture is marked by visible structural elements, geometric structures, and minimalism. In Ottawa, apartment buildings, office buildings, and the new MacOdrum Library at Carleton University all reflected this enthusiasm for brutalism. At the same time, Ottawa's Carnegie library was beginning to show some cracks in its foundation, and it was torn down. Some of its columns were repurposed as curios in Rockcliffe Park, and its stained-glass window found a new home in the new library. The new library, by architect George Bemi, opened in 1974 to great public enthusiasm. Upon its opening, the *Ottawa Journal* celebrated:

> The new main branch of the Ottawa Public Library is a stunning example of modern architecture. A standing rebuke to the notion that because a building is new and functional it need be sterile and cold. The new Library may indeed be the most successful public building put up into Ottawa since the Union Station. (January 11, 1974 in Smythe 2014) E

On the fate of the downtown branch in the 2010s, urbanist Sarah Gelbard offered this tribute to the surviving brutalist buildings in Ottawa: "They are sculptural and honest in the way they bear the marks of the geometry through which they were designed and the materials with which they were made…. They do not shy away from being actors in the scene, and dramatic characters at that. It would be a shame to draw the glass curtain-wall over them all" (Gelbard 2015). The 1974 library did not "shy away from" its function as a building for books and readers. Gelbard's comment about glass curtain-walls is a reference to the 2017 renovations to the 1968 brutalist National Arts Centre (NAC), which included an addition featuring a glass tower and glass walls.

In this era of library investment, the new National Library and Archives (LAC) was constructed at 395 Wellington Street between 1963 and 1967. This building also embodied the container/square model, with its "small punched windows" and design that reflected the "functional division of the building between stacks and public spaces" (Parks Canada n.d.). In its collection is the original British North America Act, which includes edits by John A. Macdonald; the Constitution Act signed by Queen Elizabeth in 1982 (marked with raindrops from the day of its signing); and the archive's oldest book, *De antiquitate Judaica: De bello Judaico* [*Antiquities of the Jews and the Judean War*], by first-century historian Flavius Josephus, printed in 1470 (*Ottawa Citizen* 2013). A brand-new preservation centre for LAC opened in 2022 in Gatineau. It is the largest automated storage and retrieval system in the world and the federal government's first zero-carbon building. Over eight hundred employees safeguard and manage access to a collection of ten million publications, archival music, images, stamps, and artifacts.

The future of libraries in Ottawa looks bright — spectacular, actually — shiny, and new, or these are the hopes of the politicians, designers, and supporters of the new combined LAC and main branch of the Ottawa Public Library to be opened in 2026 on LeBreton Flats. The main branch of the public library will take 61 percent of the space, and the rest will be Library and Archives Canada. The new library will be five stories high, 216,000 square feet (CBC News 2018b), and named Ādisōke — the Algonquin word for storytelling. This library will feature a green roof, ground-floor café, top-floor restaurant, and "light-filled five-story atrium called a 'town hall'" on the ground floor (Laucius 2020). Light, air, and openness will replace the brutalism of the 1970s main branch, which seems to respond to a 2015 survey of OPL patrons 80 percent citing "good lighting" as the most important characteristic of a new library (Nanos 2015, 4). There will be a recording studio and makerspace, and consumption of lattes and cobb salads are potential activities alongside reading in this new library.

The design, by Diamond Schmitt Architects, features limestone on its exterior, mimicking the Canadian Museum of History and the Parliament buildings, while "the undulating roofline will be a nod to the rolling Ottawa River" (Laucius 2020). Unlike the current LAC, with its book-like small, square windows, the new library will feature expansive windows, allowing visitors to take in views of the Ottawa River and Parliament buildings. The new library fits clearly in the realm of mega-projects designed by "starchitects" to elevate the project and enthuse the public — the Royal Ontario Museum redesign by Daniel Libeskind and the addition to the Art Gallery of Ontario by Canadian architect Frank Gehry, both in Toronto, are other examples of this trend (Bain 2015). Many cities in Canada have built dazzling new libraries in their downtowns, beginning with Vancouver's new library, designed by Moshe Safdie, in 1995.

Being seduced by starchitecture often means privileging style over substance and flipping the architectural maxim of form following function. Spectacular multifunction libraries are imagined as attractive to tourists and, key to cities' branding activities, as engines of economic development. However, is this approach towards library funding, design, and placement antithetical to the it-ness of libraries as "emancipatory spaces" (Aptekar 2019) existing outside of economic production and consumption? In the survey of OPL patrons, proximity to shops and nice views were two of the least important factors for a new library (Nanos 2015).

This shift towards spectacle reorients libraries back to the interests of elites. Instead of the religious elites catered to in seventeenth-century libraries, the elites benefiting from library spectacles will be real estate developers and other commercial enterprises betting on the future economic (rather than social) vitality of LeBreton Flats. But of course, many things can be true at once. The imagined users and types of engagement on offer at the library are both incredibly broad. The library will be a place of participation, of a variety of people doing a variety of things, some of these things may include different forms of consumption — of lunch, or perhaps spectacle.

THREATS TO THE FUTURE OF LIBRARIES

In our current context of knowledge-based economies, the internet, and shifting urban forms, is the future viability of libraries threatened?

Is the internet a threat to libraries? If magazines, journals, and entire books are available online, are libraries redundant? No. On the contrary, public libraries have been at the forefront of encouraging access to the internet, and in Ottawa, they were the first to provide free public access to Wi-Fi, in 2008, two years before Starbucks offered free Wi-Fi to its customers. The OPL system has continually expanded its online offerings — patrons can stream or download movies, TV shows, music, and e-books through their accounts. At the beginning of the pandemic, the OPL delivered Chromebooks to Ottawa's Youth Services Bureau and created a Wi-Fi hotspot at its temporary isolation centre

(Vlasveld 2020). The OPL is very attuned to issues of the "digital divide," which refers to the gaps between those who have access to the internet, communications technologies, and digital skills and those who do not (Wotherspoon 2012, 344). The rise of the internet, rather than challenging libraries' utility, has hastened the ongoing transition from libraries being repositories of materials (books) to being places to serve a range of public needs.

Despite their celebrated openness, issues emerge within libraries as patrons question and police each other's behaviours, including internet use. One such issue emerged at the OPL Greenboro branch in 2017 when two girls spotted a man at a computer terminal watching pornographic videos on a library computer. The girls' mother filed a complaint with the library. A public debate ensued that fell into predictable lines of either being for morality and children's innocence or against censorship. The library responded with this statement: "Our policy has always been to respect the sensibilities of others. The main refinement is that we will amend our policy to request that customers refrain from displaying content (text or images) that may be reasonably considered offensive in a public setting" (Reevely 2017). Of course, the immediate follow-up question is: what can be reasonably considered offensive? This issue also highlighted how public libraries respond to the digital divide. Most of the so-called "reasonable" people referenced in the library's response would likely consume internet-based pornography in the comfort of their homes if they were able. Despite these complexities, the internet and libraries seem to have a mutually beneficial relationship.

More perilous and ongoing threats to libraries than the advent of the world wide web have been environmental: fires, bats, bugs, floods, pestilence. One of the most tragic and heroic tales in Ottawa's history is the story of the Parliament building fire of 1916 and the saving of the Library of Parliament by the foresight of librarian Alpheus Todd, who suggested to the library's designers that a hallway and fireproof iron doors separate the library from the rest of the building.

The House of Commons was still in session at 8:57 p.m. on February 3, 1916, when the fire alarm was pulled in Centre Block. A fire had started in a wastebasket in the reading room and was spreading quickly. Politicians, including Prime Minister Borden, fled the building on their hands and knees (Marsh 2012). The fire burned until 2 a.m., the tower bell last rung for 11 p.m., dramatically crashed, and has sat on Parliament Hill ever since, in memorial. Seven people died as a result of the fire, the entire Centre Block was destroyed, but the Library of Parliament was saved when library clerk Michael

MacCormac shut the iron doors on his way out of the building (Public Works and Government Services Canada 2011).

Humidity, termites, bedbugs, moths, and bats have also all threatened Ottawa's libraries and archives. In the LAC collection, between 1993 and 2002, 25,000 items were destroyed by mould and dampness. In 2002, the government spent $1.5 million on the maintenance and conservation of library items in the National Library, an insufficient amount to respond to "water incidents" (Schuster 2002). Mould can only be treated by putting items in plastic bags and then the freezer. In renovations done to the Library of Parliament between 2002 and 2006, mechanized humidity controls were installed to mitigate damage due to dampness (Hilmer 2015). Large collections of paper are also vulnerable to a kind of spontaneous combustion. Assistant librarian Karen McGrath explains, "There we have flammable newsprint in an industrial building, with a corrugated metal roof which became so hot last summer that the alarm went off." After this incident, colonies of bats and mice, attracted by the heat, moved in and left droppings everywhere (Schuster 2002). Nature is a threat to the city's libraries — but it is a threat that can be mitigated by design and climate and pest control.

One of the greatest challenges to libraries are neoliberal governments that cut spending on public goods. In 2019, the city approved a budget that included modest increases to lengthen operating hours at the Ruth E. Dickinson branch in Nepean, purchase more e-books, and renovate the rural branch in Metcalfe (McDonald 2019). Also in 2019, Doug Ford's provincial budget slashed the Southern Ontario Library Service (SOLS) — which funds interlibrary loans and other services to rural libraries — in half (Jeffords 2019), impacting Ottawa's system.

Libraries, as many cities' final social safety net stopgap, are put under considerable pressure when other social services like housing, education, and immigrant settlement are underfunded. Ottawa libraries, especially downtown branches, are frequented by people who are unhoused, as a source of warmth and shelter. That the library is not respite housing was made clear in November 2019, when the main branch of the OPL stopped opening the doors to its foyer at 6 a.m., as it had been, and instead began opening the doors at 9:30 a.m., when the library opened. The library argued that the policy change was adopted in response to property damage and the library's need to maintain building security and safety. The councillor for the library's ward, Catherine McKenney, argued that the people who congregated in the lobby for warmth were poor and homeless, and this policy change was unnecessarily punitive

(Johnstone 2020). OPL board chair Tim Tierney responded, supporting the policy and argued that sheltering the city's poorest was not the library's responsibility: "The library is committed to continuing the conversation with other service providers to address gaps in the support network. These gaps are much wider than can be addressed by providing three hours of access to the unmonitored 900-sq.-ft. hallway space connecting two disparate buildings and a parking garage" (Tierney 2020).

It is unrealistic to expect any library to be a catch-all for the gaps in the city and society's social safety net. Yet, each library branch in the OPL system continues to provide all manner of technical, physical, intellectual, and social harbouring in the city. In one visit to the Sunnyside branch, I scanned the bulletin board and saw advertisements for two "teen" movie nights, a drop-in learn-to-knit group, and a book club. Beyond books and opening hours, each library branch continues to offer warmth in many ways. Libraries-as-spectacles, with the inclusion of cafés and restaurants, suggest that libraries are turning some of their focus toward consumer interests. The ability to navigate the other lesser challenges to libraries, changing digital realities, and the natural world all depend on consistent government support for the library system and the city's other social needs.

THE CASUAL COMFORT OF STRANGERS

Libraries offer a refreshing counter to so many of the other urban woes detailed in this book: the surveillance of the state, police, neighbours and parents; pressures to consume; gendered leisure spaces; the incessant drone of traffic; the demands of work. Libraries offer individuals crucial connections to so many social institutions and society more broadly conceived. Libraries provide opportunities for us to extend our hearts and minds to other people, parts of the world, ideas. Libraries nourish at the level of individual and society. A 2023 article in the New York Times by Erica Ackerberg and Elisabth Egan offered a "long overdue" love letter to libraries and concludes with this sweet meditation: "We all know that books connect us, that language has quiet power. To see the concentration, curiosity and peace on faces lit by words is to know — beyond a shadow of a doubt, in a time rife with shadows — that libraries are the beating hearts of our communities. What we borrow from them pales in comparison to what we keep. How often we pause to appreciate their bounty is up to us" (Egan and Ackerberg 2023).

Ackerberg and Egan wrote their love letter after the pandemic, and they also mused nostalgically about how during extended lockdowns people missed the "casual comfort of strangers" that is found in libraries. Libraries offer opportunities for inward reflection and outreach toward others. They encourage a refusal of indifference, and even in the context of spectacle, suggest that quiet, small, individual reflection and engagements can have outsized impact. People understand the value of libraries. In 2023, OPL reported that the number of active cardholders had gone up by 16 percent (Ottawa Public Library 2023, 11). There is hope that with the opening of the light-filled Ādisōke, and with ongoing investment in the city's many library branches, all of the best of humanity — in words and in people — continues to be within reach.

Chapter 4

WORK

IN MY PUB TRIVIA LEAGUE, there's a team with the name "Moved Here For Work." Regardless of their pub trivia successes, these trivia fans likely made some pretty good life decisions. Ottawa typically has a lower unemployment rate than other Canadian cities, with a highly unionized workforce. In 2021 the median annual income of a census "couple family" (i.e., a couple living together with or without children) was $135,800, higher than the national average of $107,000 (Statistics Canada 2024a). After offering an introduction to sociological theorizing on the structure of work, I introduce Ottawa's world of work, pursuing two main arguments: Ottawa's work world has been and continues to be structured by race and gender, and shifts in the structure of work in Ottawa have been driven both from above, in the interests of business owners, and below, through collective organizing by workers.

WORK, SOCIAL CLASS, AND INEQUALITY

In the mid-twentieth century, American structural functionalist sociologists Kingsley Davis and Wilbert Moore hypothesized that social stratification within society was the result of a collectively agreed-upon set of values. Different jobs are afforded different levels of prestige, and compensation reflects functional importance — how much a society needs that type of work — and scarcity — how easy it is to find people willing and able to do that type of labour. The Davis-Moore hypothesis suggests that different levels of prestige and compensation motivate people to pursue work that is important for society but may be difficult or unpleasant (Davis and Moore 1945). In the Ottawa Valley lumber camps, there was a clear hierarchy of occupations based on importance and scarcity. The occupational hierarchy in the bush went like this, from bottom to top: unskilled labourers, then fellers, scorers, liners and teamsters, then cooks, and finally foremen. While all the workers lived in the same cabins, ate the same food, and drank from the same water dipper, pay was differentiated based on skill and scarcity. General hands made $18–25 dollars a month and the foremen $50–75 a month (Lee 2006, 168).

While in the bush occupational distinctions were clear, there is a lot of debate broadly within society about what is valuable and what is necessary labour. Consider these four Ottawa workers' salaries: Richard Wagner, Chief Justice of the Supreme Court of Canada, was paid $413,000 in 2018. In 2020, the highest paid hockey player in Ottawa was the Ottawa Senators' defenceman Thomas Chabot, who made approximately $8 million that season. The average early childhood educator salary in 2024 was about $20 per hour, so $41,000 a year (Indeed.com 2024), similar in wages to other essential workers like hospital porters and personal support workers. Meanwhile, a fast-food worker or grocery store clerk, working full-time at minimum wage in Ontario in 2020, would make around $29,000. During the pandemic, it was only the latter two categories of workers who were considered essential to society, yet their salaries were the lowest. The definition of essential workers rebuts the Davis-Moore hypothesis, as necessary labour is often not ascribed occupational prestige nor better compensation.

Functionalist understandings of social stratification presume that those with the appropriate capabilities and motivations will be able to access the education to pursue their desired occupation, ignoring the impacts of gender, race, and class on educational and employment opportunities, including the forms of racialized streaming in schools. The social stratification of occupational prestige is also not collectively agreed upon, nor does it consider other motivations people have for pursuing certain jobs: an inclination to provide service, do good, carry on family traditions, and so on.

In the beginning, not all work in Upper Canada was freely offered or compensated. Slavery was legal and practised in Upper Canada until 1793. Peter Russell, a member of the legislative council of Upper Canada in the 1790s, hired a free man, Mr. Pompadour, but Mr. Pompadour's wife (Peggy) and children (Jupiter, Amy, and Milly) worked as enslaved people for Russell. Russell had Peggy jailed for disappearing, and he tried to split up the family. Russell fought against Lieutenant Governor Simcoe's efforts to abolish slavery in Upper Canada (Bunch 2013). While he lived in the town of York (now Toronto), the Ottawa Valley town of Russell is named after him. In the summer of 2020 the town decided to not change its name, but change its namesake to "all Russells that have had a positive impact" on the community in an attempt to distance themselves from the slavery-endorsing Peter Russell (Frizzell 2022).

Like Canada, Ottawa has been enriched by the trans-Atlantic slave trade. The main contracting firm that built the Rideau Canal was the team of Thomas McKay and John Redpath, McKay is best known today as the stonemason who built McKay's castle (now Rideau Hall) as his home; streets in New Edinburgh bear the names of his children: John, Charles, and Thomas. John Redpath, a Scot who emigrated to Quebec during the Lowland Clearances, became a stonemason in Montreal and worked on the Lachine Canal before partnering with McKay to work on the Rideau. It was later, in the 1850s, that Redpath made his fortunes in the sugar trade. Redpath was an abolitionist; however, his successes benefited the industries that were reliant on slave labour in that period. Cod exported from Canada fed enslaved people in the American South and was exchanged for commodities (salt, sugar, tobacco) and enslaved people: "The exchange of goods for slave workers and slave-produced commodities became one of the several ways in which John Redpath profited from slavery and its legacies" (Zhang 2013, 28). The Rideau-Goulbourn ward (until its 2022 renaming as the Rideau-Jock ward) and Goulbourn Street in Sandy Hill were named after Henry Goulbourn, an undersecretary of Lord Bathurst who never came to Canada and whose personal wealth came from having inherited slave-holding plantations in Jamaica (Vance 2012).

AGRICULTURAL DREAMS

Work in Canada has shifted in economic dominance from primary-sector to tertiary-sector labour (Sugiman 2012), and this pattern held true in Ottawa. From the eighteenth to early twentieth centuries, resource extraction was the largest economic driver and source of employment in Ottawa — Bytown was born through the extraction of trees. The region also employed people in a small mica mining industry in the nineteenth and early twentieth centuries in Lanark county and at Pink Lake in Gatineau Park (CapitalGems.ca 2013).

Many Americans, Brits, and French Canadians arrived to the region in the early nineteenth century envisioning bountiful fields for productive agriculture. That was certainly true of Philemon Wright. It was also true of aspirational aristocrat Hamnett Pinhey, who ambitiously settled a farming estate, "Horaceville" (named after his eldest son), on the banks of the Ottawa River in March Township in 1820. While Wright soon realized that lumber would be a much more profitable bet, Pinhey's farming plans were also quickly dashed and he pursued a government post instead. Braddish Billings, who established a farm south of the Rideau River, however, had agricultural success. Due to Ottawa's geography (including a high quantity of Leda clay and the Precambrian rock of the Canadian Shield), Ottawa and its valley are not ideal land for cash crop farming. However, to stock up for a winter in the bush, a mid-sized timber producer would buy: "825 barrels of pork, 900 barrels of flour, 525 bushels of beans, 3650 gallons of syrup, 37,000 bushels of oats,

7500 pounds of tea, 1875 pounds of soap, 6000 pounds of tobacco, 300 tons of hay" (Lee 2006, 64). Regional farmers had a steady supply of customers.

When Ottawa became the nation's capital, the city's stake in agricultural production became partially oriented toward nation building. In 1886, the federal government established the Central Experimental Farm west of the city. Minister of agriculture John Carling hired William Saunders to be the farm's first director. The farm's greatest contribution to agriculture was the development of Marquis wheat in 1907 by Dr. Charles Saunders (son of William Saunders) at the experimental farm. This frost-resistant wheat proved to have excellent yields, supported Canada during World War I, and by the 1920s, 90 percent of the spring wheat grown in Western Canada was this variety (Hinchcliff and Popadiouk 2007, 63). Today, visitors to the Canada Agriculture and Food Museum can explore Barn 76 (renamed the "Cereal Barn"), where Marquis wheat was developed.

Today there are 1,200 "agricultural operations" within the city; in fact, 40 percent of land within city boundaries is farmland. Since the 2001 amalgamation, the city has supported four agricultural fairs each fall (Metcalfe, Richmond, Carp, Navan). The National Capital Commission (NCC) has long-term leases with farmers for 5,400 hectares of farmland within the city. The nineteenth century had much more blurring of rural and urban than today. Pigs roamed Wellington Street, and city residents' milk needs were satisfied by urban cows (Elliott 1991, 45). When Eastview became incorporated as a city in 1909, one of the most onerous city jobs was that of city poundkeeper. This employee was responsible for all of the stray "horses, colts and fillies, bulls, cows or any other horned cattle, pigs, sheep, dogs" (bylaw quoted in Shea 1965, 4) in the city. Today, barnyard chickens are prohibited in Ottawa; the closest Ottawans can come to livestock in the city is the full dairy herd, goats, pigs, donkeys, beef cattle, and draught horses at the Canada Agriculture and Food Museum.

Rural Ottawa was transformed dramatically in 1958 when the NCC began creating a greenbelt. The government paid $900 an acre for farms inside the proposed greenbelt. Acres were selling for $2,000–3,000 outside of the Greenbelt. Understandably, government expropriation of hundreds of farms was not met warmly by many farmers. In 1961, the government engaged in a "blanket annexation" and for a period, the fields lay fallow and their buildings were left abandoned. By 1963, 192 of the 238 annexed farms had been leased (some to the previous owners), 43 farm houses were slated to be demolished, 363 houses were rented, and 10,000 acres were slated for reforestation (Elliott

1991, 265). Some farmers went from being owners to renters, others left and bought land elsewhere, and others moved into the city. While those farms were expropriated, the result, eventually, was reforested land.

Many of the farms that remain largely align with what food scholars Alison Hope Alkon and Christie Grace McCullen call the "white farm imaginary." This concept suggests that agriculture is imagined to be the work of smaller farms owned by white families, sustained through intergenerational career inheritance, and that these farmers then transport their products directly to their urban consumers at quaint markets. It is the imagery associated with red-barn rural tourism, the rural nostalgia that populates children's books and toys (Alkon and McCullen 2011) and the paper mâché sculpture "McClintock's Dream" in the ByWard Market building, and is sustained by prominent and cherished family farms embodying this imaginary and offering up their workplaces as sites of agritourism. Stanley's maple sugar bush in Edwards, a site with its own mascot (Stanley the Bear), has a sugar shack that still uses 1830s technology. Ferme Proulx in Cumberland similarly boasts a centuries-old production shack as one of its attractions.

Alkon and McCullen argue that on the one hand, thinking about who produces our food de-fetishizes food, connecting our understanding of food to land and labour. However, when we imagine food as being produced by small-scale, family-owned farms, food is re-fetishized, as we cherish agritourist destinations — yet the large agribusinesses and racialized seasonal agricultural labour that produce the majority of the food Canadians eat, and the land dispossession underpinning food production, are obscured (Alkon and McCullen 2011).

Other agricultural dreams are on display at private residential plots in Little Italy and Overbrook, and in the over one hundred and fifteen community gardens across the city — like Nanny Goat Hill downtown and Jo-Jos in Stittsville — where generations of people have dug into little slivers of soil to grow tomatoes, lettuce, onions, potatoes. In the 1930s, gardening was part of ensuring food security. In Eastview, men were paid in vegetables for working other people's gardens, and the mayor, Donat Grandmaitre, encouraged people to grow their own food (Shea 1965). Jim Burton recalls moving from downtown to Overbrook in 1933 because the noise, dust, and industry near their Kent Street home was making his mother ill. On their visit to a potential new Overbrook home, he writes, "my mother noticed the sidewalks and the many front gardens, some large and well-cultivated" (Burton 2022, 8). While small gardens may not be the answer to food insecurity today, they offer the tonic of doing physical, outdoor labour and, in the case of community gardens, of being with nature in community.

More common than these micro-moves towards food production are the hints of agricultural pasts now lying beneath suburban development. Anthony Tunney used to have a pasture where there is now the sprawling government office complex known as Tunney's Pasture; in the Findlay Creek neighbourhood there was, until recently, a farm owned by the Kelly family, now remembered by Kelly Farm Drive. The Place d'Orléans mall was Jean-Baptiste Dufort's farm until 1957, and the Vinette corn silo (circa 1942) stands on its own amid a development of Phoenix homes in Orléans (SFOPHO 2017). The Ontario Federation of Agriculture estimates that Ontario loses 175 acres of farmland a day to urban development (Butler 2021). This is one of the points made by the Coalition Against the Proposed Prison protesting the building of a new prison on farmland in Kemptville.

Despite the significant amount of agricultural land in and around Ottawa, this primary sector employs a minority of Ottawans. Ottawans are fed by a global food system that is, in part, orchestrated, regulated, and encouraged by politicians and bureaucrats who work in Ottawa. While the Central Experimental Farm continues to be a site for developing drought-resistant seeds and different tillage practices, Ottawa arguably impacts Canadian agriculture more profoundly through the policies developed by bureaucrats in Agriculture and Agri-Foods Canada on Carling Avenue, in the offices of Export Development Canada on Slater Street, and in Natural Resources Canada on Booth Street. Many of their policies limit small-scale farming, promote monoculture and industrial agriculture, and reign in possibilities for more sustainable agriculture.

One fall weekend in 2023, I took my two-year-old friend Teddy to Metcalfe Fair to see the sights, watch a cattle show, and admire the monstrously large pumpkins. It typified the fall fairs of my youth. The Lion's Club was there serving beef on a bun, firefighters helped Teddy climb into the firetruck on display. From one perspective, fall fairs embody the promise of a functioning rural society; the amusements are both mass produced (the corporate carnival rides) and expressions of folk culture (the baking, quilting, dancing, fiddling, and other competitions and displays). This fair brought enduring rural traditions into the future — for good (cohesive rural community, joy, intergenerational play) and for naught (the agricultural practices on display are often not environmentally sustainable). The next day, I met my three-year-old friend Isla and her parents at Just Food, the community farm on leased

NCC land in Blackburn Hamlet. We went on a wagon ride tour of a property being put to a variety of uses: there was a group of beekeepers, Gloucester Emergency Food Cupboard's Plant-a-Row Share-a-Row garden plot, the plot for KLEO: Karen Community Farm, which is farmed by Karen refugees from northern Thailand. Nine acres of the community farm are cared for by the Wabano Centre to enable movements toward Indigenous food sovereignty and giving land back. Here we were offered a vision of more sustainable and socially equitable forms of agricultural production for the future.

BUILDING A UNION TOWN

At the Billings Estate National Historic Site, Ottawa's oldest house (built 1827–1829) tells the story of five generations of Billings who lived on the estate and worked in all manner of occupations: farming but also teaching, law, architecture, politics, paleontology, etymology, piloting. One of the earliest occupations of the Billings family, done by matriarch Lamira and her daughters Sabra and Sally, was manufacturing cheese and butter. Five wooden butter molds with floral designs are on display in the museum. The exhibit informs us that this manufacturing business of the Billings women peaked in 1850, the year they produced fifteen thousand pounds of cheese and five hundred pounds of butter. Another example of artisanal manufacturing is on display in Tin House Court, between Murray and Clarence Streets. The façade of a house, crafted entirely in tin, advertised — from the early 1900s until the house was torn down in the 1960s — that the creator and homeowner, Honoré Foisy, was a tinsmith. The façade now is affixed to a contemporary commercial building, nodding to this artisanal past in the contemporary market courtyard.

Manufacturing, the secondary sector of the economy, has always had a minor presence in Ottawa, which transitioned from a primary to a tertiary economy quite rapidly when Bytown was renamed Ottawa in 1855 and became the capital of Canada and the site of the civil service in 1857. Manufacturing industries in Ottawa spurred by the lumber industry included the production of pulp and paper products, matchmaking, cabinet-building and axe factories; however, these industries were relatively small. The lack of large-scale manufacturing in Ottawa has meant that it has largely been resistant to processes of deindustrialization that have hit other Canadian cities. However, early manufacturing industries in Ottawa successfully contributed to establishing the city's labour movement.

As the city's second large public infrastructure employment boom (after the construction of the Rideau Canal), constructing the Parliament buildings required work in local quarries, lumberyards, brickyards, and Hull cement works. In total, a thousand workers were involved in the process. There was inadequate scaffolding, long hours, frequent accidents, and one worker death. In 1860, Parliament Hill construction workers went on strike for higher pay and were successful, gaining a raise of between 60 and 80 cents a day (Clavette 2001, 151). At the time, not only did labour unions not exist, they were illegal — the Master and Servants Act mandated that workers could not leave their worksites without their employer's permission, and employers could jail disobedient or absentee workers.

The Parliament Hill stonecutters led the way for union organizing in Ottawa. Historian Doris French explains that by recruiting European stonecutters to the capital they "imported a solid core of old-country artisans who were already solidly versed in the gospel of organized labour. Ottawa, during the period in which the Parliament buildings were under construction, was one of the strongest union towns in Canada, with the British workmen seeking allies among other skilled craftsmen in town" (quoted in Clavette 2001, 153). Risking imprisonment, the stonecutters unionized and staged a walkout in 1864. Two years later, typesetters unionized, forming the Ottawa Typographical Union No. 102. In part to stoke antagonisms with his staunchly anti-union adversary George Brown, John A. Macdonald led his government in passing the Trade Union Act, legalizing unions in 1872. Painters, bricklayers, and cabinetmakers all organized. In 1873, workers created the Ottawa Trades Council and contributed to the formation of the Canadian Labour Union. After the premier of Ontario cancelled the property ownership criteria for running for political office, the president of the Ottawa Typological Union, Daniel O'Donoghue, ran and won a seat in Ontario's Legislative Assembly (Clavette 2001).

Ezra Butler Eddy and his wife, Zaida, arrived in Wright's Town from Vermont in 1854. The Eddys rented a shack from Ruggles Wright and began handcrafting matches. They hired local women to join them, expanded their company, and began producing wooden buckets and washboards (Vincent-Domey 1994). At one point, the E.B. Eddy company produced 90 percent of the matches used by Canadians. By 1911, 781 of the 1,288 match workers at E.B. Eddy were women (McCallum and McLean 2016, 69). In patriarchal societies, gendered occupational segregation means that work done by women is devalued and paid less. This is not the reflection of the difficulty or the necessity of the work, but rather the gender of those employed in the profession. This was true of matchmaking: "As late as 1920, the match workers were earning an hourly rate rather than a piece rate: between $0.10 and $0.15. But it was far less than what most factory work paid, and far less than what men made in similar jobs. Wages were so low that the standard diet for the working poor consisted of bread and fat" (McCallum 2015). Matchmaking was very dangerous work. Workers kept a pail of water within reach because of the frequent fires. The use of white phosphorous in the production of matches led to a brutal, disfiguring condition known as "phossy jaw," a condition of multiple mouth abscesses. In 1911, as minister of labour, Mackenzie King outlawed the use of phosphorus in manufacturing (McCallum 2015).

The female workers (referred to as the *allumettières*) organized as the Syndicat Catholique des Allumettières de Hull and led strikes in 1919 and 1924. In 1924, under new management, one of the new owners was future prime minister Richard Bennett. The women struck because the company cut their wages by 50 percent, claiming that it did not need to abide by the labour conditions agreed upon in 1919. The company also wanted to remove female supervisors from the hiring process. After three weeks of striking, led by president of the Union ouvrières féminine de Hull, Donalda Charron, and bolstered by a supportive community that boycotted the Eddy company, the company negotiated individual deals with workers, hours and wages were restored to pre-strike levels, but the women lost the right to have a say in hiring and firing, and Charron was fired (Powell 2024).

Manufacturing began to decline nationally in the 1950s after peaking at 40 percent of the workforce (Ravelli and Webber 2010, 422). By 1971 only 8 percent of employed men and 4 percent of employed women worked in manufacturing in Ottawa (Taylor 1986, 174); this fell to only 3.4 percent of the Ottawa workforce for both genders in 2018 (City of Ottawa, Strategic Initiatives 2024). Histories of Ottawa refer to axe factories, bakeries, cloth factories. At 7 Hinton, the large white building was a wire cloth factory from 1902 until its closure in 1974. For a time, that building was also the home of Hinton Animation Studios, the company that brought 1980s Canadian children the cartoon *The Racoons* (Leaning 2003). Ottawa's current manufacturing is largely in construction and small-scale manufacturing like microbreweries. Across the city there are compelling adaptive reuses of former manufacturing sites. The Science and Technology Museum is a former bread factory; so is the Enriched Bread Artists co-operative studio space at City Centre, and the Woods Manufacturing Company (a sleeping bag company) factory at 66 Queen Street has been an office building for decades.

The tertiary (service) sector refers to a wide range of work, including tourism, education, computer technologies, child care, health care, and the civil service. In 2022, 79.3 percent of Canadians worked in the tertiary sector (Statistics Canada 2024c). Most Ottawans work in this sector, as well; in 2018, 22 percent of the Ottawa workforce worked in health and education, 19 percent in public administration, 15 percent in other services, 11 percent in professional, science and technology services, 5 percent in finance, and 3 percent in the arts, for a combined total of 75 percent of the city's workforce (Statistics Canada 2018b). The largest number of Ottawa service industry workers (145,000 people) work for the civil service (Fagan 2017); they are the focus of the next chapter.

THE FUTURE OF WORK

Exploiting the rich forests and engaging in agricultural production allowed the earliest settlers to extract many resources from the Ottawa Valley. Manufacturing set the stage for significant labour organizing, with first the stonecutters, then the typesetters and the "matchstick girls."

What does the future of work look like in Ottawa? There are many disparaging memes about Gen Z at work. The criticisms suggest that young people today are fickle and have outsized expectations. Some assume that in order to attract and retain young workers, employers must install espresso bars, on-site gyms, and team-building axe-throwing days. Ottawa's Shopify headquarters on Elgin Street (from 2015 to 2020) was outfitted with Go-Kart tracks, hammocks, graffiti art, a gourmet cafeteria, and a room called the "Bear Forest" with Muskoka chairs and bear-shaped beanbag chairs. However, sociologist James Cairns argues that millennials (and we could extend his analysis to Gen Z) are in fact quite disentitled when it comes to work, have the lowest rates of unionization of any generation, are compelled to do unpaid internships at higher rates, and must have extensive and expensive education in order to find entry-level jobs (Cairns 2017).

Young workers in Ottawa also find themselves disproportionately represented in precarious work, marked by low wages, lack of regulatory protections and job security, and lack of control over the labour process (Rodgers and Rodgers 1989). Low-wage, precarious workers include those in fast food and at Amazon warehouses, university professors with semester-to-semester contracts, and gig-to-gig arts workers. Sex workers, who are denied virtually any workplace protections, also fit this category, as do Uber drivers. Recently, the taxi drivers of Ottawa won a lawsuit against the city. The Ontario Supreme Court found the City of Ottawa negligent in the enforcement of its own taxi operating bylaw, severely impacting the livelihoods of Ottawa taxi drivers when it allowed Uber to begin operating in the city in 2014 (Raymond 2024). Organizing for improved labour conditions continues.

While Ottawa is imagined as a one-shop town, workers feature in all of the chapters in this book. Social structures produced the conditions in which people initially arrived in Ottawa to work — the immigration policies detailed in the first chapter, global structures of enslavement — and these created conditions for farming, lumbering, and large-scale infrastructure projects. Collective action — of abolitionists, labour unions, feminists — has since transformed how work is structured.

There's another team at my pub trivia league called "The Uncivil Servants"; it is their work to which I now turn.

Chapter 5

THE CIVIL SERVICE

"Here he comes now, trying to act like a normal human being," a narrator begins as a man skates on the Rideau Canal, briefcase in hand, a Viennese waltz playing as the soundtrack. The narrator continues, "but he is that most despised of human creatures. His activities have brought down upon his shoulders the scorn and outrage of history's multitudes. He is *homo bureaucratus*, the bureaucrat, and he lives in the land of paper" (National Film Board of Canada 1979). This is the opening scene of the 1979 NFB-CBC mockumentary *Paperland*. At Confederation, 2,660 civil servants ran the young country and only 354 of these workers were in Ottawa (Granatstein 1998, 19). Between 1900 and 1918, the population of civil service workers grew from 1,219 to 3,219 (Taylor 1986, 120). It grew again during and after World War II, from 12,000 employees in 1939 to 36,000 by 1945 (Bellamy 2001, 447). The civil service has fundamentally shaped the world of work in Ottawa, impacting the city's transit systems, schooling, and union density. *Homo bureaucratis* are omnipresent, but somehow little remarked upon. In a national capital region with well over one hundred monuments, there are only two to civil servants. Henry Albert Harper, William Lyon Mackenzie King's roommate, was a civil servant who drowned tragically during a skating party on the Ottawa River and is commemorated in the Sir Galahad monument at the gates of Parliament Hill. There is also a monument of Sir Arthur Doughty, Canada's second Dominion archivist, located by the Gatineau Preservation Centre of the LAC.

Sociologists have done a good job of making sense of the machinations of the civil service in the processes of approving immigration files and refugee claims (Satzewich 2015; Masoumi 2023), as well as the creation and uses of the census by Statistics Canada (Curtis 2019), yet few sociologists have asked broad questions about the functioning of the large infrastructure that is the Government of Canada. A sociologist might begin by asking: How do large and small decisions get made in different policymaking contexts? How does the civil service use consultants or engage with the corporate world? How do government departments maintain and access federal archives and libraries? But my evergreen question for every bureaucrat I meet is: after you've made your coffee and sat down, what do you do at work? This dearth of sociological research on the civil service is even stranger when you consider that a key public service job is the policy analyst, and one of the most requested academic backgrounds for entry-level policy analyst jobs is sociology. There are sociologists everywhere in the civil service. It's a bit of a cobbler with bad shoes situation.

For many, the civil service manages a large, and generally functional, society. Not knowing how it runs means that it's likely running pretty smoothly. If you are housed, employed, have safe transit, eat safe food, drink clean water, and live in a country safe from foreign invaders, it likely doesn't seem necessary to worry about how this comes to pass through the belly of the complex bureaucratic beast. Yet for others, the opacity of the civil service is by design. German sociologist Max Weber (2009, 78) defines the state as a "a human community that (successfully) claims the monopoly of the legitimate use of physical force within a given territory." A state is an organization of people that manages control over a geography (often a nation), but it can only maintain this power because people adhere to the idea that this human community manages mechanisms of violence (the army, police), who, as part of their role, can justifiably inflict violence on others. The opacity of the civil service facilitates its role — to maintain structures of domination — going uncritiqued. Drawing on Canadian sociologist John Porter and Max Weber, I offer alternate analyses of the civil service as good and, drawing on Marxist critiques, as an arm of the settler colonial capitalist state.

CIVIL SERVICE: HERE FOR THE COLLECTIVE GOOD

John Porter, in his seminal 1965 book *The Vertical Mosaic*, largely understood as the first comprehensive sociological study of Canadian society, detailed the ways in which Canadian society was hierarchically structured. Porter was the first sociologist at a new university built in town to serve a broader range of students: Carleton University. After writing the book, Porter spent the rest of his career working on projects like developing the Pineo-Porter index (a measure of socioeconomic status) from his office on the seventh floor of Carleton's Loeb building. For Porter the role of the civil service is to stabilize the government, manage military and international obligations, and to administer "the piecemeal welfare programme which has grown up over time because of electoral commitments and through federal-provincial co-operation" (Porter 2018, 417).

In his focus on the bureaucratic elite, Porter draws heavily on Weber. Weber was a child when German states were unifying under Otto von Bismarck to create a modern and highly militarized nation-state that relied on a growing bureaucratic infrastructure. The Prussian army was the first to train and equip officers in consistent ways. In his analysis of the growing military bureaucracy in his own country, Weber identified six key characteristics of modern bureaucracies: (1) fixed duties are assigned to officials; (2) there are hierarchies, and roles and powers are limited to defined realms of authority; (3) there are written rules dictating procedures, policies, and authority; (4) officials are appointed based on qualifications; (5) public and private lives are separated; and (6) the application of rules is standardized across situations (Pampel 2007, 111). Weber noted that bureaucratic rule allowed the nation-state to be effectively, efficiently, and consistently managed by qualified people. Drawing on his study, Weber argued that the most effective public service is rational, open, and *unrivalled*. Porter, in contrast, argues that the best civil service is rational, open, and *rivalled*.

Rational

A rational civil service is premised on people filling roles for which they are suited. Prime Minister Borden was instrumental in creating a rational civil service when in 1918 he passed the Civil Service Act, which required hiring through a system of competitive examinations for strictly classified jobs. By 1919, there were 1,729 classes of civil service employees across thirty-four "occupational services" (Granatstein 1998, 24). While Great Britain began reforming civil service employment in the 1850s, patronage lasted longer in Canada. In 1936, only slightly more than 50 percent of civil servant jobs were "filled through the Civil Service Commission" (Porter 2018, 418).

In Weber's rational bureaucracy, the civil servant "has no ownership rights to the things with which he works; he is subject to discipline for breaches of rules; these rules bind his actions; and his authority is limited to the defined sphere of his office" (Porter 2018, 419). This leads to some of the most vexing aspects of the civil service — like when asking for service one is routinely shuffled up, or to another department all together; officers seem to have little agency to troubleshoot problems. Translated into unaccountability, this lack of ownership can be experienced (by both civil servants and the public) as callousness (I didn't refuse to fund the life-saving surgery, it was the system!) but also as inefficiency. In *Paperland*, senior bureaucrats explain how absurdities of the civil service can be lost in the morass of the committee. A good hack, a senior executive describes, is to propose new policies or programs, get things started, and then move on to another department. The success of the new program is no longer that civil servant's success or failure to bear. Another interviewee points to the ubiquitous use of passive voice; instead of taking ownership of ideas, positions, or making declarative statements, in committee couch statements in phrases like "it might be argued that the minister consider...."

The cubicle as an architectural form underscores the notion of bureaucrats as interchangeable workers. Gréber advocated for decentralizing government buildings in his 1950 plan for the city. The result was the proliferation of government office complexes across the city — in the west end at Tunney's Pasture, in south Ottawa at Confederation Heights. The entire downtown of Hull was expropriated to build the Place du Portage and the Terrasses de la Chaudière office complexes that were opened in the 1970s.

The final scene of *Paperland* shows the offices of Statistics Canada on January 22, 1979, the day when middle managers determined that the employees were to adapt to open-concept office space; women are shown creating barriers with house plants, men assemble folding screens, an employee details on a master map how different workers will be able to see each other, thus contributing, ostensibly, to productivity. Bureaucrats' workspaces have become even more depersonalized since the pandemic. Now workers book office space on the fully rationalized desk-booking platform Archibus and are instructed to leave no traces of their humanity (family pics, mugs), behind.

Bureaucrats are unfairly understood to be part of the reason for why Ottawa is "the town that fun forgot." Or, to put this in Weberian terms, too much rationality deadens human creativity and becomes an "iron cage" (Pampel 2007, 110). Yet imagining civil servants as neither "fun" nor creative is unfair. In fact, stable, unionized employment creates a workforce with time and energy to engage in creative pursuits. Deputy superintendent of Indian Affairs Duncan Campbell Scott, clerk for the Post Office Department Archibald Lampman, and civil servant in the Department of Militia and Defence William Wilfrid Campbell were all highly acclaimed Confederation-era poets. In the 1940s civil servants were at the heart of Ottawa's Shakespeare Club and Dance Club (Granatstein 1998, 13). In 2017, filmmaker Amen Jafri produced a video series, "The Secret Lives of Public Servants," that featured National Gallery security officer Richard Wong, who cosplays around town as a superhero in his down time; Janet Hetherington, a speech writer who doubles as a comic book creator; and Marc Adornato, a civil servant by day who sculpts and bricolages radical art as sociopolitical commentary by night.

Open

For Weber and Porter, in a functional civil service authority is obtained through having the requisite skills. A bureaucracy is "open" if there is a clear means to achieve expertise (i.e., equitable access to the education and training needed for civil service jobs) and accessible means through which to be hired; "ethnic bars, religious tests, and recruiting systems based on class privileges would be irrationalities" (Porter 2018, 425).

In 1911, a civil service exam promised both rationality and openness. Yet, anti-Black racism within the civil service was brought to Prime Minister Laurier's attention when a Conservative MP asked Laurier to respond to a story of a Black man who "was the head of the examination list for the Census department, instead of being put in that position was given an inferior position by the Minister of Agriculture, looking after the black Minorca hens on the (government) farm" (Foster 2019, 104). Decades later, in the 1940s, all applicants for jobs in the civil service were still asked a question on the application form about their skin colour. Alistair Stewart, Co-operative Commonwealth Federation MP from Winnipeg, spoke out against this application process in the House of Commons in 1947, to which the minister of state, Colin Gibson, replied that this question was "to enable the commissioners, when an application is received from a member of the negro race, to place the applicant in a position which will be congenial" (quoted in Foster 2019, 114). For sociologist Cecil Foster, the idea of most "congenial" positions within the civil service for Black people reflected racial occupational segregation that had, for most of the twentieth century, limited Black men in Canada to jobs as railway porters and belied the promise of openness in the civil service. Unfortunately, racialized occupational segregation persists. A study in 2020 found that, of the 6,200 civil servants that self-identified as Black, 15 percent had experienced discrimination at work in the past twelve months, compared to 11 percent of non-Black visible minorities and 8 percent of workers. Seventy-five percent of the Black employees in this study reported that the discrimination they experienced was racial (Evelyn 2020).

The civil service elite from the 1930s to 1950s were all men — except for Mrs. Phyllis Turner, a chief of the Oil and Fats Administration in the Wartime Prices and Trade Board — and exclusively English; there were few Catholics, only one Jewish high-ranking civil servant. Despite the gender, religious, and racial homogeneity of the bureaucratic elite of this era, Granatstein erroneously concludes that "it was a meritocratic elite. If a dirt-poor boy from a Saskatchewan farm or a Winnipeg tenement could make it to university and do well, he was entitled to — and received — the same consideration for admittance to the civil service as the son of a professor or a mining-company president" (Granatstein 1998).

Then and now, the "bureaucracy can level social classes only when training is not a class privilege" (Porter 2018, 420) — only if everyone interested has an opportunity to acquire the education necessary for the position. In the early twentieth century, the school–to–civil service pipeline travelled from a small number of elite Canadian universities to the Langevin Block. Senior bureaucrats O.D. Skelton, Clifford Clark, and W.A. Mackintosh came from Queen's University, others came from University of Toronto and McGill University.

Since its inception in 1942, Carleton University has been expanding the school–to–civil service pipeline. In the early 1940s Ottawa's only institutions of higher learning were the University of Ottawa and St. Patrick's College (which would eventually become absorbed by Carleton University), both Catholic institutions. In the early 1940s many in Ottawa, including members of the local YMCA and academic Henry Marshall Tory, thought that young people in Ottawa, in the absence of manufacturing jobs, needed higher secular education to access the good government or government-adjacent jobs in the city. Carleton College began as a non-denominational junior college offering first- and second-year courses out of existing high schools (Neatby and McEown 2002), welcoming students from more diverse backgrounds.

Some of the key civil servants of the early twentieth century retired from the public service and redirected their energies toward Carleton University. Lester B. "Mike" Pearson, a University of Toronto and Oxford University graduate, became a civil servant in the Department of External Affairs in 1928 and had a varied and successful career as a diplomat. In 1948, Pearson left the public service and entered politics. As secretary of state for external affairs, Pearson was awarded the Nobel Peace Prize in 1957 for his role in the resolution of the Suez Canal crisis by suggesting a UN peacekeeping force. Bureaucrats working at Global Affairs today walk past Pearson's encased medal as they head to their offices in the Lester B. Pearson building on Sussex Drive. Pearson served as prime minister from 1963 to 1968, during which the federal government established the Canada Pension Plan and universal health care and inaugurated the new maple leaf flag, among other things (Bothwell 2011). From 1969 to 1972, Pearson was the chancellor of Carleton University, teaching courses in history and political science. Pearson's name is most often invoked when graduate students and faculty at Carleton suggest a meet-up at the graduate student pub "Mike's Place," named for Pearson's moniker. It is fitting that Pearson, who worked to expand broad access to social goods, is associated with Carleton, which has expanded access to postsecondary education broadly and to the school–to–civil service pipeline more specifically. The Norman Paterson School of International Affairs has been sending future diplomats and bureaucrats directly to the Lester B. Pearson building since the 1960s. Carleton's history program routinely supplies employees for the city's museums and Heritage Canada, and Carleton-trained sociologists, economists, and political scientists are omnipresent throughout the federal government.

The openness of the bureaucracy has also expanded because of the work of civil servant unions. In 2023 public-sector unionization was 76.7 percent; in the private sector it was 15.5 percent (Statistics Canada 2024d). Between 1968 and 1969 a twelve-storey building, solid in its red brick but suggesting some openness with its endless rows of windows and curved exterior, was built at 233 Gilmour Street to house the country's third-largest union, the Public Service Alliance of Canada (PSAC). A guide to heritage buildings describes the building poetically: "its pleasing curves express the perfect public servant … confident but not aggressive" (Palmer 2000, 172). Founded in 1966, PSAC now represents 240,000 workers. PSAC is not the only civil servant union in town, though; CAPE: Canadian Association of Professional Employees, created in 2003, represents 25,000 workers who work in economics and social science services, translation, the Library of Parliament, the Office of the Parliamentary Budget Officer, and as civilians in the RCMP. The Professional Institute of the Public Service of Canada (PIPSC), founded in 1920, represents over seventy thousand employees in the core public service and across a number of Crown corporations. The civil service gives Ottawa as a city a higher-than-average union density and a higher-than-average number of workers benefiting from the "union advantage" — benefits experienced by unionized workers, including workplace protections, benefits, and significantly, better wages, to the tune of, on average $3–6 dollars more an hour (Sugiman 2012, 374). The unionized civil service has also shaped how gender and sexuality impact labour in Ottawa.

In the early 1900s, 11 percent of working women in Ottawa worked in the civil service. Yet the deputy superintendent of Indian Affairs, Frank Pedley, suggested that women were minimally effective in the civil service, stating: "When girls enter first … they are inspired with the idea either of getting married or of something happening that they can get out of the service. They do not usually take the same interest in their duties that a man does who feels that it is his life's work and he is going to remain at it" (quoted in Taylor 1986, 120). In the 1950s, societal pressure encouraged women to retreat to the growing auto-burbs and take up the feminized, unpaid, and undervalued labour of childrearing and homemaking. Historian Patrizia Gentile explains that furthermore, in the Cold War period, the "notion of national security was linked to the idea that a strong nation is based on family, in which young men grow up to be responsible, virile citizens and young women become dutiful and submissive wives" (Gentile 2000, 132). From 1950 to 1973, beauty pageants resulted in the annual crowning of a "Miss Civil Service" by the civil service Recreation Association. "Miss Civil Service" was meant to embody the preferred qualities of a "government girl," which Gentile says was "preferably single with no children, heterosexual, well-groomed, tall, thin, and 'beautiful' with shiny hair" (Gentile 2000, 135).

While the "government girl" was celebrated for her femininity and labour, in a *Maclean's* article from this era, Alan Philips suggests that civil service work for young women was being sought for "adventure" and "independence," and single young employed women would likely drink, have sex and (gallingly!) buy things on credit (Gentile 2000, 134). Many young women that came to work in Ottawa postwar lived at Laurentian Terrace, a purpose-built residence for civil servants from which they could, absolutely, live out adventurous, independent lives.

The rational bureaucratic structure of the government — premised, at least theoretically, on merit rather than career inheritance, patriarchal prerogatives, or nepotism — and the high rate of unionization within government created a workplace where women have successfully challenged dominant gender norms. In the early to mid-twentieth century, women's jobs were not protected when women got pregnant, and no accommodations were made for maternity leave. The first job protection for women having children was British Columbia's 1921 "Maternity Protection Act," which allowed women to leave their jobs slightly before and after giving birth and made it illegal for employers to fire women for taking this (unpaid) leave, or for employers to hire women in the six weeks after they'd given birth. The 1967 Royal Commission on the Status of Women put pressure on the federal government to offer paid maternity leave for women. In 1968, and again in 1970, NDP MP Grace MacInnis put forward private members' bills to provide maternity leave to all Canadians. By 1971, unemployment insurance had expanded to fifteen weeks' coverage for women who'd had a baby, but at only a small percentage of the women's pay (Workers' History Museum 2018a).

On September 20, 1980, ten thousand members of the Clerical and Regulatory (CR) workers of PSAC walked off the job nine days before they were in a legal position to strike. Women made up 76 percent of the workers in the CR unit, 57 percent were under age thirty-five, with an annual salary of $12,815 (or $38,000 in 2018 dollars). The CR workers struck for increased wages and two weeks of additional maternity leave to supplement what was offered by unemployment insurance. At the time, PSAC was seen as "one of the country's least militant unions" (*National Post,* in Worker's History Museum 2018); clerks had never before led a strike. Within a few weeks, solidarity strikes popped up, and on October 2, twenty-thousand PSAC members marched through downtown Ottawa. The strike led to a better deal for CR members, a 24.8 percent salary increase, and a two-week maternity leave top-up. The next year, the Canadian Union of Postal Workers (CUPW) went on strike, and part of those workers' demands were also maternity leave accommodations. The win by the women of CR, PSAC was a mobilizing moment for the women of that union and contributed to larger-scale movements to improve maternity leave.

The experience of gay men and women working in the civil service reflects the limitations on the openness of the civil service *and* the current benefits of a highly unionized workplace. While women were tentatively and conditionally invited to work in the civil service until they married, gay men and women in the decades of the Cold War were actively put under surveillance, interrogated, and fired for being gay. People accused of "homosexuality" were imagined to be weak of character, vulnerable to bribes — and therefore threats to national security — and unfit for certain civil service jobs. The RCMP was tasked with identifying gay men and women in civil service jobs; they created a map of gay hotspots in the city, spied on and interrogated people and their friends, and by the end of the 1960s, "the RCMP had collected over 9000 files on presumed homosexuals, mostly living in the Ottawa area" (Lewis 2012, 296). In 2018, I went to the NGC to watch the screening of a TVO documentary, *The Fruit Machine.* It details the many ways in which members of the military and the civil service were followed, questioned, asked to "out" their associates, and fired from their jobs. The film's name was the moniker given to the interrogation device used by the RCMP. The "fruit machine," officially called the Electropsychometer, was developed by Carleton psychologist Robert Wake and measured peoples' pupils, the sweatiness of their palms, and their heart rates while being exposed to different pornographic images. It had virtually no scientific reliability and the project was abandoned in 1967 (Kinsman 1995, 158). At the end of the screening of the film, gay purge survivors were asked to stand up. Dozens of gay former civil servants stood up and received a tear-filled standing ovation by the audience.

Today the civil service is a relatively attractive workplace for many gay men and women, largely because of its unionized environment and the federal government's motivation to be perceived as an exemplary inclusive employer. The city's annual gay pride parade routinely includes participation by a number of departments of the federal government and civil service unions. Geographer Nathaniel Lewis interviewed twenty-four gay men in Ottawa between 2009 and 2010 and found that government work was a significant draw to Ottawa for gay male professionals (Lewis 2012).

Unrivalled/Rivalled

Weber understood the most effective civil service to be one that was unrivalled – that is, it has a monopoly on the nation's scientists and social scientists. Porter, in contrast, argued that a public service should be "rivalled" so that it does not become problematically immune to outside critique (Porter 2018, 424).

Porter points to the "scientific bureaucracy" to demonstrate the civil service's status as unrivalled in technical and scientific capacities in the early twentieth century. By the 1920s, the federal government was investing in science in Ottawa through the Central Experimental Farm, the Dominion Arboretum, the Dominion Astrophysical Observatory, and the Dominion Bureau of Statistics. National Research Council Canada (founded in 1916), the Atomic Energy Control Board, Atomic Energy of Canada, and the Defence Research Board (all developed in 1942) (Porter 2018, 432) are further evidence of the government monopolizing Canadian research talent. The NRC's permanent headquarters, a neoclassical building built on Sussex Drive in 1928, has been the site of significant scientific contributions, including the development of fully electric wheelchairs, the world's first cardiac pacemaker in 1950, canola, aviation biofuel, a National Building Code in the 1940s, and counterfeit technology for paper currency in the 1980s (National Research Council 2019). By the 1990s, Ottawa was home to the second-largest concentration of science and engineering jobs and filed the most patents per capita of any city in the country (Novakowski 2010). Science and innovation had begun shifting to private industries in Kanata, making the state's hold on knowledge, science, and innovation clearly rivalled.

Today there is widespread use of outside consultants at all levels of government, which could be interpreted as a civil service noting its "rivalled" status and therefore procuring outside expertise. Increased use of outsourced consultants has led some to worry that we are being managed by a "consultocracy" (Grafton 2020). In 2016 the federal government upended its payment system (before which departments had their own in-house systems), adopting IBM's PeopleSoft's Phoenix system. This led to the elimination of 1,200 payroll jobs. Immediately, thousands of civil servants complained of underpayments, overpayments, and lack of payments (Office of the Auditor General of Canada 2017). The problems with the system continue. Critics of the consultocracy could easily point to Phoenix as evidence of their critiques: outsourcing work for expediency often does not deliver (although many counterarguments vouching for the efficacy of employing consultants exist). The expanding consultocracy begs any critical sociologist to ask: who is the public service for?

THE CIVIL SERVICE AS THE FUNCTIONARY ARM OF THE SETTLER COLONIAL CAPITALIST STATE

There's a sculpture in Tin House Court in the ByWard Market by Patrick Berubé titled *Our Shepherds*. Two faceless blue men face each other while standing on top of two blue sheep doing the same. The men's noses are connected by a long rod, which, the plaque tells us, "recalls both the long staff carried by shepherds and Pinocchio's famously growing nose, suggesting an underlying discord between the shepherds' role as protectors and the clear evidence of their lies." Could this also be a playful metaphor for the civil service? Layers of security clearance demand that the public is purposely not told how the government functions, and we are led. For those committed civil servants, their role is a service, performed in the Calvinist sense — civil servants as faithful shepherds of our collective well-being. But the men stuck together in this sculpture, facing each other, beg the question: who does the civil service serve? Bureaucrats understand their role as one of influence — influencing elected officials to adopt policies to govern the population. This influence is within specific spheres and provided in specific contexts. The most influential civil servant is given the unassuming title "Clerk of the Privy Council." For some, this unassuming posturing conceals how bureaucratic rule is an exertion of power. Behind all bureaucratic rules that the public are required to follow is an unarticulated threat of violence (see Graeber 2015). Tax laws become translated into tax forms, which all seem frustrating and banal, until the incorrect fulfillment of these bureaucratic tasks translates into crimes of tax evasion, which may lead to the federal tax courts on Kent Street and facing eventual incarceration. In the context of capitalist liberal democracy, this bureaucratic power is often exerted to the benefit of the capitalist elite.

Joanne Naiman (2012), drawing on Nicos Poulantzas, James O'Connor, and Ralph Miliband, explains how neo-Marxists understand three ways in which the state functions to serve the interests of capitalism: (1) legitimation, (2) accumulation, and (3) coercion, all of which we can understand through a jaunty walk down Wellington Street.

The state legitimates corporate capitalism through "legitimating the current class structure and the right of the ruling class to rule" (Naiman 2012, 168). This is done through the state's upholding of democratic systems. Liberal democracies such as Canada's suggest that people live in a world that they've actively participated in crafting. Behold, the Parliament buildings, the workplace of officials elected by the people, an architectural cathedral to honour democratic rule. The state also legitimates and facilitates settler colonialism. The first building erected for the expanding civil service was the Office of the Prime Minister and Privy Council (formerly the Langevin Block) on Wellington Street between 1883 and 1889, a time of intense nation building, the construction of the Canadian Pacific Railway, and colonial violence represented by the hanging of Métis leader Louis Riel by Sir John A. Macdonald's government. Duncan Campbell Scott, superintendent of the Department of Indian Affairs (1913–1932) who wrote dictates expanding the oppressive power of the Indian Act, worked in this building for part of his career (Vogt 2020). Scott was responsible for adding prohibitions against wearing "traditional costumes," making it illegal for Indigenous people to hire lawyers, and sending police spies to infiltrate meetings of Indigenous groups (Francis 1992, 211). Today, public servants working in the Departments of Justice, Natural Resources, and others invest time and energy fighting legal cases demanding that Indigenous children receive the same support as non-Indigenous children, disputing land claims, and facilitating the violent suppression of Indigenous land protectors.

In other ways many departments inch toward truth and reconciliation. Civil servants are addressed directly in a number of the 94 Calls to Action that were the result of the Truth and Reconciliation Commission. Call to Action 57 stipulates educating public servants on the history of treaties and the residential school system. Calls to Action regarding Indigenous health, public commemorations, the criminal justice system, and the signing of the UN Declaration on the Rights of Indigenous Peoples also all require civil servants in order to be realized. Call to Action 80 asks for the federal government to create a national day of truth and reconciliation. This action has been achieved, and the civil service is one segment of society that experiences September 30, the National Day of Truth and Reconciliation, as a day off of work.

The second function of the state is accumulation: facilitating individuals' and corporations' abilities to amass wealth. The state is the human community responsible for the actual minting of the money we all exchange in a capitalist economy. That wasn't always the case: beginning in the 1850s the Hudson's Bay Company struck their own coins, the "Made Beaver," one of which could be exchanged for the pelt of a beaver (Gismondi 2024). Since 1908, the Royal Canadian Mint on Sussex Drive, a David Ewart-designed baronial building, has minted Canadian coins (it has been dedicated to casting collectable and commemorative coins since 1970). Since 1935 the Canadian Bank Note Company (a private company with a contract with the Bank of Canada) on Richmond Road in Westboro has printed Canadian paper (and plastic) currency. The final one-dollar bill in circulation before the arrival of the loonie in 1987 featured a portrait of Queen Elizabeth II on one side and, on the other, an etching of a 1963 photograph of the Ottawa River by Malak Karsh. In the photograph, a small tugboat is seen among a load of logs that had escaped its boom. Parliament Hill, with the Library of Parliament, the Peace Tower, and Château Laurier across the canal are all in the background. Here, the state in its neo-Gothic glory is background to the commercial functions of the city and nation in the foreground, a fitting visual metaphor for the accumulation function of the state.

The state likewise acts as a "regulator of capitalism" (Naiman 2012, 173) through crafting, enforcing, and rescinding labour laws and through taxation. Wallace Clement, a student of John Porter's, identified the interchange between the corporate elite and the bureaucratic elite in the 1970s and argued that the elite – whether bureaucratic, political, or corporate — have more fraternity with each other than with other stratum in their own realms. The state serves corporate interests through subsidies and listening to advisory councils and business associations. The state legitimates corporate capitalism and, in turn, "Because the economic sphere is accorded such an important place in modern industrial societies, it is able to determine in large part government goals and policy" (Clement 1975, 352). Many business leaders become politicians, conflating these interests even more. In 1891, E.B. Eddy, the largest employer in Hull, was also the mayor of Hull, for example (Powell n.d.c).

The federal government became quite aggressive in this regulatory role in the 1930s when it began the considerable task of establishing the Bank of Canada. A national bank is the bank of banks, the conduit between private banking and federal regulations, an institution that both stabilizes the economy for everyday Canadians and enables capitalism as a system to function. Clifford Clark, from the Department of Finance, convinced Prime Minister Bennett to set up a royal commission to study the feasibility of a national bank in 1933.

The thirty-seven-year-old assistant general manager of Royal Bank, Graham Towers, became the first governor of the new Bank of Canada, which opened on March 11, 1935. Originally, the bank was in the Grand Central Hotel (outfitted with just two chairs and a desk) before moving to the Victoria building at 140 Wellington (Granatstein 1998) and then to its current location at 238 Wellington in 1938.

Approaching Wellington Street from Metcalfe Street, you'll first see a glass wall emerge diagonally from a concrete-like bunker with "Bank of Canada" in white and purple, advertising the Bank of Canada Museum. Here, after passing the "Yap stone" (a twelve-metre-in-diameter stone disc currency from the Micronesian island of Yap), guests begin their visit by making an avatar to accompany a bracelet that they can use to log into a number of pedagogical video games that teach visitors about shifting economies, inflation, and economic history. Throughout the permanent galleries, alongside displays of historic Canadian currency, visitors are assured that the Bank of Canada has made Canada a country with a stable economy. This heavy-handed propaganda is not that necessary. The Bank of Canada, with its periodical announcements of interest rate hikes and cuts, has become so naturalized that Canadians take for granted that the state would have this level of interventionist engagement with the economy.

While the Connaught Building, another David Ewart castle and home of the Canada Revenue Agency, at Wellington Street and Sussex Drive may stir feelings of anxiety in the hearts of everyday Canadians, to typical Canadian CEOs, the Connaught is likely gazed upon fondly. Income tax works as a form of wealth redistribution: higher earners are taxed at a higher rate, and this revenue funds broad social goods (public health care, education, roads). Yet this mechanism of wealth redistribution is applied very lightly to the largest income earners in the country. For large corporations, the general federal corporate tax rate is 15 percent (compared to an income tax rate of about 33 percent for middle-income earners). Low corporate taxes facilitate capital accumulation by the ruling class, as do minimum wage laws, which continue to allow wage rates below what is considered a "living wage" (the income needed to pay for the basic requirements of life). The Weston family, which owns Loblaws and Shopper's Drug Mart and has a net worth of $7.8 billion, has lobbied against a minimum wage increase (MacEwen and Eisen 2017), using its social capital to further enhance its economic capital.

Third, the state maintains the capitalist and settler colonial order of things through coercion or threat thereof (the force of the police). For Naiman and others, this coercion is also, often, toward the ends of facilitating capital accumulation (stifling resistance so that money-making pipelines can proceed, that the import and export of goods is not curtailed). For the headquarters of these bureaucrats-with-arms, you'll have to travel to the RCMP headquarters on the Vanier Parkway, the Department of National Defence headquarters in Kanata, on Rideau Street, and on Colonel By Drive, or the Ottawa police station on Elgin Street.

BUT ... HOW ELSE TO MANAGE A NATION-STATE?

Homo bureaucratus is sometimes maligned (more often dismissed), yet is there a more suitable creature to ensure Canadians are eating e-coli-free spinach, driving on properly managed roads, have access to schools, and are able to enjoy our natural and cultural treasures? Is there a better way to ensure that public coffers have enough money for future pension payouts, that governments are building enough hospitals, kindergartens, and frigates? A third objective of the civil service identified by Porter — to manage a then-young welfare state — has expanded considerably since *The Vertical Mosaic* was written. It has also expanded since I started writing this book. Civil servants were unsung heroes during the pandemic, rolling out the CERB basic income program almost instantaneously from their dining room tables. They are also, now, busily sorting out how an expanding universal dental care program will operate and what supports for Canadian workers impacted by US tariffs will look like. The city's largest employer requires, like most things that sociologists study, nuanced analyses. The civil service is the underpinning of a settler colonial capitalist state and the mechanism for ensuring a stable economy, safe(r) natural and urban environments, and a broad range of social goods.

Chapter 6

GETTING HOUSED

In 1810, Braddish Billings got swept up in an epic storm on Lake Saint Peter while transporting a winter season's worth of lumber (Kitchen, Messier, and Sadler 1996). Shaken and discouraged, the American settler abandoned his lumbering dreams and turned his attention to agriculture. Three years later, thirty-year-old Braddish married seventeen-year-old Merrickville school teacher Lamira Dow and the newlyweds immediately settled, without title, on clergy land — Lot 17 of Junction Gore. The land was unmonitored, and as they settled in (squatted), they earned money to purchase Loyalist-owned land nearby, a decision one historian calls "most shrewd" (Kitchen, Messier, and Sadler 1996, 7). In the next few years, the Billings built a barn and cleared and planted twenty acres in wheat. After living on this property rent-free for three years, they entered into a rent-to-own agreement with the clergy, agreeing to pay three pounds, ten shillings, or twenty-one bushels of wheat in rent every year. In 1830, the Billings contributed twenty-five pounds (of the total cost of 140 pounds) to the building of a bridge across the Rideau River between the Billings community south of the river and the rest of Bytown. The Billings estate became the heart of a new community called Billings Bridge (Kitchen, Messier, and Sadler 1996, 10, 12). The Billings' house has been designated a heritage building and is now a museum, which, on its placards, quotes Lamira, who wrote immodestly in one of her diaries, "we built a world."

In the same era, east of the Billings' estate, Charles Cummings either bought or squatted on an island in the Rideau River in 1835. He named it after himself and organized the building of a bridge from the island to Bytown. The bridge had "no flooring," so people crossed the river "on the stringers." Cummings Island became the heart of a new community, with a store, post office, lumber yards, and the first telephone in the region (Breton and Lecomte 2007, 9). A metal bridge eventually replaced the Cummings Bridge in the 1890s and was named Bingham's Bridge after an alderman, but the sign with the new name was surreptitiously thrown into the river and locals continued to refer to it as Cummings Bridge (Shea 1965).

Central to the prosperity of the Billings and Cummings was land ownership. Imagined as a marker of adulthood, financial security, and proper citizenship, today homeownership is celebrated as a taken-for-granted aspiration. The success of this ideology is reflected in the high rates of homeownership in Canada: 66.5 percent of households owned their own homes in 2015, and in Ottawa the rate was 63.9 percent (Statistics Canada 2022). In his 2024 ethnography of new homeowners in the Ottawa suburb of Findlay Creek, anthropologist Eric Hitsman found that homeowners who had bought in the neighbourhood at the height of house prices (and record low interest rates) during the pandemic were driven by dominant understandings of adulthood, childhood nostalgia, promises of a child-friendly community, and financial security. However, his informants also described anxiety related to rising housing costs (driven largely by mortgage brokers who persuaded buyers to agree to variable-rate mortgages) (Hitsman 2024). This framing of homeownership ignores the basic foundational logic: houses are treated as commodities — to be bought, sold, mortgaged, and flipped — more than as homes or shelter imagined as a fundamental human right.

People living rough on the streets, student renters, long-term rooming house tenants, and those who have bought new condos in Greystone Village and mansions in Manotick are all beholden to the commodification of housing. Settler colonial urbanization underpins this logic; the state and the church led the way in dispossessing Algonquin people of this land, hoarding some and making much of it available to settlers like the Billings (and John LeBreton, Nicholas Sparks, Philemon Wright, and so on) to own. That ongoing dispossession is visible in the disproportionate Indigenous homelessness in Ottawa, the reconciliation-washing of new condo developments on Albert and Chaudière Islands, and the Missionary Oblates of Mary Immaculate's ongoing profiting off the sale of Algonquin land in Old Ottawa East.

I begin this chapter by detailing the two enduring dominant societal responses to homelessness: charity and criminalization. I offer a history of rental housing in Ottawa, from purpose-built rentals in 1930s apartment houses to contemporary rooming houses and bunkhouses. I then offer three stories of gentrification: slow gentrification (LeBreton Flats), fast gentrification (Herongate), and steady gentrification (condo-mania). I end this chapter by discussing public housing, which challenges both housing commodification and dominant punitive orientations towards homelessness.

"NO PLACE FOR A HERO":
MORALIZING AND CRIMINALIZING HOMELESSNESS

For thousands of Ottawans, being "at home" is a tenuously held condition. In 2025 three thousand people did not have a home and were either staying in shelters or part of the "hidden homeless" (people crashing on friends' couches). Five hundred people were estimated to be living on the streets (Alhmidi 2025).

The United Nations defines homelessness as "1) having no place to call home and being forced to sleep either outside or in a temporary shelter, or 2) having access to housing that is lacking in one or more of the following: sanitation, protection from the elements, safe water, security of tenure, affordability, personal safety, and accessibility to daily needs" (Walks 2015, 164). In these definitions, the UN distinguishes between absolute homelessness (having no home) and relative homelessness (access to inadequate shelter). During the construction of the Rideau Canal, workers' dirt huts meant that they were, compared to the By family living in a stone-cut home on Major's Hill Park, relatively homeless. Beginning in 1858, Poles from Prussian-occupied regions fled Otto von Bismark's "kulturekampf" — a movement led by the Prussian leader that was particularly anti-Polish — to the Ottawa Valley. The Polish immigrants settled in rough, ragged, land two hundred kilometres west of Ottawa, called the "Madawaska Highlands," then settled Wilno, the first Polish community in Canada (Blank 2016, 3). By 1911, there were 2,300 mostly single and unemployed Polish men in Renfrew County. Memoirs written by these Polish settlers detailed how some of them, living in abject poverty, took to living off the land (Grabowski 2001), thus experiencing an early twentieth-century form of chronic and absolute homelessness. A lot of relative homelessness is hidden from public view because people find precarious housing in rooming houses, poorly maintained public housing, or on friends' couches. Many people stay housed at the expense of other life necessities, like adequate food or transportation — a phenomenon known as "shelter poverty" (Walks 2015, 165).

Many Indigenous people "conceptualize home more deeply as a web of relationships and responsibilities involving connections to human kinship networks; relationships with animals, plants, spirits and elements; relationships with the Earth, lands, waters and territories; and connection to traditional stories, songs, teachings, names and ancestors" (Thistle 2017, 14). From this perspective, homelessness is understood as being disconnected from one's human and non-human kin and culture — in many Indigenous societies, known as "all my relations" (Thistle 2017, 11). Indigenous homelessness has been both the goal and the result of ongoing settler colonialism that has — with centuries of land dispossession and the creation of the reserve system and the "pass system" — been designed to remove Indigenous peoples from their homes. Clergy reserves — of St. Andrew's Presbyterian Church, which became Ottawa's "Glebe," and land owned by the Missionary Oblates of Mary Immaculate in Old Ottawa East — were part of this dispossession in Ottawa. Today, "1 in 15 Indigenous people in urban centres experiences homelessness, compared to only 1 in 128 for the general population" (Thistle 2017, 19).

Sociologists and policymakers distinguish between chronic (extended periods of), episodic (repeated times experiencing), and temporary (brief periods of) homelessness (Walks 2015). In 1900 when a citywide fire flattened much of downtown Ottawa, twelve thousand people were made temporarily homeless and were dwelling in tents on Petrie Island (Walsh 2001, 165; SFOPHO 2023, 141). Increases in chronic homelessness for settler communities have historically corresponded with shifting economic and political conditions. In the 1890s, an economic depression led to an increase in both unemployment and homelessness in Ottawa (Hamilton-Hobbs 2014). Visible street-level homelessness across Ontario increased when Premier Mike Harris severely cut social services in 1995 (Motluk et al. 2000). In 1998 the Federation of Canadian Municipalities, pushed by the grassroots Toronto Disaster Relief Committee, declared homelessness a national disaster, noting that chronic homelessness had now become entrenched in many Canadian cities (Smith 2015). The shifting economic conditions propelled by the COVID-19 pandemic twinned with ongoing austerity have further entrenched chronic street-level homelessness across Canada.

Many see homelessness as a reflection of individual failings rather than a result of structural social conditions (land dispossession, the lack of a living wage, homophobia, intimate partner violence). Charities and city and provincial governments respond to homeless people with criminalization, fear, disdain, and sometimes compassion and pity.

After a few months of delay due to a typhoid outbreak, young women from the Young Women's Christian Temperance Union, led by Bertha Cole-Harris, opened the Home for Friendless Women on January 8, 1888 at 412 Wellington Street (Cole-Harris 1892). Throughout her memoir, Cole-Harris speaks of the "friendless" women's evil — engaging in sins of intemperance (drinking alcohol), spending time in dens of vice in Lowertown, and engaging in petty crimes — as the cause of some women's perilous living situations.

Employees of the home recruited women at the city's courthouse, the prison, and "dens of vice" (Cole-Harris 1892, 45). Time spent at the home, engaged in the soul-cleansing work of doing laundry, was imagined by Cole-Harris and the other members of the YWCTU to be an important source of salvation.

This approach toward attending to the needs of poor women was oblivious to broader societal causes for the women's situations outside of the social ill of alcohol abuse, an issue that the YWCTU and other women's organizations were deeply preoccupied with. At the time of the home's opening, Ottawa was experiencing rapid population growth and timber markets were collapsing, throwing the city into an economic depression (McCrostie 1997). In 1891, like now, there was a discrepancy between the minimum wage (the legal minimum employers are allowed to pay workers) and a living wage (the amount necessary to pay for the necessities of life). Male labourers in Ottawa earned $9.80 for a fifty-eight-hour week, while the minimum necessary to pay for clothes, food, and lodging was about $10.50 a week — a shortfall of about seventy cents a week (McCrostie 1997, 7). This gap widened when you considered the lower wages paid to women, and elites' habit of slashing "jobs and salaries during the winter months" when goods were at their most expensive (McCrostie 1997, 17). Several other institutions offering church-based charity to the poor opened in this period, including the St. Vincent de Paul Society, St. Andrew's Society, St. George's Society, and the Salvation Army (McCrostie 1997).

Shaming, criminalizing, or pitying are still very much dominant approaches towards homeless people in Ottawa. A content analysis of media depictions of homelessness in newspaper stories in Ottawa between 1994 and 1997 found that none of the articles or letters troubled why anyone was living on the streets in Ottawa; the role of charities (rather than governments) in responding to homelessness was taken for granted, and a third of the articles focused on the "substance abuse" of homeless people (Klodawsky, Farrell, and D'Aubry 2002, 134–35). Overwhelmingly, news media framed homelessness as an individual problem to be addressed through the benevolence of religious or charitable institutions.

Sociologist Erin Dej argues that current approaches to homelessness are constrained and managed by what she calls the "homelessness industrial complex." Dej explains that "state governance techniques and funding models" download responsibility for housing, mental health, and social supports onto an industry that is constantly competing for meagre resources and is focused on minor reforms rather than structural changes in the housing and social sectors. The homelessness industrial complex seems to be growing in Ottawa.

In 2017, the Salvation Army revealed plans for a new 103,000-square-foot "mega-shelter" to be built in Vanier. The proposed new shelter would offer temporary shelter for 350 people and include a dining facility, employment skills training, and counselling services. The proposal required the city to approve rezoning for its new location on Montreal Avenue and would cost the city $50 million (Dickson 2017). Members of the community organization SOS Vanier argued that this shelter, which would be the largest in North America, would challenge the "traditional main street" character for which Montreal Road is zoned. SOS Vanier argued that they were not opposed to the city and the Salvation Army responding to homelessness, but they argued that the shelter model is outdated and a demonstrated failure, and the city should be supporting "Housing First" programs instead. Housing First models begin with the premise that everyone is already houseable; that you shouldn't be required to be sober, or without health issues or pets, to be housed. Yet SOS Vanier's main concerns were that the presence of the mega-shelter would lead to more crime and insecurity in the neighbourhood, an anxiety rooted in another dominant attitude to homeless people: fear (Pearson 2018).

The comfortably housed often imagine homeless people as drug-involved, violent, and criminal. However, people experiencing homelessness are more often victims of violence than the general population. One study showed that 20 percent of the homeless in Canada had experienced abuse as children (Walks 2015, 166). In 2022 there were at least three murders of street-involved people that made the news (CBC News 2023a; McSheffrey 2023). The ByWard Market has been increasingly maligned in recent years as dangerous due in part to the concentration of social service providers and its high population of drug users and homeless people. In an online petition to close a ByWard Market shelter, the neighbourhood is referred to by a business owner as "a cancer which is now terminal for those residents and businesses in their vicinity" (quoted in Dej 2020, 93).

Vagrancy laws, loitering laws, debtors' laws, and the criminalization of squeegeeing and panhandling by the Ontario provincial government in 1999 have all criminalized poverty and targeted homeless people. In December 2024, the Ontario government passed Bill 242, the Safer Municipalities Act, which made public consumption of drugs a serious offence and strengthened trespassing laws and policing of encampments of homeless people living in parks (McGrath 2024). The criminalization of the poor is felt on the streets as harassment and surveillance by police, private security, and business owners. Elijah, a homeless youth, describes how he navigates "the Block" — a stretch of Rideau Street central to the lives of many homeless people in Ottawa:

> If you look to your right you'll see a bus stop. And then if you'll notice to the right there's a telephone pole with a bus and no stopping sign? So, if you're to the left of that sign you are loitering because you are in front of McDonald's and on McDonald's property. So, cops will often come down and push everyone around and what-not. So, if you're in there they can give you a ticket for loitering, but if you're to this side of the pole you're not loitering. You're in the clear. (Kennelly 2020, 289)

Because homeless people have more interactions with the police, they are more often penalized for small offenses (like being on the wrong side of a bus stop), and subsequently become subject to more surveillance due to probation conditions (Kennelly 2020).

Sociologists Kevin Walby and Randy Lippert analyzed 530 incident reports submitted by NCC conservation officers between 1998 and 2009 in Ottawa, almost all of which reported "illegal camping," a reference to the precarious dwellings set up by the homeless on NCC land, a violation of Section 38 of NCC regulations. One report "observed a white male person stretched on a bench ... expelled (because he was not normal)." Another report details responding to a "call from a business about two squeegees camping, expelled." Another account completely objectifies an apparently homeless person when the officer refers to the targeted person as "it": "observed one vagrant sitting down in York court yard, after arguing for 10–15 minutes he wouldn't move.... Officer Love came along and removed it" (Walby and Lippert 2012, 1022).

Much disdain toward unhoused people is rooted in the imagined interests of businesses. Benches with rigid metal armrests that prevent lying down, and the ubiquitous maple leaf-shaped studs that punctuate many long ledges in Ottawa's downtown core are designed to prevent outdoor sleeping. In the early 2000s, six so-called "kindness meters" were placed throughout the ByWard Market at the behest of Mayor Larry O'Brien, encouraging people to give money to the meters with a promise that the collected money would be directed to a reputable organization. Members of the Ottawa Panhandlers' Union called the meters insulting and said the city should redistribute any collected funds directly to the panhandlers in the neighbourhood — to which city councillor Georges Bédard responded: "It wouldn't be very smart for us to collect money and then to give it back to people who are going to be using it for drugs" (quoted in Ng 2008). Disdain is infused with patronization.

In 1983, a bronze statue of Terry Fox was unveiled at the intersection of Wellington and Rideau Streets. Fox ran through this very intersection when his famous "Marathon of Hope" visited Ottawa. By the mid-1990s, the underpass had secured a reputation as an unsavoury spot because it was populated by street-involved youth. At this point journalist Shelley Page argued that Fox's statue should be moved, that this spot was "no place for a hero." Minister of Heritage Sheila Copps agreed, and in 1998, Fox was moved to a new location on Wellington Street (Bulthuis 2011) (Fox has subsequently been moved again, south on Sparks Street). Disdain towards homeless people led to imagining the presence of homeless people as at odds with the heroism of Terry Fox. An obvious site of congregation, with a wide slopping platform to sit on, and cover from the elements, since 2008 a portion of this underpass has been barricaded by a fence to prevent sitting. Surveillance cameras were added in 2010.

Overpolicing homeless people, patronizing "kindness meters," and suggesting that homeless people cannot share company with Terry Fox all express the same disdain for people reduced to one shared characteristic: the inability to find and pay for housing in the market economy. There are many alternatives to criminalizing homelessness, most of which are rooted in challenging the commodification of housing. Creating and enforcing building bylaws, making a landlords' registry, and honestly calculating what "affordable" housing costs (i.e., not making it a certain percentage below an inflated market value) are all alternatives to criminalizing homeless people, as is broadly supporting public housing.

RENTING: FROM SUGAR CUBE HOMES TO BUNKHOUSES

We haven't always imagined homeownership as emblematic of the good life. In most of the twentieth century, middle-class individuals and families lived in rental houses and apartment buildings. With his wife Agnes and pet peacocks, John A. Macdonald rented Stadacona Hall on Laurier Avenue between 1878 and 1883. Beginning with the three- and four-storey walk-ups that were built in 1905 (Rickets 2017), all apartment buildings until the move towards condominium building in the 1970s were purpose-built for renters.

The condition of rental apartment buildings in the nineteenth and early twentieth centuries ranged widely. Some apartment buildings were "overcrowded, unaffordable, unhealthy" places to live — but Toronto's medical officer of health, Charles Hastings, blamed tenants' hygiene habits and morality rather than the economic and social structures for such conditions (Whitzman 2024, 33). The closeness with neighbours was seen as an affront to collective sensibilities; there were also concerns that "apartment houses" (which were distinguished from the more stigmatized tenement houses) would affect property values in neighbourhoods. These concerns were little expressed in Ottawa, where many of the new apartment houses were built largely for the affluent (Rickets 2017, 8). The Kenniston Apartments were built in 1908 on Elgin Street (now the location of the Lieutenant's Pump and other restaurants). Here, a monthly rent of $45–55 gave you an apartment in a "court-style" building with maximum light and ventilation, amenities like an "hourly maid service," and a "first-class dining room" (Belliveau, Quinn, and Ross 2017, 22). Throughout Centretown, Sandy Hill, and Lowertown, a number of apartment buildings built from the 1920s to 1950s offered premium luxury for renters, boasting electric elevators, municipal water service, underground parking, roof gardens, courtyards, reading rooms, on-site cleaning services, and spacious living spaces. Tommy Douglas, was, for the duration of his time as federal NDP leader, a resident of the left wing of the Strathcona, a posh apartment building at 404 Laurier Avenue East in Sandy Hill. Fellow Saskatchewanian and former Conservative prime minister John Diefenbaker lived for a time in the building's right wing (Quinn 2017). In the 1930s, a housing crisis and improved building standards led to a boom of quality rental apartment houses like the Blackburn at 223 Somerset, the Windsor Arms at 150 Argyle, and Park Square at 425 Elgin Street (Ross 2017).

After World War II, the need to house returning veterans led to the creation of Wartime Housing Limited, the Crown corporation that was the precursor to the Canada Mortgage and Housing Corporation (CMHC). From 1945 to 1947, on a parcel of land near Merivale Road and Carling Avenue, Wartime Housing Limited built hundreds of nearly identical, thousand-square-foot houses that together have been described as "an endless row of sugar cubes" (Elliott 1991, 232). The petite houses, which lacked dining rooms and front entrances, were built as rental accommodation, although many renters eventually bought their properties. Historian Bruce Elliott details that "in the early years, men returning from work frequently strode through the wrong door directly into a neighbour's living room" (Elliott 1991, 232). A section of this neighbourhood has been designated a "cultural heritage character area" to commemorate the government's past investment in rental housing (Pritchard 2022).

The CMHC built a series of three-storey walk-up townhouses for returning veterans between 1947 and 1949 on Mann Avenue in Sandy Hill. Strathcona Heights housed two thousand people (Sandy Hill History 2021). In the interwar period, the Ottawa Land Association developed the neighbourhood of "Ruskin Place," known now as the Civic Hospital neighbourhood. While the majority of the new Arts and Crafts–style houses were owner-occupied, the land association designated a number of plots between Parkdale and Holland Avenues to be built as rental properties (Payne 2023, 2).

Since the 1970s affordable rental housing has been gobbled up by corporate owners; provincial rent controls were eliminated in Ontario in 1977, amid the large-scale razing of low-rent accommodation (Crosby 2020). In the 1980s, the rise of "mortgage-backed securities" led to conditions where shareholders began to own other people's homes through their investment portfolios. Now housing is an investment "frontier" (Crosby 2020, 186), built and sold in real estate investment trusts (REITS) like Brookfield, the REIT once managed by Mark Carney. As an investment, rental housing is bought, sold, renovated, torn down, and has price increases, all to maximize shareholder profits. These practices lead to a reduction in affordable housing and make more people vulnerable to homelessness. Housing scholars refer to this as the "corporate capture of rental housing" (Farha 2018 in Crosby 2020, 194). Political decisions (deregulation of rental housing) facilitate developers' and financial asset managers' ability to radically transform rental housing in Ontario. The deplorable conditions and closings of rooming houses, the building of bunkhouses in Sandy Hill, and the mass evictions in Herongate demonstrate this corporate capture.

In November 2020, a GoFundMe page, "Bring Jonathan's Cats in from the Cold" detailed the story of Jonathan Hammel, a man who had recently been killed at his Centretown rooming house. A rooming house is a house where rooms are rented out individually; each tenant has their own lease with the owner, and tenants share bathrooms and kitchens. At the time of his death Jonathan had been taking care of over twenty feral cats in the neighbourhood. The fundraising campaign was to raise money to support medical care for the cats. Within a few days, the campaign had surpassed its $6,000 fundraising goal. Hammel and the man accused of his murder lived in the same rooming house, a house in which six bedrooms were separately rented for $450 a month (Yogaretnam 2020). Not surprisingly, the welfare of the cats pulled at collective heartstrings more strongly than the ongoing issues of the rooming house tenants. Such tenants receive the same type of disdain and criminalization directed toward homeless people.

In 2021, the "shelter benefit" allocated to people receiving the Ontario Disability Support Program was $497 a month; meanwhile, the average rent on a bachelor apartment in Ottawa was around $1,000 a month. Renting a room in a rooming house cost between $230 and $570 a month (SWC and CC 2016, 5).

Rooming houses have long provided shelter for people relying on this type of meagre support. In the early twentieth century, single male Ukrainian immigrants, including future Victoria Cross recipient Pylyp Konoval, lived in rooming houses on LeBreton Flats (Horral 2016). In the 1920s Chinese men who immigrated to Ottawa on their own also lived in shared housing, known as fong-hau, around Albert Street (Yee 2005, 93). Today the biggest problems with rooming houses are their declining numbers — as they are pushed out by forces of gentrification — and their poor quality. These problems are interrelated; low-quality housing gives the alibi for their destruction, which then depletes the quantity of this type of housing. Between 2008 and 2019 the number of rooming houses declined from over four hundred to ninety houses (CBC News 2019).

The townhouses known as Osgoode Chambers, built in 1912 at 146–170 Osgoode Street, have been used as rooming houses since 1962. One-room units rented for $400–600 a month in 2020. After the buildings were bought by Smart Living, the company began evicting the tenants in the summer of 2020. Smart Living's intention was to evict the long-term tenants and renovate the units to subsequently rent to University of Ottawa students as "luxury dorm-style units" for much higher rents (Mulligan, Crosby, and Hawley 2023, 190–91). Smart Living are leaders in what housing scholars refer to as the "studentification" of housing: creating housing specialized for students (typically smaller units for higher prices) near universities and colleges. The owners presumed that after receiving the first notice of eviction the tenants would leave without fuss. While some tenants accepted the new owners' financial offers to leave, other tenants pushed for a deal that would allow them to return. These tenants and their supporters staged a rally outside of Smart Living's headquarters and, significantly, didn't leave their homes. By 2021, the tenants had had some success: "mere days before the Landlord and Tenant Board hearing for the N13s, the landlord finally offered to move the tenants into one of the unrenovated buildings. The tenants successfully negotiated new leases at the same rate they were paying" (Mulligan, Crosby, and Hawley 2023, 199).

In September 2024, a friend and I enjoyed a concert at the Rainbow Bistro, bought some T-shirts and prints of an apartment block and bold lettering that read "we live here," all to support the "Bank Block Tenants" in their efforts to challenge evictions, also at the hands of Smart Living. This movement was partially successful. The eleven long-term tenants won the right to return at their current rent; however, city council approved Smart Living's zoning changes and heritage application (the developers will build a nine-storey building behind a preserved façade) (White-Crummey 2024). However, evictions are not inevitable; affordable housing can be saved. Smart Living has since rebranded as Dwell, and the evictions — and pushback — will, I imagine, continue.

While some tenants may, temporarily and conditionally, save some affordable housing through sustained collective action, the housing that they are saving is often neither safe nor healthy. In many Ottawa rooming houses there are broken windows, exposed pipes and electrical wiring, broken floorboards, mould, dirty kitchens and bathrooms, cockroaches, bedbugs, and poor ventilation. These conditions exacerbate the poor health of many rooming house tenants, who have high rates of chronic bronchitis and emphysema. Rooming house tenants have a life expectancy ten years shorter than average (SWC and CC 2016, 7). Osgoode Chambers tenants submitted complaints to bylaw about poor living conditions and a lack of heat in February 2021. City bylaw emailed Smart Living about these complaints, and when the landlords said they hadn't heard any complaints, the city did not push this issue (Mulligan, Crosby, and Hawley 2023).

Rooming houses rarely provide adequate privacy. Tenants must constantly negotiate the use of shared bathrooms and kitchens; food theft is a common complaint. In Ottawa, 50 percent of rooming house tenants have at least one diagnosed mental health condition like substance abuse, anxiety, bipolar disorder, PTSD, and schizophrenia; these conditions are worsened by fraught close contact with other renters. Safety is another problem for rooming house tenants. Tenants experience abuse from landlords, illegal evictions, mail interference, harassment, violence from other tenants, negligence in repair requests, and broken locks (SWC and CC 2016, 6). "Home takeovers" occur when rooming house tenants are pushed out of their homes by drug dealers. A participant in Dej's study, Mac, described his experience living in an Ottawa rooming house: "Like where I live now, it's just swamped with drugs. There's people banging on my door all night long with drugs. They put it on the tenants.... I've been beaten with bats, pipes, you name it, so they can deal out of my place" (Dej 2020, 67). But because they have these problems, does not mean that they are not an important part of the housing landscape. Political will to respond to complaints, at minimum, to increase building code inspections, and to implement easy rooming house requirements (working locks on each door, a mini-fridge in each room) would be a meaningful start to improving this housing stock.

The studentification of housing in Sandy Hill involves replacing Victorian homes with cheaply built and cramped but highly profitable bunkhouses for University of Ottawa students. Bunkhouses are buildings that include multiple bedrooms with their own individual locks and individual leases; they are similar to rooming houses yet are unregulated and built for a higher rental market. Where previously a house might be rented by four students who each have a bedroom and share a living room, kitchen and bathroom, now that same size house could include up to six individual bedroom lease arrangements, a kitchen and bathroom, but no other shared living space. For students, bunkhouses can offer potentially affordable housing and the flexibility and autonomy of not needing to coordinate housing with roommates. The main benefactors of bunkhouses, however, are the landlords. Unlike their Victorian neighbours, bunkhouses are austere, grey bunkers with tiny sad windows and no lawns, landscaping, warmth, porches, or curtains. The designs reflect how little the builders think of the intended residents. And unlike university residences, there are no common rooms, residence "fellows," opportunities for community building or low-key socializing; they are little boxes for sleeping.

Action Sandy Hill has argued that bunkhouses have led to increased garbage, noise, and the destruction of heritage buildings. Action Sandy Hill has been accused of being anti-student; however, spokesperson François Bregha argued that the group wanted a "commitment to create incentives and tighter regulations, which would encourage developers to build two- or three-bedroom apartments" (CBC News 2018c). The group has put pressure on the city to establish stricter building bylaws that would stop the construction of new bunkhouses, and it has pressured the University of Ottawa to build more student residences.

TCU is a real estate development firm that has become the ire of Sandy Hill residents. In 2017, city councillor Mathieu Fleury invoked a rarely used power to force TCU to appear before the planning committee when they were planning on transforming a house at 70 Russell Avenue into a building with four units and twenty-one bedrooms. Fleury described the group as having "built some of the worst bunkhouses in Sandy Hill" (Chianello 2017). TCU, despite touting a "human-centric" approach to real estate (MacLaughlin 2021), is an investment company that, in its pitch to investors, details how mixed-use developments are "trendy" building ideas that will maximize investments. This single-minded profit orientation was demonstrated again in 2021 when TCU planned to pave a portion of Sandy Hill's Besserer Park to create a path to three parking spots for a building that TCU was planning to build on a bit of urban forest it had acquired. The park was only saved through the activism of Action Sandy Hill (Shah 2021) The park has since been renamed Herbert and Estelle Brown Park, in honour of two people we meet later in this book.

Both rooming houses and bunkhouses are modes of rental housing that squeeze maximum profit out of their properties, extorting tenants marked by limited economic and social capital: the very poor (rooming houses), and the young and inexperienced students (bunkhouses). However, the early history of rental housing in Ottawa shows that treating renters as merely profit generators to be maligned is not an ahistoric absolute. Living in rental housing has also been a broad, acceptable, and publicly supported way to make oneself at home in Ottawa, with renters living in safe and well-designed apartment houses in Centretown, "sugar cube" houses in Carlington, and townhouses in Strathcona Heights.

GENTRIFICATION: SLOW, FAST, STEADY

The shifting political context for the housing market in the 1970s led to the corporate capture of rental housing and the rise of condominiums — selling individual apartments as owner-occupied homes. Condo-led gentrification began to transform many downtown neighbourhoods. Ruth Glass first coined the term "gentrification" in 1964 to refer to the process of the "gentry," the property-owning class, moving into working-class urban neighbourhoods, displacing working-class people, and qualitatively reshaping urban spaces (Smith 2000, 294). The influx of condominium buildings (homes of the "gentry") leads to a net loss of many types of rental housing, but it also impacts leisure spaces, orientations toward community and toward strangers, and how homes are imagined and sold to women. The various contours of this phenomenon will be explored through detailing slow gentrification on LeBreton Flats, fast, recent gentrification of Herongate, and the condo-fied gentrification in many neighbourhoods that has been ongoing.

Slow Gentrification: LeBreton Flats

In 1821, John LeBreton bought a parcel of land at Richmond Landing for 499 pounds. When learning of the government's canal-building plans, LeBreton offered to sell the land to the government for three thousand pounds. Outraged by LeBreton's real estate speculating, Lord Dalhousie refused the offer and made a better deal to acquire land from Nicholas Sparks east of LeBreton's land. By 1900 the land owned by LeBreton, now known as LeBreton Flats, had become a vibrant working-class neighbourhood (Jenkins 2020). The Flats were the location of the city's first train station, school, and hotel, and the terminus of the city's first road. After the fire of 1900 destroyed all of the buildings in the Flats, the community rebuilt, again as a working-class neighbourhood (Walsh 2001). It was the neighbourhood where future businessmen and inventors Thomas Ahearn and Warren Soper struck up lifelong friendship as children in the early 1900s. By 1950, when Jacques Gréber gazed upon the neighbourhood, it was full of busy homes, laundry strung on lines, taxi stands, mechanic shops, and restaurants.

While many of his peers fled to North America, Gréber stayed in France during World War II and worked for the fascist Vichy regime between 1941 and 1943. The Vichy administration "facilitated internment and deportations that 'made the Germans' task easier when it came to the final solution'" (Picton 2010, 308). Gréber created the urban plan for the French city of Marseille in the 1930s; this plan focused on slum clearance, zoning based on class and income, and the removal of "dangerous and unhealthy homes." In January 1943, 1,949 Jews were rounded up from the Old Port of Marseille and sent to death camps. Geographer Roger Picton offers this analysis: "while Gréber is not directly responsible for the expropriation, an arc of knowledge stemming from his original regional plan ultimately resulted in the destruction of Marseille's Old Port." When Mackenzie King invited Gréber to Canada after the war to create a plan for the national capital, Gréber drew on his Vichy administrative experience (Picton 2010, 309–10).

In the early 1950s, different levels of government in many North American and European cities were embracing large-scale so-called urban renewal projects that involved mass land expropriations, the demolition of housing, and the building of highways. So-called slums were interpreted as unhealthy blights within cities that had to be "surgically removed to stop further infection of the city" (Picton 2015, 134). The period between 1949 and 1968 saw "slum clearance" that led to large-scale public housing projects (Silver 2011, 34).

The Gréber plan included the entire expropriation of LeBreton Flats (Picton 2010, 310). Plate 178 in the plan shows "a series of generously-spaced buildings interspersed across what looks to become a bucolic green landscape" (Miguelez 2015, 239). Appraisers commented on dust, noise, and "noxious odours" and concluded that this historic and dynamic neighbourhood did "not represent a desirable community" (Picton 2015, 137). On April 17, 1962, the federal cabinet approved a proposal from the National Capital Planning Committee to legalize and finance the expropriation of fifty-three acres of LeBreton Flats, twenty-nine acres along Nepean Bay, and the adjacent rail yards. Within twenty-four hours, 270 property owners received notices that they were going to be bought out by the federal government and forced to move (Picton 2010, 316). Picton notes that by 1961, the population had increased by over 10 percent to 2,292 largely French-Canadian but also Irish, Italian, and Lebanese residents (Picton 2015, 138). The government's plan was to create a complex of six million square feet of government office space, including one million square feet for the new headquarters of the Department of National Defence (DND), in time for the 1967 Centennial (Picton 2015, 131). The expropriation was a rare federally led postwar urban renewal project (Picton 2010, 310).

The expropriations worsened the city's housing issues, angering Mayor Charlotte Whitton, who was also concerned that this expropriation would distance workers from their workplaces. She saw the expropriations as evidence that the federal government privileged city beautification over the housing needs of people living in Ottawa. The NCC general manager, E.W. Thrift, replied to Whitton's concerns by saying that the NCC, the largest landowner in the region, had "little available or likely to be available" for the city and that contributing land or housing would be "too costly" for the land commission (Picton 2010, 317).

The DND found cheaper land elsewhere to build their headquarters and from 1962 to 2005 the Flats became a meadow, used periodically for events like Ottawa's Bluesfest. Since 2005, the Flats have been the site of the Canadian War Museum, a few Claridge condominium buildings, and the Mill Street Brew Pub. While slow, the story of LeBreton Flats is the story of full-scale residential and cultural displacement of a working-class community with a community of condo owners and amenities aimed largely toward tourists (the new community still lacks a grocery store).

Fast Gentrification: The Mass Eviction of Herongate

In 2018, 89 percent of the residents of the south Ottawa neighbourhood of Herongate were people of colour, 44 percent of the residents were Somali, and many of the households were headed by single mothers (Herongate Tenant Coalition 2018, 5). Between 1988 and 1996, 55,000 Somali refugees moved to Canada as Somalis fled the Somali Civil War (OCASI 2016). Seven thousand Somali refugees settled in Ottawa (Abdulle 2000); however, they did not receive the warm welcome that the Vietnamese and Laotian refugees received in 1979. Somali refugees were only 2 percent of the Government-Assisted Refugees in Canada between 1993 and 2001, increasing to 4 percent between 2002 and 2009. The violence in Somalia and the issues experienced by Somali refugees in Canada remained off the radar for most Canadians. This disinterest transformed into more explicit forms of rejection with the passing of an amendment to the Immigration Act (Bill C-86) in 1993 that required applicants to have "satisfactory" identification to land in Canada. This amendment was put in place to dissuade applicants from destroying travel documents; however, the

Ontario Council of Agencies Serving Immigrants explains that the collapse of the Somali government made acquiring satisfactory ID nearly impossible. This amendment also prevented Convention Refugees from reuniting with their families, accessing social supports, leaving and re-entering Canada, or applying for certain jobs. While 90 percent of Somali refugee claims were accepted between 1990 and 1993, after the passing of this amendment, the acceptance rate dropped to 57 percent (OCASI 2016, 1–2).

In the 1990s, Herongate offered a good place to live for Somali refugees because the townhouses accommodated large families and rent was below average. As more Somalis settled there, it became a hub for community and social resources. There are numerous Somali restaurants in the area, as well as the Somali Centre for Family Services. However, in 2012, most of the housing in the neighbourhood was bought by a single landlord, Timbercreek. Timbercreek and its supporters saw only empty land, broken windows, and a prime opportunity to increase profits through razing these homes to build higher-rent properties.

In 2015, Timbercreek demolished eighty townhouses (Kestler-D'Amours 2018). In May 2018, over four hundred residents received eviction notices requiring them to vacate by September 30 as the landlord planned to continue the process of what they called reinvigoration but the Herongate Tenant Coalition's lawsuit called "hyper-gentrification." Timbercreek's plan was to build a "resort-style" community of rental homes that would "reflect the premium nature of the community" (Delamont 2019).

The evictions in 2012 and 2018 were bolstered by a few myths of gentrification. Timbercreek argued that the homes had to be demolished because they were beyond repair; however, the company did not see their responsibility for these maintenance issues. Tenants argued that they had been complaining for years about water damage, inadequate garbage collection, broken windows, cockroaches, and a general lack of upkeep, but to no avail (Kestler-D'Amours 2018). Herongate embodies the corporate capture of rental housing and how this process kills affordable housing while maximizing shareholder profits. The Herongate homes were bought by TransGlobe, "one of the worst corporate slumlords in Canada" in 2007. The Herongate Tenant Coalition contends that "Herongate appears to be part of a larger national campaign to slumify people's homes, with the long-term goal of redeveloping neighbourhoods, turning housing into investment funds, and pushing working-class folk out" (Herongate Tenant Coalition 2018, 7). This process was possible because of the long erosion of renters' rights in Ontario's provincial landlord and tenant laws. At the municipal level, Mayor Jim Watson, and the city councillor responsible for the ward, Jean Cloutier, routinely stated that it was beyond their jurisdiction to intervene in the Herongate evictions; meanwhile, both Watson and Cloutier received campaign donations from Timbercreek in 2014 (Herongate Tenant Coalition 2018).

Gentrifiers imagine pre-gentrified spaces to be like uncolonized spaces — *terra nullius* — empty land. That was certainly true here, as Timbercreek, a blasé city government, and Timbercreek's supporters did not see the community and culture that existed at Herongate. While the vision put forth by Timbercreek — now called Hazelview — of creating a mixed-income rental neighbourhood has not been realized, what has happened, however, is the largest mass eviction in Canadian history. And Hazelview's stockholders have done fine: in 2025 its investments had net assets of $95,431,698 (Hazelview n.d.).

Steady Gentrification: Building Condo-land

In late summer 2019, I joined a few of my friends to spend a leisurely evening on the luxuriously spacious patio of James Street Feed Company, a much-loved pub in Centretown. The evening was marked with sadness because it was our farewell visit; the pub closed that fall. Just weeks later I was hit by another gut punch when, attending my local gym in the Glebe, the proprietors told us that the gym was being forced to relocate — the owners of the building, Minto Properties, were tearing out most of the 1980 red-brick commercial building to build an eight-storey condominium. The renovations led to the closure of many businesses, and it also removed the "Fifth Avenue Courtyard," a quasi-public indoor space that provided a welcome hangout place that was warm in the winter, and cool in the summer. The James Street Feed Company closed because the property had been sold to a condo developer in 2010 (Hoytema 2019).

Pro-gentrification advocates argue that gentrification leads to economic growth, which creates goods for the existing community, and that gentrification increases tax revenue for the city, allowing the city to invest in social services and community assets. They suggest that gentrification allows for demographic heterogeneity as existing working-class residents and incoming gentrifiers live side by side. These arguments support what Loretta Lees refers to as "emancipatory social practice": understanding gentrification positively as a process that creates "opportunities for social interaction and tolerance" (Lees in Slater 2004, 1193). Condo living contributes to urban intensification rather than sprawl. Furthermore, condos are smaller spaces to cool and heat and require people to share green spaces. In Ottawa, the footprint of newly built condos has shrunk from 1,104 square feet for condos built in the 1990s to 891 for those since 2017 (Hayashi 2023). Increased possibilities for using active modes of transportation suggest that condo living should be more ecologically sustainable than other residential modes.

Critics of gentrification argue that gentrifiers (including individuals, real estate developers, and the governments that enable these processes), privilege middle-class housing and middle-class understandings of culture in ways that make invisible all of the vitality already existing in pre-gentrified neighbourhoods, but lead to a net loss in affordable housing as rental buildings are converted into condos and other rental housing is razed. Speculative real estate developments displace family-run small-scale retail as commercial rents increase, and small ethnic retail and grocery stores (SERGs) are threatened.

Years before my friends and I toasted farewell to the James Street Feed Company, the bar hosted a meeting of Toronto-based developers Urban Capital who were promoting their plan to brand a stretch of Bank Street "South Central." The company's David Wex positioned his group as "pioneers" in the classic language of gentrification and referred to this part of Centretown as empty, a "location [that] was really a nowhere between the city and the Glebe." The community rallied in response, disrupted the event, and scrawled defensive graffiti on the South Central billboards. One woman stood in front of the James Street Feed Company with a sign "this deadzone is our home" (Media Co-Op 2012). Centretown was an already inhabited and very dynamic neighbourhood — like LeBreton Flats and Herongate.

Speculative condominium building is enabled by city governments that waive development fees, are lenient with existing building standards, and are persuaded to amend existing zoning laws. The city entices developers to include affordable housing units in their plans for new buildings, to mixed ends. In a study of the rapid intensification of West Centretown, urban geographers found that of the thirty-five new developments built and approved between 2015 and 2021, only five "committed to making a portion of their housing offerings affordable," and often the notion of "affordable" was simply "below market rent" — a dubious definition considering the extremely overpriced rental market (Imeri, Sumanth, and Hugill 2022, 29). Developers offer "community benefits" in exchange for exclusions from height (or other) building restrictions. Yet these benefits — contributions to the ward's parks or community gardens — are often offset by waived development fees. Condo-intensification leads to a net loss of relatively affordable rental housing.

Many of the environmental benefits of high density that come with condo living are lost in the interest of maximizing profits through building flashy but energy-inefficient window walls, installing cheap but inefficient HVAC systems, and relying on environmentally damaging and unhealthy VOCs (volatile organic compounds), found in treatments like laminate flooring. This indifference toward the environment is not inherent in the ownership model of condos — in fact, many early condominiums from the 1970s were well-designed, properly insulated, and are living long lives. The rise of corporate, rather than individual, developers has led to the proliferation of ostentatious but cheap and unsustainable design in condos with smaller square footage. Condo developers, unlike owners of rental buildings and public housing, have no stake in how buildings age. After a condo is sold, if window walls crash onto the sidewalk below, or if the condos routinely flood, have bursting pipes, or exorbitant heating and cooling costs, these are not the developer's problem.

Critics argue that despite the location of condos in potentially heterogeneous urban settings, condo living contributes to social polarization and homogeneity. This contradiction — craving heterogeneity while creating homogeneity — is in play when looking at how condos are sold to women. Condo life is portrayed to women as a form of emancipation from the binds of patriarchal nuclear family arrangements and an escape from feminized poverty. Yet, there is a long history of single women living on their own in cities before the arrival of condos. Unattached women have lived in rooming houses, workplace dormitories (like Laurentian Terrace and workers' quarters in hotels), but also in their own apartments and houses as renters and as owners. In 1930, six of the thirty renters of the luxurious Windsor Arms were women, presumably with their names on the leases, and they were unattached (Ross 2017, 36). The heroines of single living in Ottawa were the formidable Billings sisters Sabra and Sarah (Sally) Billings. These two women inherited the Billings Estate after their parents died and divided the farm house in half. The eldest, Sabra, insisted on occupying the side of the house that included the kitchen, and she had access to the well. Sally built her own kitchen. Cosmopolitan Sabra spent much of the year travelling in the United States. She was also a deeply devout woman who facilitated the building of Gloucester Township's first church, the Free Church of Scotland, and was a supporter of the temperance movement. The more reserved Sally was committed to the operations of the farm and supported the establishment of a Methodist church. The sisters shared the house until their deaths, both well into their nineties.

Condos are also sold to women as fortresses with many security features, protecting women from the dangers of the city (Kern 2010). Indeed, the Minto complex "Fifth + Bank" that supplanted the Fifth Avenue Courtyard sells its units in part through advertising on their website "peace of mind" features that include "security-controlled access, concierge service, facial entry, digital key entry, virtual concierge, smart package lockers, 24-hour emergency service, online amenity booking." Kern argues that a generalized fear of the "Other," which includes sex workers, non-white people, and poor people, is invoked when selling condos to women. A focus on external threats reinforces what scholars call the paradox of women's fear: women are socialized to fear strangers when the greatest threats to women are people they know (Kern 2021, 145). The irony of selling freedom and security to women through the allure of condominium ownership is that gentrification is a process that disproportionately displaces women and racialized people, groups that have less money to participate in homeownership and middle-class leisure pursuits.

The irony of selling social heterogeneity when marketing condo living is also on display at the Zibi developments on Albert and Chaudière Islands in the Ottawa River. Since 2013, Ottawa-based Windmill and Toronto-based Dream have been developing thirty-seven acres of the islands to produce a so-imagined sustainable community to house five thousand people and employ six thousand, featuring "complete streets," and waterfront office spaces (Williams 2017). The development, which the developers named "Zibi," has been contentious since its beginning. The Pikwakanagan First Nation, encouraged by Windmill's plan to build healing circles and an interpretive centre, supported the project (Paine 2015). However, the Kitigan Zibi community rejected the appropriation of the word (and spelling) *Zibi*, an Algonquin word for river used specifically by the Kitigan Zibi community (other communities use *sibi*) without consultation (McKay 2015). In 2015, nine Algonquin chiefs filed a resolution arguing that the rezoning of this property for mixed residential and commercial use denied Algonquin rights to this sacred land (Macdougall 2015). A decade later, anti-Zibi protest signs that read "Free the Falls! No condos on Stolen Algonquin Land" have been scattered to the wind, and four condo and townhouse complexes have units for rent or sale; a two-bedroom, two-bath townhouse was listed in 2024 for $750,000.

Condo building in Old Ottawa East does not attempt any reconciliation-washing of the history of colonial violence underfoot. In 2014, the Missionary Oblates of Mary Immaculate sold twenty-six acres in Old Ottawa East for $32 million. Since then, eQHomes and the Regional Group have been developing Greystone Village, a community of townhouses and condos that boasts access to the Rideau River, bike paths, units for seniors, and affordable housing. Despite profiting off of this land, Oblates pled poverty when requested to commit to the $25 million that a group of Catholic churches agreed to pay to a fund for survivors of residential school abuses in 2006. Collectively, the groups only managed to contribute $3.9 million to the fund (Ireton 2021).

The building and branding of condos has happened within a context of divestment from rental housing, disparaging of renters, and a neoliberal focus on individualism that nourishes its inverse: a suspicion of others. This is the context in which "facial entry" and citadel-style downtown living have become desirable. Political decisions that trade green space for campaign contributions allow developers to build higher and closer together, with little regard for existing tenants, the environment, or community needs. Condo developers profit off of "stranger danger" while simultaneously creating homes that are likely to leak, require expensive unsustainable heating and cooling systems, fuel antagonism toward neighbours, and are under-insulated (I shudder still for the pains of the Metcalfe Street, Kent Street, and ByWard Market glass-walled condo dwellers that suffered Convoy honking in February 2022). Of course, it is #notallcondos — owners and residents in various buildings develop community despite the individualist logic built into condo living. Many buildings have active party rooms where neighbours hang out and knit, have board game nights, curate their own libraries, host piano recitals. In my building, we celebrate all of the major holidays, the change of seasons, and most importantly: our building superintendent's birthday.

PIERRE TRUDEAU LIVES IN PUBLIC HOUSING

Since 2022 there's been an art piece on Cambridge Street in Chinatown by artist Sujin Lim. A white gate on to a residential street takes the shape of an outline of a house topped with puffy clouds. On the grounds of city hall there has been an art piece called *Living Room* by artists of Urban Keios: many aluminum chairs, open doors, and a large empty television are sprawled on the lawn. Both of these art pieces are public expressions of something very domestic and intimate: home. They might inspire some to ask: what if housing and access to a home is similarly imagined as a public good rather than an individual responsibility or asset to rent or own?

In the early 1970s, public housing activist and writer Dorothy O'Connell created a series of buttons that read "Pierre Trudeau lives in public housing" as part of a fundraising campaign for the Ottawa Tenants' Council. The council sold the buttons for fifty cents, twenty-five cents for people living in public housing. O'Connell sent a button to Trudeau, who promptly was seen wearing it on TV. When the CBC called O'Connell to solicit her response, she just replied that Trudeau owed the Council twenty-five cents (Garrett 1990, 36). Trudeau was, of course, living in public housing, as were many other high-ranking elected and appointed Canadians in Ottawa. Beginning with Louis St. Laurent in 1951, prime ministers and their families (except for Justin Trudeau and Mark Carney's families) have lived in Gorffwyfa (Welsh for "rest"), which is the official name of a building more simply known as 24 Sussex Drive. Prime ministers also have access to an estate on Harrington Lake in Gatineau Park. Since 1950, beginning with George Drew, the leader of the Opposition and their family (with the exception of Bloc Québécois leader Lucien Bouchard in the 1990s) have lived in Stornoway, a thirty-four-room mansion in Ottawa's Rockcliffe Park. There are even more mansions–as–public housing in the national capital. The governor general has lived at Rideau Hall since 1867, when Canada's first governor general, Lord Monck, moved in. The speaker of the House lives in a state-owned farmhouse on Mackenzie King's former estate, "Kingsmere," in Gatineau Park. Yet most public housing in Ottawa is less opulent.

Investment both nationally and in Ottawa led to significant growth in public housing between the 1960s and 1980s. The decade 1964–1974 saw the number of public housing units across the country grow from 10,000 to 115,000 (Silver 2011, 34). In the 1970s 35,000–40,000 nonmarket homes were built each year in Canada; 25 percent of all new homes built were for "regulated affordable-housing programs" (Whitzman 2024, 31–32). In Ottawa, public housing investments were made in the traditionally working-class neighbourhoods of Little Italy and Lowertown.

Italians first immigrated to Ottawa starting in 1900; by 1911, seven hundred Italian families lived in Ottawa, mostly in Lowertown. To serve the growing population, St. Anthony's of Padua was built in 1913 on Booth Street, confirming the Italian migration from the ByWard Market to what became Corso Italia. Another wave of Italian immigration happened after World War II (Kent 2024). In Little Italy between 1964 and 1966, 1,100 households were uprooted from their homes, seen by the city as "cancerous pockets of deficient housing," and in their place 111 brick-clad rowhouses were built. A passion project of Mayor Charlotte Whitton, it was named "Rochester Heights" (Smythe 2018). It was here that Dorothy O'Connell lived with her family. After the stunt with the buttons, O'Connell and Trudeau struck up a correspondence, and at one point Trudeau and his children were given a tour of Rochester Heights by O'Connell (Egan 2020).

Public housing complexes were built in Lowertown in the 1970s. Anglesea, a federal-provincial 1972 public housing development at 330 Murray, is an eleven-storey complex with an enclosed green space to encourage community gathering and children's free play. Friel Towers, at 200–201 Friel Street, included Le Corbusier–inspired two-storey maisonette apartments and was designed to house 155 families that had been displaced by earlier razing (Belliveau, Quinn, and Ross 2017, 73). This type of thoughtful design marked a high moment in investment and care for public housing, although it was not built without resistance. Between 1967 and 1977, the NCC expropriated and forced the relocation of 1,400 families; the affluent moved to the suburbs, but French and Irish churches and Jewish synagogues closed, and the forcibly relocated complained of inadequate compensation, high rent in new homes, and inadequate support for displaced seniors (Historical Society of Ottawa 2023).

Since the 1970s, public housing has been downloaded first from the federal government to the provinces, then to more cash-strapped municipal governments (Whitzman 2024). Today the City of Ottawa's Housing Services branch owns and manages 22,500 social housing units. The city also offers housing allowances, rent supplements, and owns rent-geared-to-income units (which set rent at no more than 30 percent of the renter's income). These initiatives, while helpful, do not stop landlords from charging unaffordable rents and do little to improve available rental housing in the city. The socially supported housing that is available is insufficient. In 2021 there were twelve thousand people on a wait list for public housing; some people wait on this list for up to five years (Williams 2022).

Ottawa Community Housing (OCH), an arms-length organization of the City of Ottawa, is the largest provider of public housing in Ottawa, responsible for 32,000 tenants. OCH inherited many properties from the provincial government in 1999, during the province's offloading of housing responsibilities onto city governments. A 2008 study calculated that OCH buildings required $211 million in repairs. The neglect is noticeable by residents, who complain of drafty windows, leaky roofs, and bedbugs. Furthermore, in 2021 OCH received more than 44,000 community safety calls (Williams 2022). Because of the wait list for public housing, tenants often feel incredibly stuck, unable to move out of unhealthy and unsafe homes, kept in conditions of relative homelessness.

Some public housing complexes have remained vibrant, and others have converted into other forms of non-commercial housing. A public housing complex since 1982, Strathcona Heights in Sandy Hill is now, in part, a housing co-operative. The neighbourhood O'Connell raised her children in is changing again. The City of Ottawa and OCH have already started to build the city's newest public housing project, Gladstone Village, which is slated to include over three hundred affordable housing units in one eighteen-storey and one nine-storey tower. The village will also include commercial retail spaces, green space, an expanded Plouffe Park, bike paths, and a rejuvenated Plant Bath community centre.

Different organizations within the city have taken up Housing First strategies to address homelessness and the affordable housing crisis. Non-profit organization Options Bytown boasts that 88 percent of the people they've placed through their Housing First program have remained housed two years later (Options Bytown 2024, 12). Erroneously, the Salvation Army — the provider of the city's largest shelter — also boasts a Housing First program. Churches, the historic providers of charity and engines of land dispossession, are increasingly shifting their orientation toward more sustainable investments in affordable housing. St. Luke's Anglican Church built forty-four rent-geared-to-income units, and renovated the institution guided by the "Greening Sacred Spaces" renovation model. In 2008, Kingsway, Northwestern, and Westboro United Church congregations amalgamated and Westboro United Church was sold and developed into a mixed-use space including low-rise affordable townhouses, office space for Bluesfest, and the Bluesfest School of Music and Art (Martin and Ballamingie 2016, 83). In summer 2023, the First Unitarian Church and Ontario Aboriginal Housing Services began working together to build fifty affordable housing units on the church's expansive parking lot (CBC News 2023a).

Another model of securing affordable housing in Ottawa emerged in 2021 in the form of the newly created Ottawa Community Land Trust (OCLT). Born in the midst of the pandemic, an affordable housing crisis, and an emerging enthusiasm for land trusts across the country, the OCLT does not build but preserves existing affordable housing. Mike Bulthuis, executive director of OCLT, explained that for every new unit of affordable housing built in Ottawa, thirty-one units are lost through evictions and rent hikes between tenants. Without any renovations, units can shift from being affordable to unaffordable housing overnight (personal communications, February 9, 2024). The OCLT's mandate is to — through government funding, private investment, and selling community bonds — buy existing affordable housing with the express intent of keeping it affordable in perpetuity.

THE HIERARCHY OF THE HOUSED

The hierarchy of what makes a good home is historically and culturally specific. At the top of this social imaginary of the housed are homeowners, the gentrifiers, the smiling condo owners sipping mojitos on the deck of a rooftop pool. These folks are courted by developers, seduced by advertisements for the sustainable urban living on offer at Greystone Village, the Zibi developments, or the Claridge condos at LeBreton Flats. This is a vision that emerged in the 1970s but has accelerated. In creating these idealized homes, neighbourhoods are razed, reconfigured, the Oblates make millions, developers profit off of Algonquin words, and thousands of people on LeBreton Flats, Herongate, and Centretown are displaced. Condo-steady gentrification is the latest iteration of two hundred years of land dispossession from Algonquin people.

Next in this home-making hierarchy are renters, although "renter" is an extremely broad class. Historically (and today, in some luxury rental contexts), renters were not maligned as an underclass. Politicians and senior civil servants rented apartments in luxury apartment houses in Centretown, Sandy Hill, and houses in Ruskin Place. Yet broadly, renters are today imagined as a transient, vulnerable, underclass. The renters of townhouses in Herongate, students renting rooms in bunkhouses in Sandy Hill, and the very poor tenants of rooming houses all suffer at the whims of profit-motivated homeowners that neglect then raze their properties.

If renters are generally dismissed and pushed around, those without a home face more violent forms of societal disdain. Homelessness in Ottawa has long been impacted by both shifting and stubbornly constant societal attitudes. White settlement in the region is premised on structural Indigenous homelessness; as the capital of a settler colonial nation-state, Ottawa is a site of designing this structural homelessness and is also home for displaced Indigenous people from other parts of the country. Street-level homelessness has risen since the 1980s, a reflection of the divestment from public housing. Consistently, people without homes have been imagined and treated as criminals, moved out of public spaces, their possessions destroyed by NCC conservation officers.

There are alternatives that disrupt this hierarchy of homes and their dwellers: public housing. While also disruptive (like in the 1970s Lowertown public housing development), and not necessarily safe and happy housing (for example, many experiences with OCH today), public housing developments offer a challenge to imagining that housing must be profit generating. Public housing also has the potential to deliver what gentrifiers promise: heterogenous communities that can be sustainable, diverse, healthy, and safe.

Chapter 7

SUBURBIA

The Museum of Nature, an iconic castle-like building originally built as the Victoria Memorial Museum between 1905 and 1911, occupies prime real estate in downtown Ottawa. This spot was central to the landholdings of Bytown settler, shopkeeper, and politician William Stewart, who bought this plot in 1834 (Burns 1978). Stewart's land extended from the Rideau River in the east to Bronson Avenue in the west, Gladstone Avenue to the north, and Isabella to the south — much of contemporary Centretown. Stewart built a bucolic summer home here, a place to get away to from the urban hustle bustle of Rideau Street two kilometres away. He cultivated over ninety fruit trees and grew oats, wheat, peas, potatoes, and clover. William died in 1856, and in his will he requested that a better house be built on his property for his wife, Catherine. The result was Appin Place, a Victorian stone house with gabled roofs and elaborate trim surrounded by a high cedar hedge. In 1871, Catherine divided part of the land into city lots. The city laid streets that were named after the Stewart children: Flora, Florence, William, Williamina, Isabella, McLeod, Archibald, Ann, and John. One street — Catherine — is named after the Stewart matriarch herself. The region became known as Stewarton, and by 1877 it had a population of 250, its own post office, a general store, and Scrim's Florist (which still exists at its Elgin Street location). No longer the rural outskirts, Stewarton was becoming one of Ottawa's first suburbs. The City of Ottawa annexed Stewarton in 1889. After Catherine died in 1900, Appin Place was torn down in anticipation of the building of Canada's first national museum.

Since the late nineteenth century, Ottawa has suburbanized in ways typical of North American cities, beginning with the annexation of police villages and continuing with streetcar suburbs in the late nineteenth century, publicly built suburbs in the interwar period, developer-built auto-burbs postwar, the growth of "edge cities," and ongoing suburban sprawl today. Today, eighteen of the twenty-four wards are suburban or rural; only 241,000 of the city's million people live in downtown wards. Spatially, politically, and socially, Ottawa is a suburban city.

Richard Harris offers six characteristics of suburbs. First, suburbs are residential spaces of low density. Second, they include mostly detached or semi-detached family homes that are located at the urban fringe. Third, suburbs are marked by a high degree of homeownership, and fourth, suburbs are largely populated by the middle or upper-middle class. This is true of interwar and postwar suburbs, where the homogeneity of the homes and their prices attracted people from similar class backgrounds. This demographic homogeneity leads to Harris' fifth characteristic of the suburbs, which is that this population is politically distinct. Harris' sixth characteristic of suburbs is that they are largely residential, thus requiring a commute to access workplaces and places of leisure and commerce (Harris 2004, 18–19).

Together, these characteristics have given rise to a distinct way of life: suburbanism. Sociologist S.D. Clark wrote in 1966 that suburbanism turned families "in towards themselves.... Not a society in which people were alert to the important issues of the world" (quoted in Harris 2004, 7). For sociologist Ondine Park, echoing Clark's sentiment, a defining feature of suburbanism is an ideological and material interiority. Drawing on Walter Benjamin who was writing about nineteenth-century Paris, Park argues that domestic interiors are an individual's etui (small case of personal goods), and "the implication here is that the interior holds, contains, and collects together all the smallest traces of the individual's existence so they might not get lost." While the role of domestic interiors was not born with the Enlightenment, the Enlightenment's focus on individual freedom and private property transformed domestic interiors into "a fundamental component of self-fulfillment: without privately owned property — in particular, without access to a private interior — one could not truly fulfill the conditions of achieving selfhood" (Park 2016, 67–68). In suburban environments rooted in private property ownership, the focus on the interior as a space to produce and reflect one's individuality becomes outsized, especially in the context of homogenous house designs and strict community standards dictating that exteriors conform to a neighbourhood aesthetic.

Suburbanism is not a free choice of the majority of Ottawa's suburbanites; it is a choice structured for them and into which they are socialized by broad historical processes of suburban development, ongoing political and economic decisions, and ideological persuasion. Suburban homes are what is available and broader society (government, media, mainstream education) idealizes homeownership. Individual commitment to suburbanism, even when day-to-day realities suggest that suburban living is expensive, lonely, and inconvenient, embodies what sociologist Sut Jhally understands as the paradox of the "good life." Jhally detailed how advertising shifted in the early twentieth century from a focus on the use value of commodities for sale — or the item at the level of its literal use (denotation) (e.g., this bra clasp is strong and flexible) to selling commodities through their connotative signifiers (e.g., this bra will make you seem like an angel). This shift proved extremely useful for consumerism. Now, items were being sold as things that could provide for buyers an ever-promised but elusive good life. The result of this type of advertising was that consumers were encouraged to endlessly consume. If the good life was achieved, shopping would stop (Jhally 1990). This logic applies to all sorts of consumer goods, including houses. Geographer Dolores Hayden describes suburbia broadly as "the site of promises, dreams, and fantasies. It is a landscape of the imagination where Americans situate ambitions for upward mobility and economic security, ideals about freedom and private property, and longing for social harmony and spiritual uplift" (Hayden 2003, 3). Selling suburbia as an embodiment of the good life was made very explicit in the branding and selling of "Happiness Homes" in Long Island in the 1920s (Hayden 2003, 6).

Today the average Ottawa house is 1,948 square feet, almost double the 1,000 square footage of the postwar "sugar cube" homes of Carlington (Raymond 2023). These growing homes — and their lawns — are perfect containers for the accumulation of other consumer goods that are helpfully available at suburban box stores and through which suburbanites can attempt to achieve the good life.

The good life is also interiorized. Park, drawing on Hannah Arendt, argues that interiorization emerged at a time of broader alienation from "larger historical, political, and social forces, as well as from the pace and relentlessness of change under conditions of modernity and particularly of rapid industrialization." Retreating is a balm for the anxiety of engaging with a broad, and seemingly threatening, public. Leisure has also become privatized and interiorized as people outfit basements with video games and backyards with pools, making visits to arcades and community centres seem less necessary. The comfort and individualization offered by a domestic interior also promises the "good life, even if the conditions are ultimately annihilating." These conditions are annihilating because, as Park notes, again drawing on Arendt, a private life is one marked by "privation — a lack, an insufficiency." While surrounded by stuff, without the social — neighbours, friends, community — people are "socially dead" (Park 2016, 75). It may be a good life, but it is a small life.

In this chapter, I offer a history of Ottawa's suburbanization, from the nineteenth century annexation of police villages to the 2001 annexation of edge cities. I then analyze the paradoxes of suburban nature, the suburban lawn, and the "man cave," detailing how what suburbanism promises (nature, happy families) is at odds with what it delivers. Throughout this chapter, the tension between structure (designed neighbourhoods, with houses demanding or suggesting specific family formations and ways of living) and agency (the desires and behaviours of suburbanites) is clear.

SUBURBANIZATION: FROM POLICE VILLAGES TO EDGE CITIES

Settlers established a small number of police villages (with a minimum population of 750 to be incorporated as such) in the vicinity of Ottawa in the early nineteenth century. People built homes over time on the lots they had purchased, and villages would then outfit these communities with slowly expanding infrastructure. This owner-built development led to the slow building of communities heterogenous in demographics and architectural styles.

Annexations of police villages were premised on being win-win deals for the villagers and the city. For the residents, annexation promised improved infrastructure: paved roads (with newly developed tar macadam), firefighting services, sewers, and city rates for the local hospitals. For the city, annexation expanded their tax base. Ottawa annexed Rochesterville in 1887, Stewarton and Mount Sherwood in 1889. Some villages rejected annexation. Archville (now Old Ottawa East), was confident in its own water services so this village opted instead to become incorporated as the village of Ottawa East (Elliott 1991).

A compelling early planned development in this period was Rockcliffe Park. Thomas Keefer, son-in-law of Thomas McKay and inheritor of the sprawling McKay's Bush, was a gifted engineer; he designed timber slides and the city's waterworks. He also adhered to landscape science of the late nineteenth century. Motivated by the need to settle debts for the McKay estate, Keefer sold McKay's house to the colonial government (to become Rideau Hall) and laid out a grid on the property for development. In 1864, he divided the parcel into Park (which remains Rockcliffe Park), Villa (the toniest of houses in the city), and Village (what is now New Edinburgh). Industry was banned from this planned neighbourhood, and the influence of Frederick Olmstead on Keefer's plans can be found in the naming of Mariposa Avenue, Prospect Road, and Beechwood Avenue — all references to three projects of Olmstead's in Chicago (Edmond 1993).

Industrial-era suburbanization was motivated by citizens of all classes wanting more space, fresh air, and opportunities for healthier and happier living. In 1891, suburban development followed the streetcar line south to the Glebe, land that was being primarily used for recreation at the Aberdeen pavilion, lawn bowling, and tennis clubs (Gordon 2015). Development east was hindered by the Rideau Canal and north by the Ottawa River. West of downtown, the established working-class neighbourhood of LeBreton Flats impeded middle-class settlement (Newell 1995, 22). These geographical realities led to the land west of LeBreton Flats — what became Hintonburg — as the next region to develop.

After a career as a shopkeeper in Richmond, Joseph Hinton moved to join his son Robert on farmland south of the Ottawa River and west of Ottawa in 1868. In 1874, Robert divided the farm into 263 lots and named the village "Hintonburgh" (Leaning 2003, 20). In 1891 the village became more accessible and thus desirable when the electric streetcar line was extended, going along Holland Avenue and stopping at the western edge of the Central Experimental Farm (Newell 1995). Investors in the Ottawa Electric Railway formed a syndicate called the Ottawa Land Association (OLA), which, by the 1890s, owned the Holland-Hinton lands, linking transit and land development (Leaning 2003, 20). When Hintonburg incorporated as a village in 1893, the area of less than five hundred acres supported a population of 750 people, and by 1896, there was a town hall, police station, fire services, and four churches (Newell 1995, 4). After its 1907 annexation, Hintonburg became a classic streetcar suburb. New Edinburgh and Rockcliffe grew when the streetcar was extended to those neighbourhoods in 1894 (Edmond 1993).

Land in Hintonburg was marketed by the OLA to both middle and working-class buyers. In 1891, the neighbourhood's residents were mostly labourers — only 5 percent were civil servants. By the 1920s civil servants, an accountant, and an optometrist lived on Byron and Kenora Avenues, while Stirling Avenue continued to be home to labourers and carpenters. Plots on Stirling were narrower, with little street frontage, and became populated by cheaper wood houses. West of Holland Avenue was developed by middle-class homeowners (Newell 1995). This development was characteristic of streetcar suburbs that were generally heterogenous in social class and consisting of owner-built homes (Harris 2004).

Many Ottawa suburbs were designed to reflect "Garden City" principles. In the 1890s, British landscape architect Ebenezer Howard, who developed this urban design model, understood cities as acting like "magnets," drawing people into their core to work and access resources. He also understood that people and human society needed access to nature to thrive. In Howard's plan the ideal Garden City was built on six thousand acres, with one thousand acres dedicated to city life, which would ideally support a community of thirty thousand people. The city would have a public garden in its centre, surrounded by public buildings with six tree-lined boulevards radiating towards the edges, where the factories, warehouses, and timberyards would be. Frederick Todd's 1903 plan for Ottawa was informed by the Garden City movement. Central Park in the Glebe and Dundonald Park in Centretown were designed by Todd. In Howard's plan human waste would be transported to the agricultural sections of the city and, optimistically for the 1890s, Howard wrote, "The smoke field is kept well within bounds in Garden City; for all machinery is driven by electric energy" (Howard 2003, 106). Neither the vision of all-electrical energy or human waste as manure came to pass in Ottawa's process of suburbanization; however, Andrew Holland rented some of his land to farmers and unsuccessfully attempted to broker a deal with the city to dispose of its waste (emptying outhouses and cesspools) onto the fields in the late 1800s (Allston 2017). In a conversation with a city employee at the 2024 "Doors Open" event that was the big-city-trucks-a-palooza at the city's baseball diamond, I learned that in the processing of human waste, the wastewater released back into the river is a tea-like hue, and the — ahem — "remainder" is powdered and sent to farmers to use as fertilizer. Howard and Holland's dream has been partially realized.

Lindenlea, a suburb built by the Ottawa Housing Commission between New Edinburgh and Vanier beginning in 1919, was informed by Garden City principles. In this period, there was a housing crisis alongside the postwar return of veterans. One of the advocates of the Garden City movement, Thomas Adams, became the town planning advisor to the federal government's new (established in 1909) Commission of Conservation. Adams' report encouraged the federal government to build more housing for returning veterans and working-class people and to provide interest-free loans to individuals and cities to build housing. Adams designed Lindenlea as a model to inspire other government-led developments in Canada. The houses, on 168 lots, took the form of five or six designs from which homeowners could choose. In the end, the neighbourhood included brick and stuccoed two-storey houses with verandahs, side porches, and second-storey balconies and large windows to encourage ample fresh air. The houses included consolidated bathrooms (tub, sink, and toilet in the same room) and built-in closets, both new design features (Delaney 1991). Unlike future suburban development, this community was publicly built for a working-class population. However, Adams' focus on design and quality construction led to houses that were financially out of reach for working-class Ottawans, so the neighbourhood was inhabited largely by middle-class civil servants. Interwar suburbanization also gave rise to Ruskin Place, which included single-family homes, purpose-built rental housing, and the publicly built suburban "sugar cube" houses of Carlington, marking the beginning of homogenous suburban development.

The post–World War II development of large suburban developments with larger homes, privatized green spaces, and single-use zoning was influenced by a growing middle class that could afford buying their own homes. Furthermore, the 1944 National Housing Act (NHA), which followed the Dominion Housing Act of 1936, offered long-term, low-interest mortgages to Canadians, a move that greatly increased access to homeownership for the middle class (Hercules Stevenson 2013). The Canada Mortgage and Housing Corporation, a Crown corporation that emerged from the NHA, favoured suburban building by developers who could contribute upfront investment in developing the infrastructure — water, sewage, etc. — and then transfer those costs to the home buyers (Harris 2004). This practice began with the building of Don Mills, Ontario, a development outside of Toronto, and by the end of the 1950s, it had become the norm. The Ottawa equivalent of Don Mills was the development of Manor Park, a community just east of Rockcliffe Park. Gloucester township expropriated the land and sold it to Manor Park Reality in 1944. They in turn subdivided the 225 acres and planned the community to include single-family dwellings (offered in a limited number of designs), an elementary school, a shopping plaza, and a park (Hercules Stevenson 2013).

This model of corporate suburban development led to homogeneity in the suburban landscape because it was cheaper for developers to build a series of identical homes, leading to what Richard Harris refers to as "creeping conformity." This process greatly enriched developers, who would build with upfront capital then transfer costs onto individuals, who would pay for their homes (and the embedded infrastructure) over time with long-term mortgages. Developers would, in turn, back politicians who supported their plans to annex and develop more land. Meanwhile the large-scale adoption of private automobiles (the number of cars on Canadian roads grew from 1.1 million in 1945 to 4.3 million in 1961), meant that more land became devoted to highways, parking lots, angled and underground parking, gas stations, and race tracks (Harris 2004, 143, 129). The corporate suburbs were planned with presumptions of car ownership, giving these developments the name "auto-burbs."

Unlike streetcar suburbs, postwar suburbs were specifically oriented toward middle-class families. Historian Veronica Strong-Boag explains that an expanded welfare state and high employment inspired people to work toward "the lifestyle of comfortable homes and new products advertised since the 1920s in the continent's popular media" (Strong-Boag 1991, 474). In Ottawa, the expanding civil service — with its solidly middle-class white collar and largely male workforce (Andrew and Doloreux 2012, 1293) — offered the perfect clientele for the city's growing auto-burbs.

In the 1950s different construction companies bought lots and built homes in the new subdivisions of Faircrest Heights, Applewood Acres, Ridgemont, and Elmvale Acres on what had been Rideau Park, part of Billings' estate. Campeau Construction developed Applewood Acres, building 350 homes, seeming to draw on the designs of CMHC houses (Svirplys 2011). Much of this neighbourhood, which became Alta Vista, was sold as single lots and built on by individuals; developer-led suburbanization was not yet fully established (Alta Vista Community Association 2024).

An image of all-white suburbs emerged in the postwar United States when practices of mortgage discrimination and "white flight" led to racially homogenous suburbs. In Canada, there is a paucity of data on the racial composition of postwar suburbs or on experiences of mortgage discrimination. Yet, postwar suburbs, homogenous in social class demographics, were likely shaped by the racial composition of Canada in this period. Immigration policies before the 1960s were structured to encourage largely white immigration to Canada. In 1961, less than 3 percent of Canada's population of eighteen million people was non-white (Breton 1998, 85). Today, older postwar Ottawa suburbs like Beaverbrook continue to have racialized populations lower than the city average. But not significantly — 26 percent of Beaverbrook is racialized, compared to the citywide average of 32.5 percent (Ottawa Neighbourhood Study n.d.).

Bill Teron was also a fan of the Garden City movement. Teron bought 1,200 hectares of land west of Ottawa in the 1960s to build a model community designed to include mixed-density living, commercial and residential spaces, and large open spaces. In 1964, Tiffany Crescent was built in what was then its own city, Kanata. Teron divided the city into smaller communities, including Glen Cairn, Bridlewood, Katimavik, Hazeldean, Morgan's Grant, and Kanata Lakes, each of which was to have its own commercial centre. In an interview, Teron described the landscape he was crafting into Beaverbrook to work with the natural environment: "This was the rugged romantic. The houses are meant to be cottages in the woods. They're not meant to be peacocks" (Laucius

2018). Teron imagined Kanata to be a complete community; homeowners immediately became members of the community association, and Teron built tennis courts, a golf course, a riding stable, and a swimming pool. The community was designed to include townhouses, single-family homes, and apartment buildings (Laucius 2018).

Despite Teron's ambitions, Kanata has become a low density, car-dependent suburb with large Minto and Richcraft homes and little regard for the ecological consequences, embodying postwar "suburbanism." Kanata developed as an edge city beginning in the 1960s and then most explosively embraced this status in the 1990s. An "edge city," as defined by Joel Garreau in 1991, is a city that emerged after the 1960s, had over five million square feet of leasable office space, 600,000 square feet of retail space, and "more jobs than bedrooms" (Garreau 1991, 6). In the 1990s, at the height of the tech boom, one in nine employees in Ottawa was either a scientist or an engineer (Novakowski 2010, 556). In Kanata, the sprawling 367-acre Carling Campus (which was first acquired by Bell Canada and Northern Electric, the precursors for Nortel, in 1971) was, at its peak in the 1990s, the workplace for ten thousand employees. Barrhaven, developed in the 1960s by Mel Barr on land outside of the Greenbelt, also exploded in growth in the 1990s when Nortel and JDS Uniphase set up shop in the growing suburb (Andrew and Franovic 2020, 310). Nortel went bankrupt in 2009, sold their Kanata campus to the federal government, and from 2000 to 2016, the tech industry workforce in Ottawa shrunk, from 73,000 to 42,500 (Bagnall 2016). The Department of National Defence began moving into the old Nortel buildings in 2017. Kanata, which today has three million square feet of office space at the Kanata Research Park alone, its own expansive shopping centres, and the Bell Sensplex Arena, was a quintessential "edge city" until its amalgamation with Ottawa in 2001.

In 1969, Ottawa was part of the Regional Municipality of Ottawa-Carleton (RMOC) which was the upper tier level of municipal government; below it were sixteen lower-tier municipalities, although several annexations reduced the number of lower-tier municipalities to eleven in 1974. In this arrangement, the RMOC was responsible for a number of municipal services and for 80 percent of the tax base; the lower governments were responsible for 20 percent of municipal taxes. In the 1990s, urban amalgamations were imposed on cities across North America. In 1999, Premier Mike Harris ordered four regions in Ontario to "come up with a restructuring 'solution' to lower taxes, enhance services, reduce the number of local politicians, and increase accountability" within ninety days (Rosenfeld and Reese 2003, 59). Amalgamations were the solution. Between 1996 and 2002, 566 municipal governments were amalgamated to create 198 larger municipalities in Ontario (Rosenfeld and Reese 2003). In the Ottawa region, twelve local governments were amalgamated into three. The post-amalgamation Ottawa included: Ottawa, Gloucester, Cumberland, Nepean, Kanata, Vanier, Rockcliffe Park, the townships of West Carleton, Rideau, Goulbourn, Osgoode, and the Ottawa-Carleton Regional Municipality. Overnight Ottawa became a city that suddenly included rural fairs, pumpkin patches, new industries, thousands more voters, schools, more garbage to collect, and thousands more kilometres of roads to manage.

According to a study by the Fraser Institute that focused on the period between 2010 and 2012, municipal amalgamations in Ontario did not achieve their objectives; instead they led to higher property taxes, higher employee costs, and increased long-term government debt. Costs went up when cities were required to make quick decisions when consolidating services, rush negotiations with labour unions, and harmonize services across large rural and suburban areas (CBC News 2015).

If we consider Harris' fifth characteristic of suburbanization, that suburbanization leads to politically distinct neighbourhoods, the 2001 amalgamation has had a considerable impact on municipal politics. Of the twenty-four councillors on the Ottawa City Council, eight represent urban wards; the remaining sixteen councillors represent suburban or rural wards. Urban governance in Ottawa is largely driven by councillors who endorse the logic of suburbanism — two ways of life that are at odds in many ways. Frequently (like in the 2025 budget that included massive cuts to public transportation), the few urban councillors stand alone in defence of the needs of the urban core. The "creeping conformity" in house styles identified by Harris has also been supported by *and* fostered a conformity of political views within the suburbs.

Since the 1990s sociologists have referred to Canadian suburbs with concentrations of racialized populations as "ethnoburbs." Today, the Ottawa neighbourhood with the highest percentage of racialized people is the inner suburb of Ledbury-Heron Gate (69.2 percent), followed by Chapman Mills (62.7 percent). The suburbs of Findlay Creek (57.8 percent), Stittsville East (52.6 percent), Emerald Woods–Sawmill Creek (57 percent), and the far eastern suburb of Portobello South (45.2 percent) all have racialized populations that are well above the city average of 32.5 percent. Ethnoburbs are created when racialized immigrants arrive to Canada and move directly to suburbs. This is partly a result of immigration shifts beginning in the 1960s, when the Canadian government began privileging educated, middle-class immigrants from around the world rather than exclusively white immigrants from Europe. New immigrants are drawn to the available space in suburbs and to settle near family and friends. This has led to new suburban landscapes that include the concentration of new places of worship, grocery stores, and other shops that cater to racialized immigrants (Addie, Fielder, and Keil 2015). Merivale Road has become celebrated for its bounty of more than twenty South Asian restaurants and multiple grocery stores that have opened in the last few years, a process the *Ottawa Citizen* referred to as the "desi-fication" of Merivale. The stores and restaurants also cater to the many South Asian international students who study at the nearby Algonquin College. Nisharg Gangwani, the proprietor of the Indian grocery store, expressed that having his store within customers' walking distance was a priority for him (Hum 2023). A walkable, racialized suburban neighbourhood contrasts with the auto-burbs of the postwar period.

What does suburbanism look like in Orléans, Stittsville, and Barrhaven? Ottawa suburbs, I argue, offer three compelling paradoxes to forward the overall suburban paradox of the good life: the paradox of suburban nature, the paradox of suburban lawns, and the paradox of the "man cave."

THE PARADOX OF SUBURBAN NATURE

In the late nineteenth and early twentieth centuries, suburban nature was imagined as offering a regenerative counterpart to the overcrowding and industrial grit of urban life (Newell 1995). After a typhoid epidemic in 1913, the new suburb of Woodroofe Gardens, which boasted its clean well water saw 28 percent growth in one year (Elliott 1991, 201). Yet, suburbanism has a paradoxical relationship with nature: suburban life is sold to people as increasing access to nature, yet urban sprawl gobbles up of all sorts of nature (agricultural lands, forests, wetlands, streams) and structures a dependence on environmentally destructive cars.

On a bright February weekday in 2023, I visited my friend Hollis and her baby in her new home in the south Ottawa neighbourhood of Blossom Park. We all bundled up to go for a walk around the neighbourhood. I'd expected a brisk winter walk through suburban residential streets, so I was surprised and delighted when Hollis' dog quickly led us onto a wooded path along a creek. I showed off some of the new trekking skills I had learned recently at a workshop in Blackburn Hamlet, pointing out the bunny tracks in the snow. Hollis pointed out some trees that had been downed by the derecho the previous spring. This, I learned, was Sawmill Creek, a tributary of the Rideau River, a precious bit of nature for the neighbourhood. Plans for a transit development in the late 1970s that would have led to filling in the creek had concerned environmentalists, who pointed out that the creek was an important natural environment, home to at least two owls, beavers, and other wildlife (MacLeod 1978). The creek was not filled in, but it was neglected, and in the early 1990s neighbours noted the smell and sight of oil in and around the creek each spring. Increased development in the region seemed like an obvious source (*Ottawa Citizen* 1991). The smell has subsided and today, Hollis, her family, and her neighbours retreat to the creek for daily walks and playful everyday adventures.

The Leitrim Wetlands no longer provide such a natural retreat. In 2003, after vigorous opposition by environmental groups, Leitrim — a unique ecological site in south Ottawa — was drained and a community of fifteen thousand people hunkered down in newly built Taggart houses in a development called Findlay Creek. The wetland, layered in ancient peat, and with its own unique variety of flora and fauna was almost entirely destroyed by the development. Naturalist Dan Brunton explains that "the vegetation and the … tightly balanced systems on the north side simply died out. Now they're replaced by really common plants and invasive stuff" (Mills 2024). In its place residents and visitors can walk the Findlay Creek Boardwalk, a five-hundred-metre stroll that offers a bit of a museum-like whiff of a lost landscape.

In June 2024, the city embarked on a six-month, $50 million project to expand two kilometres of Bank Street from two to four lanes at Findlay Creek (Szperling 2024). When ecologists again sounded the alarm for disruption to the natural environment, Brunton quipped, "there's nothing left. It's been transformed from any shred of naturalness" (quoted in Mills 2024). Despite this mournfully dead ecosystem, and the economic pressures of living in conditions of being "house poor" that many new homeowners in Findlay Creek find themselves (Hitsman 2024), the neighbourhood is bursting at its seams; Findlay Creek's elementary school has twenty-three portables (as of June 2024) and three schools are slated to open in the neighbourhood.

A new suburban development in Ottawa's south end — Tewin — will also require expropriating large tracts of a complex and rich ecosystem. Tewin is the collaboration of Taggart and the Algonquins of Ontario Realty Corporation; *Tewin* is Algonquin for "home" and the development is being promoted as a move toward reconciliation (although many Algonquin people argue that AOO does not speak for them), being carbon neutral, and designed according to Algonquin principles. When the city allows new parcels of land to be developed it begins by "scoring" parcels for their viability. These scores are based on access to existing infrastructure (water, sewage, transit lines) and viability of the land itself. The Tewin properties scored −8, compared to other plots that scored up to 70 points. Despite the low score, the development is being allowed as "a sign of reconciliation" a decision that caused "First Nations chiefs to speak out in protest" (Porter 2021). The plot, 445 hectares, was added to an expanded urban boundary in 2022.

In 2023, in the middle of the night, Taggart and AOO clear-cut seventy hectares of trees on the property, in violation of a tree-cutting bylaw, and created a "green screen" by leaving a row of trees closest to the road. Initially, Taggart and AOO argued that they were clear-cutting to clean up from the derecho — but then they said no, it was to use the uncultivatable wetland property for farming (Hendrickson 2023). One of the critiques of this development is that the land is made of Leda clay, deposits from the ancient Champlain sea. When met with fresh water, the clay liquifies and becomes unstable. A Leda clay foundation is what led to the sinking of the central tower of the Museum of Nature in 1915 and the dramatic Rideau and Wellington Street sinkhole of 2016. Residents in the area caution that many people have had house foundation issues. All new houses in the Tewin development will require sump pumps, and low-rise buildings will need reinforced supports (Porter 2021). Taggart and AOO argue that developments across the city also are built on Leda clay, and there are many building techniques that make these developments feasible. In any case, this development on land far removed from other suburbs will require significant investments in road and infrastructure building — meanwhile trees have already been destroyed and wildlife displaced.

THE PARADOX OF SUBURBAN LAWNS

Suburbs gobble up wetlands and farmland, and developers and suburbanites replace these landscapes with lawn monocultures. While aesthetic conformity in houses and lawns is the design of suburban developers, the logic of conformity is embodied by residents and enforced formally through bylaws and informally through neighbourhood pressure (a neighbour coming over to look at your un-mowed lawn and saying in only half-jest, "you don't want to be that guy"). A cursory survey of Ottawa suburban garden stores (Home Depot, Lowes, and Canadian Tire) found Scotts' "EZ Seed" (a combination blend including Kentucky Bluegrass and Golfgreen Nitrogrow) to be popular varieties for Ottawa suburban lawn-tenders. Kentucky Bluegrass is not indigenous to Ottawa. In fact, it is best suited for the west coast of North America. Ottawa lawn-tenders are participating in the "lawn industrial complex" that emerged in the United States in the late 1920s, driven largely by one seed seller — Orlando McLean Scott of Scotts Seeds. Ted Steinherg details that by the 1950s the well-tended American lawn had become an image of "domestic tranquility" (Steinberg 2006, 44).

Beginning in the 1920s, labour-intensive grasses were sold as preferable to clover — a grass that productively takes nitrogen out of the air and into the soil and requires no fertilization. Clover also attracts bees and is slippery when wet — both characteristics that were framed as unfriendly to children. The suburban lawn that is pristinely manufactured and groomed offers few ecological benefits. Lawns epitomize the paradox of suburban nature. This investment in private slices of nature has the appearance of the love of nature, yet the watering and fertilizing of huge monocultures has many negative consequences. The pesticide 2,4-D contaminates groundwater, impacting aquatic life, and phosphorus runoff from fertilizer has led to algae blooms. Overwatering, and growing lawns that need so much watering, deplete cities' water supplies. And then there are leaf blowers, the worst assaults on our sonic landscapes and machines that have been described as the "dirtiest engines on the face of the Earth" (Steinberg 2006, 166). (My new friends from truck-a-palooza 2024 assured me that the city uses low-frequency leaf blowers to limit this sonic violence.)

It is no longer legal for private homeowners to use large classes of herbicides and pesticides on their lawns. However, golf courses have exemptions to these bans in Ontario's Pesticides Act provided they submit an annual report on the pesticides used and limit their use to spaces of golf play. In a review of the twelve Ottawa golf courses that submitted an annual report in 2022, a number of herbicides and fungicides were used, including Triticonazole, Pyraclostrobin, and Propiconazole. The most popular chemical treatment in 2022 was Chlorothalonil; 702 kilograms of the fungicide was spread on ten suburban Ottawa golf courses in 2022 (IPM Council of Canada 2024). Chlorothalonil is toxic to fish and aquatic life and a significant contributor to honey bee decline by making bees that come in contact with the fungicide vulnerable to a gut parasite (Pettis et al. 2013). A quintessential suburban engagement with nature — playing golf at private clubs — gets specific permission to, and takes license to aggressively kill, precious pollinators.

Steinberg notes that lawn care quickly became gendered as lawns became individual outward expressions of success and neighbourhood expressions of order and respectability. Through lawn care, men could "act out their male fantasies for self-assertion — rooted in an earlier tradition of competitive individualism — by firing up the power mower and cutting down the grass" (Steinberg 2006, 57). The suburbs are imagined as heteronormative family places where women (mothers) attend to the interiors and men (fathers) the exteriors. The interior plans of the houses, with their standard larger primary bedroom and smaller other bedrooms, likewise suggest that the houses will be occupied by a couple with two to three children. However, the presumed heteronormativity of the suburbs is changing. In a study on gay men in Ottawa, a participant described this experience:

> Friends of mine actually put it very nicely in that they bought — they built this giant house in [suburban] Greely and you know, they dug up a big lawn, and at the end of the day, nobody really cared if they were two fags, they were more upset about the fact their lawn wasn't perfect.... And once they fixed their lawn, they were nice neighbours again. (Quoted in Lewis 2012, 304)

It was lawn normativity, not heteronormativity, that impacted the couple's experience of the suburbs.

Suburbs are still attractive for those seeking access to nature, and for many who live in suburbs that flank the Greenbelt, nature is available. Those living in Stittsville, who have lawns backing onto Old Quarry Road, are snug between nature and a shopping complex. My friend who lives in Barrhaven routinely walks and paddles in the nearby Chapman Mills Conservation Area, and I have learned so much about local nature from my romps in the Greenbelt land and former pine plantation in the suburb of Blackburn Hamlet. Yet a century of suburbanization, with its single-use low residential density and reliance on automobility, has had a net negative impact on the forests, wetlands, and farmland of Ottawa. Furthermore, suburbanism and its attendant logic of interiority has nourished a lawn industrial complex that extends to a golf course habit that encourages polluting the groundwater and sickening bees. However, this is not the only option for suburban nature. Even within existing suburbs, new "suburban imaginaries" (Park 2016), are possible and buds of more ecologically sustainable suburbs are visible. In my forays into suburbia, I've witnessed locals enthusiastically enjoying the Sawmill Creek path, a young girl picking wildflowers in an unfenced backyard along the Old Quarry Road trail, and a carefully rewilded front lawn in Kingsview Park.

THE PARADOX OF MAN CAVES

The 1920s Edwardian period was the era of the "new woman"; women experienced expanded work opportunities as nurses in World War I and in the growing civil service. However, they faced backlash in the interwar period, as government policies and popular discourse encouraged women to return to traditional domestic pursuits. Feminist backlash met the "city scientific" movement of urban planning and the rise of home economics as a discipline to reimagine home-making as a professional, legitimate, scientific (yet still unpaid) pursuit. Houses of Lindenlea were designed in line with the latest understandings of health and with the latest domestic technologies, which ironically demanded more, not less, work from women. The large second-storey windows designed for airing out houses also led to the need for constant cleaning and dusting (Delaney 1991, 160).

Corporate auto-burbs developed in the context of the baby boom of the 1950s. Women on average had 3.7 children, compared to the current average of 1.26 (Statistics Canada 2024b; 2018a). Larger families were seen to need larger houses and women were encouraged to return to more intensive child care responsibilities. As single-zoned residential spaces, the suburbs are imagined as feminine spaces: they are the private sphere. In contrast, the city — the public sphere — is imagined as a masculine space. During Ottawa's period of rapid suburbanization post–World War II, as the civil service was expanding, the civil service was also becoming a more masculine work environment. It was presumed that upon marrying, women would secure their place in the domestic realm in the growing Ottawa suburbs.

In the 1950s there was a boom in the availability of kitchen appliances and convenience food, yet "even convenience foods [had to] be slaved over to show love" (Marling in Neuhaus 1999, 5). Jell-O, the delicious gelatinous dessert, was much improved by adding cottage cheese, pineapple chunks, and whipped cream to become Jell-O salad. The convenience of the postwar era was burdened by gendered ideologies that demanded women spend time in the kitchen, yet now freed from tasks like churning butter, they had to trot over to the Westgate Mall grocery store to stock up on Jell-O and its accompaniments.

In 2008, after Robert Wang lost his job at Nortel, he redirected his focus. Wang imagined that during the ongoing recession people might become more interested in home cooking. His invention, the Instant Pot, hit shelves in the summer of 2010 and became an immediate hit (Robin 2016). While its name promises technological assistance, like Jell-O, the Instant Pot also implies more labour: making one's own yoghurt, making chili from dehydrated beans, feeding the whole block a dinner of pulled pork. Born in Kanata, the Instant Pot can be seen as an emblem of contemporary intensive gendered labour. Like the scientific design of the houses of Lindenlea, scientific innovations in Ottawa suburbs continue to contribute to — rather than alleviate — women's domestic burdens. The Ottawa suburbs are full of larger houses (to clean), more remote from community amenities and workplaces (to commute to), and new, innovative(!), domestic tasks (making your own yoghurt).

While auto-burbs emerged in the context of growing car ownership, most families had one car and women were often left at home all day with their children and little to walk to but new malls — and "once visitors got there, new plazas, lacking free public space and cultural amenities, offered them little beyond a community based on common commitment to purchase" (Strong-Boag 1991, 494). Today, suburbs with poor transit connections and the feminization of poverty that continues to restrict women's transit options mean that suburban women experience greater time poverty than men or urban women (Rose 2015). Amid ongoing suburbanization and a stubbornly unequal gendered division of domestic labour, larger houses and the cultural demand to engage in intensive motherhood suggest that suburbs contribute to women's oppression.

Despite men's show of dominance expressed through lawn care, suburbs are paradoxically read as emasculating. In the 2010s, people started naming renovated corners of their suburban homes (usually parts of the basement) "man caves." A man cave is a refuge for men, a place for their hobbies that may include a gaming system, a mini-fridge full of manly beverages, a raggedy man-chair. I know "man cave" is still a relevant cultural reference because Ottawa-based burger chain The Works has a burger called "Obi-Wan Kobe's Man Cave," a burger topped with caramelized onions, bold B sauce, Monterey Jack cheese, and bacon. "Man caves" suggest that because the suburbs are feminine, men are reduced to claiming just a small corner of their home, a home that presumably they have contributed to paying for, inferring that men are poorly served by suburban living. However, this is the pernicious nature of patriarchal messaging, which ignores that while women are encouraged to take ownership of the rest of the house, they are discouraged from holding power in the rest of the city or society. The "man cave" ideology reinforces the idea that the private sphere is for women and the public sphere (where power and influence lie) continues to be for men. If interiority is "small life," this life-shrinking disproportionately impacts women, who are expected to revel inside large suburban homes.

The man cave also contributes to the interiorization of leisure. My friend in Kanata, when asked to describe the man caves that he's visited, explains to me that many include kegs, so the homeowner can enjoy beer on tap, at home, making a visit to one of the prime suburban leisure opportunities — going to Moxie's or Milestones — no longer necessary. Yet, while suburbanism encourages the privatization of leisure — both through consumption-based leisure (going to the mall) and through the privatized parks of backyards and private pubs in basements — in the postwar period, suburban women created community through participation in parent-teacher associations, church activities, community groups, demands for libraries, and advocating for improved public transit (Strong-Boag 1991). Women continue to create community in Ottawa's suburbs today. The Diane Deans Greenboro Community Centre — a 2006 complex that includes the community's library and a full recreation centre — exemplifies the accomplishment of establishing spaces for shared leisure. My friend Hollis drops her tween son there many Friday nights for "youth night" and for teen cooking classes, indoor soccer, and so that he can play video games with his friends. She visits every Saturday morning for Zumba and the weekly coffee shop and book sale. The space offers an alternative to the "man cave" or a femininized and fetishized domestic interior while also challenging the dominant logic of suburban interiorization, as social supports, time, and leisure are enthusiastically and publicly shared.

THE SUBURBAN GOOD LIFE

Ottawa has been suburbanizing since the late nineteenth century, first through the annexation of police villages and the development of streetcar suburbs, then through interwar experiments in Garden City creation. Postwar suburbanization, initially informed by Garden City principles, quickly morphed into the auto-burbs found in other Canadian cities. A provincially imposed amalgamation in 2001 required the city to gobble up the "edge city" of Kanata, the city of Orléans, and a number of other rural and suburban communities. Ongoing government policies supporting corporate suburban house building and expanding the urban boundary reinforce this growth.

Such material conditions perpetuate and reinforce the dominant and paradoxical ideologies of suburbanism. The desire for nature that motivated the Garden City movement has been distorted into sprawling residential neighbourhoods of individualized backyards, planted with foreign grass varieties that demand endless water, herbicides, and pesticides. The fresh air, clean water, and gardens promised by Ottawa's earliest suburbs have been replaced by Barrhaven homeowners requesting permission to pave over their entire front lawn to create more parking (Mills 2022) and by crowded highways that pollute the air with exhaust, noise, and lights. Suburbs cultivate myopic family-centric orientations at the expense of engaging with broader communities. Suburban "man caves" suggest that this arrangement somehow alienates men, yet the focus on women as consumers and producers (of lunch, of family schedules, of happy children) further entrenches a patriarchal division of labour.

Yet it is not all structure and no agency. Suburbanites embrace their local, protected, natural green spaces, organize seed collecting and composting workshops, and advocate for environmental protections in city laws and policies. Suburbanites also challenge the logic of interiorization by forging community in various spaces and by organizing and participating in annual community fairs like Findlay Creek's Bazaar in the Park and Convent Glen's annual community barbeque. The suburbs are also shifting in form. Neighbourhoods in the College and Bayshore wards are full of rental apartment buildings, and intensifying condominium buildings are being built in Manotick, Stittsville, and Richmond. Suburbanism is like the Kentucky Bluegrass planted in Kanata lawns: labour-intensive, ecologically devastating, but with the perpetual promise of the good life. Yet, also like the Kentucky Bluegrass, this imported logic also requires close maintenance and can therefore also die out, leaving room for new imaginaries on how to live in community with nature and each other.

Chapter 8

TRANSIT

Here's a fun fact about this book: I wrote it, in its entirety, while waiting for the #7 Carleton.

Like many Canadian cities, Ottawa's early transitways were its waterways: the Ottawa and Rideau Rivers. In summer, Algonquin people navigated these waterways in elegant, lightweight birchbark canoes. During the lumbering era, in spring, the Ottawa River provided a fast-rushing transit system for felled logs, workers navigating the river in specially designed pointer boats, steamships, and timber slides to transport timber and bypass rapids. In the winter people travelled by sleigh on the rivers' frozen waters. The first road cut in Ottawa was Richmond Road, which was built in 1818 and went from Richmond Flats (now LeBreton Flats) to the military outpost of Richmond. Throughout the Ottawa Valley in the nineteenth century, roads were developed to facilitate the timber trade. Towns on the Quebec side of the Ottawa Valley (Low, Kazabazua, Gracefield) are eighteen to twenty kilometres apart, the distance of a day's horse-drawn carriage ride (Lee 2006, 67). Opeongo Road was built in 1854 and went from Bytown to Renfrew and south to Barry's Bay (Blank 2016). After the passing of the Public Lands Act in 1853 by the Legislative Assembly of the Province of Canada, settlers who cleared twelve acres, built a house, and resided on the land for five years would receive title to the land. Over 1,600 kilometres of colonization roads were built in the 1840s and 1850s to facilitate the granting of this land (Shragge and Bagnato 1984). Early roads were the crucial infrastructure that facilitated settlement and extraction of natural resources from the region.

Transit systems have enabled great flourishing of neighbourhoods, cities, and nations, and they have also killed neighbourhoods, cities, ecosystems, and been central to settler colonialism. Transportation networks are also a series of social spaces that require interactions that are both formalized (rules of the road) and informal (codes of courtesy on a crowded bus). A nickname for Ottawa used derisively by cycling and pedestrian advocates is "Auto-wa," referencing the city's seemingly endless devotion to the needs of cars. Sociologist John Urry argues that "automobility" is not merely a mode of transit, it is an ideology that "stemmed from the path-dependent pattern laid down from the end of the nineteenth century" (Urry 2004, 27). This devotion was not inevitable, though, nor must it last, although structures of path dependency and induced demand make automobility seem stubbornly entrenched.

For Urry, automobility involves six components. First, at the heart of automobility is a "manufactured object" — the car — produced through a small number of firms dedicated to the system's ongoing strength. Second, automobility, while it is a system supposedly designed for a collective, it is rooted in individual consumption; automobility is a privatized mode of transit.

This privatized model did not *entirely* begin with the car — the automobile was such named in reference to other mobiles — carriages that could not move on their own but were pulled by prized and likely fetishized horses. In Bytown's early days, the transit options were walking or taking a horse and carriage. There was no organized transit, although accommodations were made for horses; there are nods to this in Ottawa's downtown. The York Street fountain, installed in 2000, is modelled off of a fountain that stood at George and Clarence Streets in the 1890s. It features a small basin, a street lamp, and a drinking trough for horses. East on York Street, tucked away past a row of vintage clothing stores and across from cocktail bars, are Cundell's Stables, where Belgian draught horses and miniature horses are housed to this day. Cundell's provided horses for the city's snowplowing, fire, and garbage services beginning in 1890 (Mercer 2017). Many of the horses of Bytown, including the horses of the police and parliamentarians, were trained by one of the city's earliest Black residents, Paul Barber, who settled in the region in the 1880s. Barber also trained horses for the horse races that took place on the frozen Ottawa River (Lim 2017).

In the nineteenth century, horse transit became somewhat regulated. Horses had speed limits and were not allowed to trot over Sappers' Bridge. Bytown's court records tell the story of Dr. Edward van Cortland appealing a trotting ticket in the 1840s by arguing that first, he could not control his horse — anyone who knew his mare could attest to that — and second, he brought to court a witness, his patient's husband, who testified that had he not trotted over the bridge, he would have not arrived in time to save his wife's life. It is unclear whether or not the doctor was required to pay the one-dollar fine (Moffatt 1986).

Since the mid-twentieth century, cars have become fetishized and imagined as an index for freedom, accomplishment, sexiness. However, fetishizing cars was not obvious or instant. Many high-ranking civil servants from the 1930s to 1950s walked to work from their New Edinburgh homes (Granatstein 1998, 11). William Lyon Mackenzie King famously walked to work from his apartment at the Roxborough on Elgin Street, and Mayor Whitton insisted that a new city hall be built on Green Island because it would be a convenient walk to work — for her! Today, however, car ownership even among the working class is presumed and the fetishizing of cars is on display in Little Italy's annual Ferrari Festival, devoting downtown space to the Audi dealership in Lansdowne Park, and approving a $2.9 million tax break for creating a Porsche dealership on Montreal Road as part of its "Community Improvement Plan" (Pringle 2021).

Urry notes that automobility, while premised on private ownership, requires a complex of "social and technical interlinkages." Federal and provincial governments invest significant public money in highways and roadside amenities, and private businesses serve the mechanical needs of cars, taking up resources and space at the expense of communities and nature. While the early twentieth century was a period of significant investment (and innovation) in developing a streetcar system, by the 1950s, the public investment had turned almost exclusively to the building of roads and highways for cars. In 1950, Gréber's plan included creating ample parking spots set back from the street and removing electric streetcars.

The removal of the train lines along the Rideau Canal in the 1960s led to the creation of Colonel By Drive and Queen Elizabeth Driveway. Sociologist Rob Shields suggests that one of the impacts of the creation of Colonel By Drive is that by connecting people to Parliament Hill, the Rideau Canal, and other "crown" jewels via a driveway, Colonel By Drive naturalizes automobility by quite literally putting cars alongside nature. Colonel By, and other parkways — like the Kichi Zibi Mikan along the Ottawa River — present the car as the ideal way in which to experience the capital city and its natural spaces. Shields notes that such roads celebrate a human (and national) domination over nature. Colonel By Drive and Queen Elizabeth Driveway are parkways that follow the Rideau Canal — a man-made and controlled waterway: "an unusually satisfying 'passage' through a space in which nature is disciplined and precisely controlled: here and there the grass grows taller, but only as decreed by the picturesque conventions of landscape architects" (Shields 1996, 30).

The Queensway is not subtle in its domination of nature. In the 1950s, New York City urban planner Robert Moses orchestrated the mass destruction of neighbourhoods in New York City in the interest of highways, a move that inspired considerable citizen resistance, led in part by urbanist Jane Jacobs. In the 1960s, Jacobs mobilized locals to protest the proposed Spadina Expressway in Toronto. This era of highway creation and resistance also impacted Ottawa. On a visit to Canada in 1957, Queen Elizabeth II detonated dynamite from her perch on Hurdman Bridge, thus inaugurating the beginning of the creation of the Queensway. This too was part of Gréber's design; he envisioned a cross-town east-west parkway to be created along the old CN lines (Miguelez 2015). The Queensway (named by royalist Mayor Charlotte Whitton to soften the negative feelings toward expressways) opened in stages beginning in the east and ending in the west between 1960 and 1966. In the process, neighbourhoods were bisected, land was expropriated, and over 150 houses were demolished or moved between Island Park Drive and Bayswater Avenue alone (Allston 2015a). The grid was reorganized, streets were renamed with north and south designations, remaining houses were permanently jiggled by the explosive highway creation — some bathroom doors were never again closeable. In the 1960s there were plans to create an expressway on King Edward Avenue; the plan was shelved in response to outcry from the residents of Sandy Hill (Miguelez 2015).

Parkways and the Queensway have entrenched the car as the idealized mode of transit in Ottawa and have facilitated suburbanization and the development of suburban office parks and warehouses. Meanwhile, highways are significant contributors to light and sound pollution, their shoulders are routinely and fatally occupied by nesting turtles, and their pollution contributes to many health conditions, including dementia (Yasin 2022).

One of the correlates with path dependency is what transit scholars call induced demand: new transit infrastructure leads to new transit uses (El-Geneidy, Patterson, and St-Louis 2015). Induced demand means that as people choose trips by car they would not have otherwise chosen, this new "demand" leads to justifications to open up more land for urban development (as seen in the Bank Street widening in Findlay Creek). In 2019 the city budget included $100 million for 3.3 kilometres of road widening for Strandherd Drive (approximately $30 million dollars per kilometre) in Barrhaven (OttawaStart. com 2019). This widened road will quickly fill up with more cars. While induced demand is frequently noted when it comes to road widening, similar insights are less frequently levied in relation to improved active transportation infrastructure. Yet, when bike lanes and active transitways are created, they are also quickly populated. The immense success of the Flora Footbridge connecting Old Ottawa East and the Glebe, and the opening of Queen Elizabeth Driveway to active transit during the pandemic, offer two examples. Today, roads and highways are a considerable use of space. In 2017 the City of Ottawa maintained 5,661 kilometres of roadways — approximately the distance from St. John's, Newfoundland, to Edmonton, Alberta — $10 billion in infrastructure.

Fourth, Urry argues that automobility subordinates all other forms of transit, leading to a disinvestment or ignoring of the needs of public transit users, walkers, and cyclists — three modes of transportation to which I now turn.

In 1866, the City of Ottawa and Parliament approved the creation of the Ottawa City Passenger Railway. This horse-drawn streetcar system took passengers throughout the downtown on a seventy-minute, four-mile round trip. There were no regular stops, passengers flagged the streetcar and paid their five-cent fare. While the system was immediately popular, the streetcars were cold with hard wooden benches, and they often got stuck in spring mud and winter snow. A lucky passenger would hold the horses' reigns when the conductor collected fares (Hendricks and Philpott 1985). The streetcars were stopped in their tracks in October 1872, when nearly all of the city's horses were stricken with a horse flu, in an epidemic dubbed the "Great Epizootic" that was devastating North America; the flu didn't have a high mortality rate, but it did make the horses sick and unable to pull streetcars, fire engines, or carriages for a while. Veterinarians offered the remedy to this public transit crisis: mushy oat porridge, apples, and carrots to encourage the appetites of the flu-stricken horses (Powell n.d.d).

In 1891 Warren Soper and Thomas Ahearn created the Ottawa Car Company, which exported streetcars across Canada, and the Ottawa Electric Railway (OER). The OER led to Ottawa's earliest electric streetcar service, which began with four routes, travelling from Broad Street station on LeBreton Flats, to Albert Street, then down Bank Street to Lansdowne Park (Hendricks and Philpott 1985). With its cheap three-cent fares, OER ridership was high, peaking in 1921 at 336 rides per year per capita (almost a daily ride per citizen!) (Davis 1999, 351). Ottawa electric streetcars were the first in North America to have floor-mounted electric heating units and boasted polished oak interiors and plush red seats. In 1900 the OER introduced Sunday service, an addition that allowed many Ottawans to access green spaces and leisure opportunities by taking riders to the West End Park, Britannia Beach, and Lansdowne Park. In the Holt report of 1915, the authors note that streetcar use had Ottawa-specific rush hours: the regular morning and after-work rushes, and a rush hour between 11:30 a.m. and 2 p.m., on account of civil servants going home for a hot lunch (Holt et al. 1916, 126).

After its ridership peak in the 1920s, many factors led to the death of

Ottawa's streetcars: not enough investment in new tracks; the company cancelled the universal fare; car ownership was picking up, and this increased traffic was impacting streetcars' efficiency. Finally, OER labour strikes in 1918 and 1919 led to the emergence of jitneys (unlicensed shared-ride taxis). In 1938, Ahearn declared that the era of Ottawa streetcars was over and that OER would henceforth only invest in buses (Davis 1999). In 1946 the City of Ottawa bought the Ottawa Electric Railway and created the Ottawa Transportation Commission in 1948. The last full day of streetcar service in Ottawa was April 30, 1959.

The Ottawa Transportation Commission was mostly funded through passenger fares. In 1972, the transit commission, now known as OC Transpo, was taken over by RMOC and service expanded to surrounding municipalities (Canada, Bureau of Management Consulting 1977). OC Transpo implemented region-wide fares, new suburban routes, and overall service expansion, all moves that increased ridership. In 1978, the city began constructing a bus rapid transit (BRT) system to include thirty-one kilometres of bus-only transitway, bus lanes on highways, and two one-way downtown streets (Albert Street and Slater Street) dedicated to the BRT. The first stage of the BRT opened in 1983. By 1985, the BRT had reached its peak ridership and was seen globally as a model system. The system capitalized on the existing high OC Transpo ridership, the economic crunch of the 1973 oil crisis that motivated people to use cheaper public transit, and the federal government's cancelling free parking for its employees and staggering its work start times, offering considerable incentive for the largest workforce in the city to use the bus. All of these factors led to a "decade-long 'virtuous circle' of rising patronage and improving service, backed by supportive policies in road space allocation and parking prices" (Al-Dubikhi and Mees 2010, 417).

By the late 1990s, though, the province reduced then cancelled its subsidies, fares increased, services were cut, and transfer stations were cold with exposed concrete and little shelter. Despite neoliberal austerity measures that had led to an erosion of the quality of the BRT, ridership was still high and buses were at capacity (ten thousand passengers an hour in each direction). In the 2006 census, Ottawa had the lowest driving mode share for work commutes of Canadian cities, at 60.4 percent, compared with 65.4 percent in Montreal and 67.3 percent in Vancouver (Al-Dubikhi and Mees 2010, 409), for which Al-Dubihki and Mees (2010) credit the innovative and highly successful BRT system. To respond to the system's operation beyond capacity, in 2008 the city began the long (and ongoing) process of creating a light rail transit system.

The bus system, even in its heyday, had significant limitations. It was primarily designed for civil servants with routes to and from the downtown core. There were much fewer routes for people, including the increasing population of immigrants, who lived and worked in the suburbs. Getting from downtown to the suburbs, or within suburbs, outside of peak hours (for shift work and non-work activities) was difficult, a limitation disproportionately impacting women and racialized people engaged in care work and working in the suburbs (Andrew and Franovic 2020). Women are more likely to use public transit because of the gendered nature of poverty (Rose 2015). In Ontario, 57.6 percent of public transit commuters are women (Cruikshank 2017). Women are also more likely to make trips to more places — work, home, daycare, school, grocery stores, arenas, and so on — and are poorly served by systems designed for primarily work-to-home trip patterns (Rose 2015). A 2018 study by the Healthy Transportation Coalition and the City for All Women Initiative (CAWI) on public transportation recommended that to make public transit more equitable, OC Transpo should implement a family transit pass, lower the cost of the EquiPass, improve rural access, build more bus shelters, improve GPS for bus schedules, extend length of time for bus transfers, implement online booking for Para Transpo, and increase the number of bus routes for the suburbs (Lambert 2018). Poor suburban public transit also does a great disservice to teenagers. At a recent visit to a sociology class at St. Peter High School in Orléans, in a discussion of personal troubles as public issues, I learned that route #13, a key way many students got to school, had been recently changed, worsening many students' commute.

Transit systems enable or disable people from participating in civic and social life. The "social model of disability" argues that impairments — inabilities to walk, see, hear — are located in the body, but disability is produced socially through our environments: workplaces, schools, media, and cities (Landsman 2009). Ottawa's public transit system has made efforts to make the city more accessible. OC Transpo's policies stipulate that it is to accommodate assistive devices, including wheelchairs, canes, and service animals. Yet disabled users have long voiced concerns about safety and facing violence on the bus system as well as the lack of a plan for disabled passengers when the LRT requires emergency evacuation (Lythall 2023). Frequently, automatic doors and elevators in transit stations fail to work, preventing people with disabilities from accessing the entire system. There are reduced fees for people with disabilities; OC Transpo also operates Para Transpo, a service that will pick up people at their homes. Yet there are severe limitations to this system, including issues with online booking, wheelchair-accessible taxis that require wheelchair users to sit at dangerous and uncomfortable angles, consistently late bus service, and, most gallingly, despite the relentless work of disability activists, users of Para Transpo must call or book online a day before the ride is needed (Crawford 2023).

Public transit has also faced deprioritization and disinvestment with inter-city travel. For those not as enamoured with Ottawa as this author, one of its enduring appeals is that it is less than two hours from Montreal and not too far from Toronto. But what if you cannot get out of Ottawa? Inter-city transit has been greatly reduced (i.e., it is horrible!). Greyhound, the premier inter-city bus company, shuttered its business in 2021. Taking the train remains both expensive and slow. Those without their own car are left with few options. This isn't a new phenomenon; passenger transit in and out of Ottawa has never been a priority. Early train transport was designed to transport logs rather than people. In 1848, a group of businessmen met in Bytown to coordinate the building of a train line to Prescott, a town 60 kilometres to Bytown's south; the result was the Bytown and Prescott Railway (B&PR), whose lines connected to those of the Grand Trunk Railway that travelled Toronto to Montreal and south into the United States. The first trains left the B&PR station in New Edinburgh on Christmas Day, 1854. In 1855 the company was renamed the Ottawa and Prescott Railway (Lee 2006, 99). In 1859, the Brockville and Ottawa Railway established a route from Chaudière Falls to Carleton Place to export lumber from the Ottawa Valley. In 1870 the Brockville and Ottawa Railway built a line that carried lumber from a station at LeBreton Flats to the St. Lawrence River at Brockville, ending at one of Brockville's enduring tourist attractions: Canada's oldest train tunnel! In 1895 J.R. Booth built a train station south of Rideau Street, on the east side of the Rideau Canal for his railway company Canada Atlantic Railway (CAR). CAR was created in 1879 to ship lumber and grain from Georgian Bay to Ottawa and Montreal, and it was eventually sold to Grand Trunk Railway (Lee 2006). In the nineteenth century, downtown Ottawa was a tangle of train tracks.

In 1910 the Grand Trunk Railway acquired land at Elgin and Wellington Streets to build the city's grand new Union Railway Station. From its opening in 1912 until it stopped operation in 1966, the station was at the bustling heart of downtown Ottawa, and it delivered passengers but also mail and goods to nearby department stores, and food to ByWard Market shops. In April 1954, a delegation of thirty-four Black men and women — representatives of the Negro Citizenship Association — and supporters from Canadian Jewish communities chartered a sleeping car and arrived in Ottawa to have audience with Prime Minister St. Laurent's government and spread their conviction of being (as their motto stated): "Dedicated to the making of a better Canadian citizen." The delegation was largely made up of Black railway porters who, through their work, and the social capital nourished through expansive Canadian travel, mobilized to challenge the anti-Black racism in the existing immigration system (Foster 2019, 34).

In a 1939 plan for the downtown core, Gréber suggested removing the loud, polluting, and numerous freight trains from downtown. Gréber envisioned passenger rail arriving into the Rideau Street station, connecting visitors to downtown and the streetcar system. However, by the 1960s, the majority of visitors were arriving by car, the streetcars had disappeared, and the government decided to build a new train station in the inner suburbs (Gordon 2015). The current train station, located in an eastern suburb three kilometres south of Union Station, designed by architect John Parkin and opened in 1966, has been celebrated as an icon of Canadian modern architecture. The government was intent on razing the old Union Railway Station to create a parking lot. Fortunately, saving this Beaux-Arts building would become one of Heritage Ottawa's first successes. In 1969 the station became the Government Conference Centre (Heritage Ottawa 2017).

In 2021 Greyhound Canada announced that it was ceasing all operations in Canada and selling off its stations. The Greyhound station that had been on Catherine Street since 1972 has already been demolished; the site now is surrounded by scaffolding for a new condominium development. Many Ottawans remember — if not fondly, at least fairly neutrally — the Greyhound station as a reliable place to wait for buses, pick up visitors, enjoy one of the last remaining photo booths, and wait for a taxi after arriving late at night. An earlier inter-city bus company, Colonial Coach Lines, offered bus trips in and out of Ottawa beginning in 1928. The company was bought by Provincial Transport Company of Quebec in 1930 and then became Voyageur bus line. Their station, marked with a vertical marquee, was at the intersection of Albert and Bank Streets. In a *Lost Ottawa* article, Joan recalled in 1957 making thirty-five cents an hour as a clerk on Sparks Street and paying $1.10 in return fare to take the Colonial Coach bus to South March (*Lost Ottawa* 2019).

Since 2021 a few different bus companies have emerged to fill the gap. Yet the lack of a bus station as a reliable and safe place to wait for the bus, inquire about buses, and sleep through a layover has left a considerable gap in Ottawa's transit system. The emerging bus services find convenient (to them) places to pick up and drop off passengers, usually mall or big box parking lots. People are dropped off all over the city, in places not necessarily connected to the city's public transit system. As of 2024, one of these companies, FlixBus, was picking up and dropping off passengers at a makeshift stop by the still-in-construction National Library. Claude A. Lachance wrote a letter to his city councillor detailing the many problems with this arrangement, including noisy idling, diesel-spewing buses from 5:00 a.m. until midnight daily, passengers being dropped off with their luggage in between two LRT stations, a lack of garbage bins, and passengers having to weave in between delivery trucks to board their bus. As Lachance concludes, "this is the City of Ottawa, the capital of the country. Yet this so-called terminus has the feel of being a bus stop to a small village. And please don't wait until someone is seriously hurt because of the traffic congestion on Commissioner Street" (Lachance 2024). Being dumped on the side of a road is, indeed, not a fine or helpful welcome to the city. While inter-city bus transit is in decline, a new shiny system is on the rise: light rail transit!

I remember the September day in 2019 when my friend and I, both living in the Glebe at the time, walked up to Lyon and Queen Street to the station of the newly opened light-rail transit system. We rode the whole east-west length of the line and saw things we had never seen before — not extraordinary things, but little slices of the Ottawa landscape. Sadly, the shine on this new system quickly dulled. Months later, taking the LRT from my new Centretown home to Carleton on my way to a morning class, the LRT got stuck at Lyon and we were all kicked off the train. I emerged from the depths of the station, surveyed my options, and just as I was reconciling that I would have to walk and then inevitably wait for the notoriously unreliable #7 Carleton bus and potentially be late for my own class, I heard a small voice say: "Professor Davidson?" A student in my class was on the same stalled train; we jumped in a shared Uber and commiserated about our shared circumstance. This delay was the beginning of the LRT troubles. The LRT has since been afflicted by doors that closed on people, trains derailed by a loose gear box and stalled by ice, stations falling apart, and a lingering foul smell at the Rideau station. The system shut again in July 2023. The culprit blamed this time? Big crowds during Bluesfest.

Why is the LRT a mess? Is it the French Alstrom trains untested for Ottawa's climate? The tracks? The labour shortage during the time of its creation? Was it the system of procurement? The lack of local representatives on the Rideau Transit Group (RTG)? Perhaps it was Mayor Jim Watson's insistence on cheap and fast, and therefore not good? Journalist James Bagnall (2020) suggests this: "For a city with no recent experience in building an LRT system, insisting on speed was a risk." Mayor Watson's city council voted against an inquiry into the LRT disaster in October 2021. A provincial inquiry identified the following as key issues with the Ottawa LRT: off-loading financial risks on to RTG through the public-private partnership model, using unproven vehicles, a lack of coordination among contractors, the disruption brought on by Rideau Street sinkhole in 2016, subcontractors promising completion dates they knew could not be met, the city and RTG lowering functionality criteria when they knew the criteria could not be met in 2019, a fact that the city manager didn't share with city council (Hourigan 2022). The LRT on the north-south Trillium line, including its spur to the airport, is up and running now. However, regardless of how reliable the LRT is, it shares a limitation of the BRT. The considerable investment in these LRT lines has led to the cancellation of a number of bus routes, making getting around in the many parts of the city not easily connected to the LRT even more difficult.

Transportation systems structure and require interactions between strangers. Sometimes these interactions are very close, as elbows jab your back and backpacks of strangers fall on your lap on a crowded OC Transpo bus. One of my most shameful memories is the time, approximately twenty years ago, when I got fries at the chip truck at the corner of Sunnyside and Bank then jumped on the #7 St. Laurent. While I held onto the strap, the grease from my fries dripped on an unfortunate passenger's dress pants. Eternal apologies, fellow transit user. While there are many environmental impacts of automobility, Urry argues that there are also social impacts to automobility through the weakening of neighbourhood vitality, and lost opportunities to practice civility, which are available on public transit. Urry explains that drivers on a shared road engage in a formal civility based on "shared rules" and "communicate through common sets of visual and aural signals, and interact even without eye-contact in a kind of default space or non-place available to all 'citizens of the road'" (Urry 2004, 29). However, road civility is distinct from interacting with others face-to-face as pedestrians or bus riders. Urry suggests that being ensconced in powerful yet anonymized machines decreases civility as drivers are no longer fully human, more hybrid. Furthermore, eye contact from cars is more difficult and sometimes impossible. The subtlety and intimacy of eye contact is replaced, via automobility, by the aggressive horn as a form of interaction. Automobility also necessitates parking — the most antisocial of land uses.

Urry's fifth characteristic of automobility is that it aligns with other ideologies that imagine a narrow scope of what constitutes the good life (Urry 2004). Cars are celebrated in coming-of-age movies, children's cartoons, leisure activities (the contradictory logic of demolition derbies — are they a challenge to, or a conspicuous celebration of automobility?). But, like the promise of the good life sold through suburbanism, this promise is also full of paradoxes. The owning and driving of cars is a large expense, requires specific embodied capabilities, and is only experienced as convenient in the absence of a robust, reliable public transit system. These paradoxes are revealed when we look at the under-celebrated joys and benefits of walking and cycling.

Ottawans love to walk, absolutely. If you find yourself on some of the 150 kilometres of trails in the Greenbelt in any season you will find crowds of families, pensive solo hikers, walkers with pockets full of bird seed for the chickadees, folks snowshoeing, and people checking birding apps. This walking is celebrated, similar to the sojourning promoted in the nineteenth century to Victorian middle-class men (Urry 2007). However, this appreciation of walking as leisure does not translate to pedestrian-friendly transit planning. In late nineteenth-century Europe, aimless walking was medicalized as a form of "fugue" compulsion and then criminalized through anti-vagrancy laws (Urry 2007, 82). Department stores had such an appeal in early twentieth-century Ottawa because of how they offered a rare space for women to walk unbothered in public, reflecting how walking the streets was dangerous and seen as morally suspect for them. Many factors impact walkability: tree canopies, sidewalk quality, zoning that influences the variety of things to see and do on walks, conspicuous policing, and feelings of safety. Yet the greatest threat to walkability is automobility.

In Ottawa's Pinecrest neighbourhood, children are bused to school from across the highway. Their school is close, but still a terrifying and impossible walk for children of Pinecrest Public School; the school is separated from the neighbourhood children by the 417 Highway. Jaywalking continues to be criminalized and where people can walk is structured by material infrastructure (highways, sidewalks, street trees, curb cuts), but also social and moral conventions. Yet walking can be rejuvenating (even, or especially, in Ottawa's winters), allowing access to nature, neighbours, and surprising small enchantments. Walking is a joy, in part, because of the "pauseability" of walking as a mode of transit (Urry 2007, 74), the ease of slowing down or stopping for a conversation or a coffee. Pedestrians are most likely to enjoy street art like the murals of Centretown, the fire hydrant sculptures in Hintonburg, the cartoon sculptures in Chinatown, and are more likely to drop into stores, chat with neighbours, get to know the neighbourhood dogs, join a protest, and participate in the perpetual search for missing neighbourhood cats.

Cars are taken for granted as the transit of freedom, yet auto-oriented cities require certain embodied capabilities that shut out a lot of people with disabilities and are tested formally for everyone over eighty years old. In car-centric cities, old people move through the city less. In one Hamilton-based study, old people who relied on driving saw their distances travelled shrink more than old people who relied on public transit (Biglieri, Hartt, and Channer 2021). Car-centric cities are also more fatal to the old. The Ottawa Road Safety Report published by the City of Ottawa details that between 2014 and 2020, forty-two pedestrians were killed by vehicles on Ottawa streets. In Ontario, 63 percent of pedestrian fatalities at intersections are people over the age of sixty-five (Yasin 2022, 23), in part because the time given to cross an intersection is calculated based on an able-bodied, middle-aged norm. Managing shopping bags and perhaps a toddler, or a cane, and walking off of a bus into a snowbank is also very treacherous. In Stockholm, the city has begun to adopt a "gender-equal" snow removal policy by plowing the bus stops and sidewalks first, schools, and then bike lanes, recognizing that there, like in Ottawa, women are more likely to walk and take public transit (CBC News 2018d). Not only is this approach gender-equal, it is also one that facilitates the mobility of the very old and the very young, those who use mobility aids, and active transportation. Urban seniors are up to three times more likely than their suburban counterparts to meet the recommended daily physical activity level (Biglieri, Hartt, and Channer 2021) and are more likely to meet up with friends, be able to navigate heatwaves, visit the library, and access other resources.

Many North American cities, Ottawa included, are made less walkable by the lack of public washrooms. This is a need that cuts across all of humanity but is more likely to limit the urban mobility of people with disabilities, people who menstruate and are pregnant, people engaged in care work (disproportionately women), young children, and the elderly. Researchers have found that, among the elderly, people move throughout the city limited by the "bladder's leash": their awareness and confidence in being able to access a public washroom (Lowe 2018, 83). During the pandemic, many flooded the Queen Elizabeth Driveway to walk, and the NCC supplied porta-potties along the route (unfortunately these were closed during the week). Public washrooms are few, and publicly accessible washrooms are often unmarked. This issue is the focus of the Gotta Go! campaign, a social movement focused on encouraging the City of Ottawa to invest in more public washrooms. A 2016 audit of Ottawa's public washrooms commissioned by the Gotta Go! campaign sampled the quality and accessibility of a sample of ninety-two public washrooms in Ottawa. Of those washrooms, 45 percent of the washrooms were closed, either seasonally or for daily closure, only 21 percent were gender-neutral, and only 63 percent were deemed "wheelchair accessible" (CBC News 2016). The Gotta Go! campaign gained early success when they convinced the city to include washrooms in some of the new LRT stations, inclusions that exceeded the minimal building code requirements (Lowe 2018). One cost-effective and easy suggestion forwarded by the Gotta Go! campaign is that the city publicize existing publicly accessible washrooms (i.e., washrooms in city facilities, museums, libraries). Notably, the extensive renovations on Parliament Hill include an already available, easily accessible public washroom behind West Block.

Finally, automobility is the "single most important cause of environmental resource-use," one-third of all carbon dioxide emissions, and the cause of many wars (Urry 2004, 26). Partially in response to the ecological devastation wrought by automobility, cities have begun, since the early 2000s, to redesign urban throughfares as "complete streets" — streets designed to facilitate walking, biking, and driving. Since 2013, O'Connor Street, Churchill Avenue, Main Street, Campeau Drive Extension in Kanata, Robert Grant Drive in Stittsville, and sections of St. Laurent Boulevard and Queen Street have become complete streets.

A key element of complete streets is the creation of separated bike lanes. Considering the age of the wheel (very, very old), biking is a relatively recent invention. The Science and Technology Museum's exhibit *Freedom on Two Wheels* has suspended over a dozen bikes and over a century of biking history in a circle (cycle) on the ceiling. The earliest bicycle was a hobby horse — a bicycle with no wheels, a toy for rich adults, which was designed in the 1820s and didn't help with commuting at all. In the 1860s, the velocipede was born; this device had pedals on the large front wheel, iron wheels, and was colloquially known as the "boneshaker" — in reference to the comfort it provided. Bicycle design really picked up in the 1870s with the design of a bicycle called "the Ordinary" featuring outsized front wheels, improved comfort and speed, but requiring some skill and agility to mount. This period also saw the development of the adult tricycle that featured hand pedals to operate the back wheels. With its easier mounting, this device was marketed to women. The museum's collection includes the "Ladies Singer Tricycle" from 1879. Finally, the "safety bicycle" was developed in 1884 and it takes the form of today's bicycle — two wheels of the same size, gears, chains. With this bicycle, it was now possible to bike for leisure and for transit, and unlike the early days of the hobby horse, cycling is a relatively cheap mode of transit. Yet in Ottawa biking has historically been imagined merely as recreation to be limited to specific recreational paths.

In a city designed around the logic of automobility, cycling is often understood as deviant and risky (Scott 2016). This riskiness often translates into cycling being a gendered practice. In the early history of cycling, biking was imagined as unfeminine, and in fact, the practice of women biking was seen as potentially leading to the health condition of "bicycle face" — a look of constant strain brought on by the exertion. The *Freedom on Two Wheels* exhibit details that, despite this, and despite the designing of tricycles for women, by the 1890s, a third of cyclists were women, and accommodations — specifically a "skirt guard" for the bicycle's back wheel, were designed to facilitate women cycling.

Today there is a permanent "ghost bike" (a bike painted white) affixed to a gate in front of city hall as a memorial to ongoing cyclist deaths; the safety of cyclists is not prioritized in Ottawa. In the 1980s, in the wake of a cyclist death, citizens formed a group, Citizens for Safe Cycling, to encourage the city to invest in transit infrastructure that would improve cyclists' safety (Scott 2016). In 2010, the NCC committed to "Copenhagenize" Ottawa through the creation of segregated bike lanes. The first manifestation of this plan was on Laurier Avenue. The local business improvement association was concerned about the lane taking away parking spots, impacting business and causing an impediment to delivery trucks. In response, cycling advocates pointed to research that shows that cyclists stop and shop more easily and frequently than drivers do. Sociologist Nick Scott argues that segregated bike lanes also impact who bikes, acting as "democratic beachheads for inviting more kinds of cyclists into cities such as Ottawa, where cycling trips are dominated 2:1 by men." After its completion, Laurier Avenue saw a tripling of its cycling volume and was named one of the "top ten biking facilities in North America" (Scott 2016, 29). Today, cyclists continue to encourage city planners to see cycling as a mode of transit. In 2023, city council approved a transportation master plan that would increase bike lanes by 50 percent by 2046, adding crucial "missing links" to the bike path system so that cyclists aren't stranded between paths, and developing a bike network that would connect rural parts of Ottawa like Kars and Manotick to the rest of the biking network (Glowacki 2023).

POST-CAR FUTURES

Today, Ottawa is more Auto-wa than ever. In the 2022 election, mayoral candidate Catherine McKenney's plan for an expansive bike lane system became a stubbornly divisive issue, and the candidate that promised lower taxes and more suburban dog parks won. The 2023 city budget included cutting $47 million from public transit, while money was earmarked for plans to expand the road to the airport that will run alongside the new LRT extension. Despite the council's commitment to automobility, new transit systems are emerging: while it is rarely possible to "skate to work on the canal" as was promised at my Carleton job interview, the winter streets do seem to be populated with more fat tire winter bikes than I have seen before, and summer e-scooters are very popular.

Let me tell you about a few of my favourite Auto-wa spots. Flora Hall — a former garage-turned-popular microbrewery, bar, and restaurant on Flora Street at Bank — is the "Cheers" for many that live in the condo complex across the street, and it is one of only a few fully accessible bars in the city, taking advantage, as it does, of the garage-style door to the patio. Another gem is the Gladstone Theatre at Gladstone and Preston Streets. This theatre was originally a truck-repair garage and is now a vibrant performance venue, offering shows like the holiday concert of *Tone Cluster: A Very Queer Choir*, the *Sponge Bob Musical*, and *Hamlet*. A third favourite spot: at the corner of Island Park Drive and Wellington Street is my favourite gas station — the Island Park Esso. It is pretty off-brand for me to have a favourite gas station, but this is one rare full-service station, and when you get an oil change, they always run your car through the car wash. Along with that friendly service, another appealing aspect of this gas station is its original 1938 art deco style. It is the building's beautifully maintained design that inspires me to ask: what if this spot, could, like Flora Hall and the Gladstone Theatre, live on in new post-car functions, as a café, art gallery, or seed library for gardeners? If automobility requires a complex of "social and technical interlinkages," as Urry suggests, imagining a less car-oriented Ottawa will require envisioning new systems of transit and new lives for these interlinkages: reimagining garages, single-zoned suburbs, mall parking lots.

Chapter 9

SECURITY

It's Friday, February 18, 2022. A nice winter day, sunny, –12C. Nice weather in my favourite season, yet the city has been under siege for three weeks by people referred to as the "Freedom Convoy," fighting to get the federal government to repeal a vaccine mandate for truck drivers, but also fighting more broadly to overthrow the democratically elected Trudeau government, buoyed by the energy of pandemic frustrations. In the first few days of the siege, there was a stockpile of propane tanks under a tarp in Confederation Park. I left the city for the first two weekends, avoiding most of the honking and exhaust coming from trucks that had jammed Metcalfe, Kent, and Wellington Streets. During the week, I watched police officers casually walk past a group of protesters who had parked their vehicles, and themselves, at Confederation Square by the National War Memorial, music and generators blaring. But on this Friday, Ottawa — and more specifically, my otherwise comfortable downtown neighbourhood — became the site of a total police occupation. Ottawa police were joined by RCMP and police officers from other cities. I lived in the "securitized zone." Even though it was all happening just blocks away, I watched the police close in on the protesters on TV from the safety of my apartment. By the end of the day, peace — seemingly — had been restored. Many local sociologists and criminologists joined the broader public in amazement at this display of lawlessness and what appeared to be police collusion that allowed the occupation to last as long as it did. Indeed, the three weeks of disorder and the federal government's application of the Emergencies Act to forcefully remove the occupation would necessitate a national inquiry and inspire reams of still-not-fully-tapped academic scrutiny. For many, the initial underpolicing of the Convoy highlighted how crime, policing, and the law are all deeply political.

Italian scholar Cesare Lombroso, understood as the founder of criminology, like many nineteenth-century proto–social scientists, rooted his understanding of social behaviour in biology. For Lombroso, the heat of the summer agitated humans' criminal impulses, and human skull shape could be used to predict and explain criminal behaviours (Hassan and Lett 2023). Many schools of criminology emerged, starting with Lombroso, that questioned why people committed crime and focused on interventions to prevent it, but they had little to say about the role of power in determining what a crime was and in responding to them. In the 1960s, that biologically determinist understanding of crime became challenged by critical criminology, a theoretical orientation toward crime that began with the premise that collective definitions of deviant and criminal behaviour reflect power relations. People and institutions (the ruling class, patriarchy, white supremacy, etc.) define what is legal/illegal and how violations should be addressed. A leading thinker in this era, William Chambliss, explained how vagrancy laws created in the fourteenth century forced workers back to work; the laws were designed to facilitate capitalist accumulation (Walby and Gorkoff 2023). The Master and Servants Act worked the same way in nineteenth-century Bytown. The power relations embedded in laws are classed, but also gendered, racialized, and heteronormative. On Bank Street in Centretown there's a commemorative bench that details the story of Everett George Klippert, the last person incarcerated for homosexuality in Canada. Klippert was convicted as a dangerous sexual offender and jailed from 1966 to 1971 (Ibbitson 2016). The bench features an image of Pierre Trudeau talking to the press, ostensibly saying, "there's no place for the state in the bedrooms of the nation," the line he gave when his government passed Bill C-150, which decriminalized homosexuality in Canada in 1969, two years before Klippert was released. The policing (or underpolicing) of the Convoy, the legal powers embedded in the Emergencies Act that facilitated the eventual policing of the Convoy, the criminal cases, and subsequent incarceration are all expressions of power relations.

At the crux of many tensions in crime, policing, and incarceration is a debate about what political scientists refer to as the "social contract" between the state and citizens. There is a rich history of social contract theorizing — including that of John Locke, Thomas Hobbes, and Jean-Jacques Rousseau, who suggest that citizens and the state engage in ongoing power relationships, citizens consent to giving up power in exchange for protection, and as a result, are freed of life that would otherwise be, according to Hobbes "brutish, nasty, and short." The nature and content of this contract, and understandings of human rights and freedoms, are constantly negotiated. Ottawa is central to negotiations of our national social contract — it is here that Canada's criminal laws are drafted, debated, and passed by Parliament, upheld and challenged before the Supreme Court of Canada. Laws are upheld locally through policing, too — the state exerting its force to control individuals' behaviours and bodies.

SECURITY FOR WHOM?
POLICING THE TOWN AND CROWN

In 1827, Bytown's council appointed Alexander Frazer as the young town's first constable. In these early days, the closest courthouse was in Perth (85 kilometres but a long, bumpy carriage ride away), and many minor crimes were not prosecuted because the trip to Perth was difficult and generally deemed not worth the trouble (Craske 1992).

In 1837, during an unemployment crisis after the completion of the Rideau Canal, the young city was hit with its first experience of organized crime. The Shiners' War (1837–1845) was led by Peter Aylen, a man described as a "run-away sailor, timber king, ambitious schemer." Aylen's goal was to organize the Irish and "drive the French Canadians off the river and thus guarantee jobs and high wages in the timber camps to the Irish" (McTaggart in Taylor 1986, 34). The Shiners, who acquired their name either from how they shined their hair or from the French word for oak, *chêne*, attacked the rafts of French lumbermen. They took over the Union Bridge, "threatening travellers and demanding payment" (Gordon 2015, 57). John Taylor explains that "there were clearly many reasons for the Shiners' War, but probably at bottom were economic imperatives" (Taylor 1986, 34). It was a proletariat war, as two working-class groups fought for access to limited employment opportunities. Joseph Montferrand was one of the French folk heroes of this war. He could, according to lore, take on multiple Shiners at once, and in one instance, flung them off a bridge. The Shiners' War also inspired the creation of the city's first citizen police force, the Bytown Association for the Preservation of the Public Peace (Gordon 2015, 57). A third outcome of this war was the entrenchment of anti-Irish sentiment among the elites and other non-Irish working class in Bytown (Taylor 1986, 34).

Today, there are 1,480 police officers, five police stations and twenty community policing centres in Ottawa, a presence many want to expand; in fact, Mayor Mark Sutcliffe has already realized one of his campaign pledges, and the new Police Services Hub opened in the Rideau Centre in 2024. In the 2023 budget, policing was the largest expenditure, with a budget of $401 million, a $15.2 million increase over the previous year (Anand 2023). This is the budget for just one level of policing in the city. There are four layers of policing in Ottawa: the Ottawa (city) police, the Ontario provincial police (provincial highways), the RCMP (Parliament Hill, Crown lands, diplomatic events, national emergencies), and Parliamentary Security Services (Parliament Hill).

Security for the City

Ottawa is policed in ways typical of North American policing. The poor and racialized are overpoliced. In summer 2023, in a letter to the Ottawa Sun editor, Desmond Mills describes a walk along the Rideau River, observing weeds, dirt, and a "homeless encampment that had set up a bonfire." He concluded, "The city should abide by the broken windows theory. If visible signs of decline are allowed to fester and general standards are allowed to fall, so, too, will new problems arise" (Mills 2023). Mills is referencing an influential theory of criminal behaviour developed by James Wilson and George Kelling in 1982 that has become adopted as a form of folk wisdom today. The "broken windows" theory argues that minor signs of social disorder, like broken windows, rowdy teenagers, or panhandlers, are pre-criminal behaviour that, if not addressed, will create a context in which more serious criminal behaviour can flourish (Wilson and Kelling 1982). The impacts of accepting this type of theorizing are that cities have condoned policing that relies on the criminalization of poverty (ticketing panhandling or loitering), and racial profiling. The look of certain types of (racialized, poor) people and other non-criminal but non-normative behaviours (sleeping in public, for example) are often read as pre-criminal behaviours and policed as such. Decades of criminologists have detailed how this theory is unfounded. Bernard Harcourt details how Wesley Skogan analyzed the relationship between multiple crimes in multiple American neighbourhoods and "signs of disorder" (like broken windows) between 1977 and 1983. Skogan found a correlation between one crime (robbery) and broken windows in five Newark neighbourhoods, but no similar correlation in the other thirty-five neighbourhoods in other American cities and no correlation between signs of disorder and other crimes. Harcourt notes that while Skogan does not assert a causal relationship between disorder and crime, his conclusion is, however, that "disorder needs to be taken seriously" (Harcourt 2001, 63).

The overpolicing of poor and racialized neighbourhoods often is underpinned by "broken windows" logic. Broken windows are the result of poverty and often negligent corporate landlords (ahem, Timbercreek), and the higher rates of criminal charges laid on people living in neighbourhoods with broken windows is largely the result of more police officers hanging around laying charges for minor violations. Neighbours also contribute to the policing of "signs of disorder" by calling the police on non-criminal but subjectively interpreted "suspicious" activities or people. It is not a theory, but a self-fulfilling prophecy rooted in a criminal justice system founded on supressing the rights of workers and poor, Indigenous, and racialized people. Excessive policing of "signs" of sex work does not lead to a reduction in sex work but does lead to police violence against sex workers. The overpolicing of poor and racialized people and neighbourhoods leads to more anti-Black, anti-Indigenous police violence that has a long history in Ottawa.

The social contract between the police — whom we collectively allow to legitimately carry arms — and the citizenry is frayed when police overstep these rights. The Ottawa police have been, in recent years, critiqued for their excessive use of no-knock raids — police violently entering the homes of citizens where there is suspected criminal behaviour (e.g., possession of drugs or firearms). These raids have been criticized because they are traumatizing (using devices like "flash-bang" grenades), ineffective, and a violation of Charter rights. In 2020, twenty-three-year-old Anthony Aust jumped from his apartment balcony to his death in the midst of such a raid (CBC/Radio-Canada 2021b; Yogaretnam 2021). News reports, inquiries, and Supreme Court judgments all negotiate this violent clash between individual rights and liberties (to be secure in one's home) and the power of the state. In August 2023, news sources reported that no-knock entries by the Ottawa Police had declined between 2020 and 2021, from fifty-nine no-knock entries in 2020 to just two in 2021 (CBC News 2023b).

The Ottawa Police Service has a history of misogyny that is expressed through violence toward women who are arrested, are victims of crime, and are female officers. In the period in which I've been preparing this book (2021–25), a number of officers with Ottawa Police Services have been charged with misconduct (taking photos and videos of people in custody), rape, uttering death threats, criminal harassment, pointing a gun at a victim, and sexually harassing female constables. Some were convicted, some acquitted, most officers were put on paid leave (CBC/Radio-Canada 2021a; Trinh 2021). Of Ontario police officers on paid leave between 2013 and 2024, 35 percent of the 435 officers had been charged with gender-based violence, sexual assault, or intimate partner violence (Ireton 2024).

Like police forces in other North American cities, the OPS also has a long history of anti-Black violence. On the morning of July 24, 2016, workers at the Bridgehead coffee shop in Hintonburg called the police. Thirty-seven-year-old Somali-Canadian Abdirahman Abdi had been acting odd, harassing women in the shop and on the street. According to witnesses, the first officer on the scene, Dave Weir, tackled, pepper sprayed, and beat Abdi with a baton. Abdi attempted to defend himself with a rubber bolt retrieved from a construction site and tried to run into the apartment building where he lived. A second officer, Daniel Montsion, arrived and, after delivering many blows to Abdi's head while wearing assault gloves, Montsion pinned a motionless Abdi on the ground and handcuffed him. At 9:52, the cops called the paramedics. By the time he was seen by a doctor he'd already died. Within two days of Abdi's death, members of Ottawa's Somali community staged a vigil at the apartment building where Abdi had been killed and they established the group Justice4Abdi. The Ottawa Muslim Association paid for Abdi's funeral. Montsion was charged with manslaughter and tried, but he was not convicted. During the 2017 trial, Montsion's colleagues wore wristbands with Montsion's badge number to support their colleague. Anti-Black police violence was not new to Ottawa, or even to Montsion, who had been charged and acquitted of assaulting another Somali man in 2014 (Cole 2022).

Misogynistic and racist violence at the hands of the police significantly frays the delicate social contract and leads many to argue that perhaps this form of policing is not the way to ensure security for all. Women have organized their own systems to respond to gender-based violence in public spaces, like Project SoundCheck and the Hollaback! Ottawa campaign. Black and racialized communities organize to speak back to the police — as demonstrated in the Justice4Abdi campaign — and for other non-police means of assuring community safety. During the Convoy — when the police seemed, for local residents, to be indifferent at best, or pals with the unruly visitors who were waving flags of deeply racist groups at worst — many were not surprised and distrust in city policing deepened.

Policing of Ottawans is also facilitated by everyday surveillance through store cameras, neighbours' cameras, and people who post about "suspicious" activity on neighbourhood Facebook pages. In 2019, Mayor Watson proposed a series of closed-circuit television surveillance cameras (CCTV) to be installed in the ByWard Market in a project dubbed the "Ottawa Public Surveillance Project." The program's stated goal was to "contribute to the safe environment of the downtown areas; assist as one of the components of the downtown area's revitalization efforts; and improve the ability of the Ottawa Police Service and community to respond to crime and anti-social behaviour occurring in the downtown areas" (Watson quoted in Cave 2022, 68).

Sociologist Diana Cave drew on media accounts and interviews with interested parties to parse the dominant frameworks of support for and opposition to this project. A "law-and-order" framing saw people deemed as potential criminals through an "us vs them cognitive schema" that privileged the "middle-class, white, property-owning community members" as the "focus of *who* to be cared for, and *how* is through increasing enforcement and monitoring of those deemed as an *other* or deviant" (Cave 2022, 117, emphasis in original). This was the framing endorsed by city politicians, members of the ByWard Market BIA, and other advocates for the CCTV plan.

The "resistance" framing was adopted by an advocacy group created precisely to oppose this project: the Coalition Against More Security (CAMS). CAMS argued that surveillance is not a deterrent to crime, especially the petty crimes most common in the market. Furthermore, the impacts of CCTV would disproportionately impact people already overpoliced and people already denied privacy and dignity by being unhoused. Frontline workers and criminal defence lawyers argued that the market needed investments in harm reduction rather than expensive cameras (Cave 2022). Furthermore, the only possible impact of cameras would be increased incarceration. One research participant, market resident Alex, commented, "It might be a lot easier to convict criminals. But that wouldn't stop them from being criminals.... So, I think that it could be useful if all you want to do is put people in jail" (Cave 2022, 127). CAMS was very effective in disseminating this resistance framing, detailing both the uselessness and the potential negative and unfair impacts of a CCTV project. In April 2020, the city abandoned the project (Cave 2022), an effective expression of ongoing state-citizenry negotiation.

The omnipresence, use, and contestations of everyday surveillance (private and public cameras) demonstrate ways in which the citizenry engages with and in policing in the city. The Convoy occupation in 2022 nourished widespread enthusiasm for different types of citizen-led security. Many remember proudly, will tell their grandchildren about, and bought the T-shirts for the "Battle of Billings Bridge." Ottawans who had been dealing with the Convoy for weeks heard that a new convoy was planning to restock the supplies of those occupying downtown. This resupplying Convoy's route was to arrive at Parliament Hill via the southern highway exit at Billings Bridge. On February 13, 2022, a few dozen — and by end of day, nearly a thousand — Ottawans arrived by bike and foot to block Billings Bridge. The blockade stopped thirty trucks from passing, allowing them through eventually when they agreed to surrender their jerry cans of fuel (Hutt 2022). It was a direct-action citizen security success (for some).

Months later, in August 2022, in the ByWard Market at St. Brigid's — a decommissioned Catholic church that was being rented by a group called The United People of Canada (TUPC) — another community-led form of security organized. TUPC was a Convoy-affiliated group in the process of purchasing the decommissioned church to become an "Embassy." They created what they referred to as a "lawful security force" to securitize the building. One of the directors of the group said it was prepared to "ensure the rule of law is upheld within our lawful authority"; however, Lowertown neighbours were worried that the group was organizing its own militia. The group was not approved by Ontario's Ministry of the Solicitor General; it was working without a licence (Taekema 2022). These two expressions of vigilante security were politically in direct opposition, but both expressed a deep distrust in policing by the state.

Security for the Nation

During the summer you can tour the RCMP stables at the Canadian Police College in Rockcliffe, see some antique carriages, and meet the RCMP musical ride horses, including the black Hanoverian, Carter. Carter doesn't perform in the musical rides, but he does pull carriages and very sociably sticks his nose through the gate of his stable to say hello. This tourist attraction offers a subtle reinforcement of prominent narratives that the RCMP are a police force marked by "responsibilisation, respect, professionalism," the words written on the stable walls. Many criminologists are critical of what they call "copaganda": pro-police propaganda that takes the form of friendly pro-cop television shows (Brooklyn 99, Law and Order, the Disney-fied version of the RCMP Mountie), social media campaigns, and, one could add Carter to this list.

Critical criminologists argue that the history and ongoing practices of the RCMP demonstrate how state-led security serves the interests of the political and capitalist elite while suppressing Indigenous sovereignty and engaging in similar types of misogynist and racist violence found in the OPS. In 1873, the federal government created the North West Mounted Police with the express purpose of patrolling Western Canada and suppressing Indigenous peoples. Macdonald's government outfitted the force in red, a reference to the British army, and designated them as a paramilitary force, giving them governing powers in Western Canada. The force was renamed the Royal Canadian Mounted Police in 1920 (Gerster 2021). Since 1873, many large and small moments have challenged their promise of "responsibilisation, respect, professionalism" and instead reflected the force's oppressive paramilitary origins. This has been clearly documented in the RCMP's approach towards Wet'suwet'en land defenders in British Columbia that have been protesting the construction of the Coastal GasLink pipeline since 2019. In a legal suit where protestors accused the RCMP of violence, complainants offered audio recordings of police referring to protestors as "ogres" and "orcs," mocking their red palm face paint (a symbol protesting the high rates of murders of Indigenous women) (McKay 2024b), and using radio transmissions of "what sounded like children" who "sang the nursery rhyme Ring Around the Rosie, along with other disturbing noises, including a voice saying, 'I know where you are. I'm coming to get you'" amid large-scale, militarized arrests of protestors (McKay 2024a). Moreover, in 2021, a class-action lawsuit filed by a number of female RCMP officers against the force for allowing a culture of rampant sexual violence led to a $125 million settlement (Walker 2023). The RCMP have headquarters in Ottawa, police the parliamentary grounds, and are called to action in rare moments of political violence. The RCMP, of course, also have their stables in Ottawa, and historically there were performances of the musical rides on the parliamentary grounds. Despite their practices as a paramilitary force involved in all sorts of violence against Canadians, the RCMP are portrayed in Ottawa as part of the imagery of Canada as a peaceful nation.

Parliamentary security can be a metonym for public security more broadly; security should keep people safe *and* able to express individual freedoms of movement and expression. In the beginning, parliamentarians were well protected symbolically, but not actually. Since 1867, the sergeant-at-arms has been charged with keeping order in the House of Commons and throughout the Parliament buildings. They carry the mace, symbolic of the Crown, into every session of the House of Commons, and pragmatically they are responsible for the security of the Parliament buildings. Yet, the sergeant-at-arms could do little to protect MP Thomas D'Arcy McGee on April 7, 1868. On this evening, McGee was jingling his keys at the door of the boarding house he was staying in on Sparks Street after a late-night session in the House of Commons, when he was shot in the back of the head. It was Canada's first political assassination. The death mask of McGee's hand (his face being too badly wounded) became a prized artifact at the Bytown Museum. This shocking murder of a parliamentarian did not immediately lead to strengthening security within the parliamentary district, though. In fact, between 1930 and 1935, George Black, a Yukon MP, routinely shot rabbits from his office window, calling the media to report when he'd had an especially good day (Dance 2014, 175). Securitization of Parliament Hill has expanded considerably since then, slowly prompted by a few dramatic security breaches. The Hansard of May 18, 1966, reads that that day a "loud explosion was heard in the chamber." In the men's washroom, only a few feet from Prime Minister Pearson's office, forty-five-year-old Paul Joseph Chartier was found "lying in a pool of blood, and exhaling his last breath" — a bomb strapped to his chest had killed him (Hewitt 2019, 47).

By 2014, when an active shooter entered Centre Block with his rifle, the grounds were being protected by sergeant-at-arms Ken Vickers, the OPS, the RCMP, Communications Security Establishment Canada, Ottawa Paramedic Service, and Ottawa Fire Services. The following year the Parliamentary Protective Service was consolidated, a security force that answers to the Speaker of the Senate and the Speaker of the House of Commons (Thibedeau 2015).

Parliamentary security was originally designed to protect parliamentarians from a potentially aggressive monarch and from the people they were representing. It also needs to ensure that parliamentarians are not prevented from doing their work, especially from voting on bills in the House of Commons, while allowing the public to access Parliament Hill to "help democracy flourish." Vickers (sergeant-at-arms from 2006 to 2015) explains here his approach to his job: "Number one, is it going to make [the Hill] safer? Number two, what does it do to intimidate or not intimidate people to come here?... I think it's fundamental to our democracy.... This is a House of Commons, and it's for the commoners" (Dance 2014, 171, 185).

Security forces were put to the test when the Convoy occupied Wellington Street in front of Parliament Hill. This was the site of the infamous hot tub protest party. In the aftermath of this occupation, the federal government offered to buy Wellington Street from the city and make it car-free as well as their security responsibility; the city rejected the offer (Pellerin 2023). Incidentally, Gréber had suggested the closure of Wellington Street to functions "exclusively reserved" to the needs of Parliament (Gréber in Miguelez 2015, 261).

Ottawa is where all manner of national security infrastructure is created, maintained, and amended. These security measures dance on the edge of the social contract by maintaining security, sometimes at odds with citizens' rights. The largest of this complex of national security, the Canadian Security Intelligence Service (CSIS) can trace its origins to a red brick low-rise apartment building on Somerset Street across from Dundonald Park. Here, on a September evening in 1945, Russian cipher clerk Igor Gouzenko anxiously paced in his apartment while his wife and young son watched. Gouzenko had noticed that men wearing suits were standing in Dundonald Park looking up at his window. As a twenty-three-year-old lieutenant in the Red Army, Gouzenko was sent to Canada by the NKVD (the Soviet secret police) in 1942. In September 1945, Gouzenko left the Russian embassy with 109 documents, evidence of Russian espionage, and began a clumsy journey attempting to alert Canadian authorities. He first took the documents to the offices of the *Ottawa Journal.* Met with disinterest, he continued to the Department of Justice on

Wellington Street, but there was no one there to talk to. He returned the next day with his wife and son, waited patiently for two hours to talk to officials, and finally told a woman in the Crown attorney's office about the papers in his possession before returning home (Kavchak 2004). The men watching him from Dundonald Park were not from the NKVD, as Gouzenko feared; they were RCMP officers who had begun to take Gouzenko's claims seriously. One of the effects of Gouzenko's defection from the NKVD was the creation of the Security Service in the RCMP (a force that would later become CSIS). Gouzenko's role in the beginnings of the Cold War is significant. Igor Gouzenko's books, *This Was My Choice* (a nominee for the Nobel Prize for Literature in 1955) and *The Fall of a Titan* (winner of the Governor General's Literary Award in 1954) are on display in the Cold War exhibit of the Canadian War Museum.

While undoubtably useful for maintaining all manner of national security, Ottawa locals have been impacted by living and working in such close proximity to national security infrastructure (CSIS is headquartered in east Ottawa on Ogilvie Road). The Cold War, with its anxieties about communist infiltration in all aspects of Canadian society, inspired large-scale spying in Canadian universities, including Carleton University (Hewitt 2002). Thousands of queer men and women lost their jobs in the military and civil service through the twentieth century in the name of national security, as discussed earlier, and Indigenous land defenders are still targets of much ongoing government surveillance (Crosby and Monaghan 2018). The decentralization of government buildings during the Cold War, originally suggested by Gréber, was in part intended to make the federal government less of an obvious target for an attack (Martin 2013). The spectres of Cold War anxieties are most explicitly on display in Carp at the "Diefenbunker" — the concrete bunker and fallout shelter that is now Canada's Cold War Museum. And all of these Cold War security activities began, in a sense, here, across from Dundonald Park.

While the pushback of citizens to state powers is our right, is expected, and can be effective in readjusting the state/citizenry dynamic (as seen in the success of the CAMS movement), pushback from the state — which may be acting in the interests of other factions of society, competing understandings of freedom, or conflicting understandings of societal priorities (infrastructure, the economy, the environment, capitalist profit, Indigenous sovereignty) — is often experienced as excessive coercion. The state's use of more-than-usual policing powers is justified and partially accepted when it invokes what political scientists call "emergency powers." Political scientist Nomi Lazar explains that, in fact, "most liberal democracies have standing constitutional or special legal powers to derogate rights and the rule of law for the sake of order in times of crisis" (Lazar 2009, 1). In Canada, the War Measures Act of 1914, which became the Emergencies Act in 1988, has provided these mechanisms.

There have been two moments in Canadian history where the federal government has used emergency powers in peace time, both of which took place, in part, in Ottawa. In October, 1970, following the kidnapping of British trade commissioner James Cross in Montreal and the kidnapping and murder of Quebec's minister of immigration and labour, Pierre Laporte, by members of the Front de libération du Québec (FLQ), the federal government of Pierre Trudeau invoked the War Measures Act. This act allowed the police to arrest and detain people without a warrant. The military was deployed to protect government buildings and officials. On October 13, Pierre Trudeau, on the steps of Parliament, was asked by a journalist just how far he would go to keep Canadians safe, to which he famously replied, "just watch me" (McIntosh and Cooper 2013). While most of the focus of the exceptional use of the Canadian military and powers granted to the police was in Quebec, the Third Battalion of the Royal Canadian Regiment set up camp in Rockcliffe Park Public School, escorted then–minister of justice John Turner's daughter to school, patrolled the streets of Rockcliffe, and set up protections outside of the homes of former prime ministers Pearson and Diefenbaker (Edmond 1993).

After what is now known as the "FLQ crisis," outcry over the use of the War Measures Act resulted in an inquiry and the 1981 McDonald report. The McDonald report led to two major outcomes: revising the War Measures Act and taking spying powers away from the RCMP. This second outcome was achieved in 1984 with the establishment of CSIS. The War Measures Act was replaced in 1988 with the Emergencies Act. The new legislation was compliant with the relatively recently installed Canadian Charter of Rights and Freedoms and contemporary understandings of human rights. It also required that an inquiry with a robust investigation, including debate in the House of Commons and review by the courts, would follow each time it was used (Holthuis 1991). This added layers of accountability to the state's potential use of emergency powers and thus reflects another moment in the ongoing negotiation of the social contract between the state and citizens.

Fifty-two years after the FLQ crisis, some Ottawans (especially those living downtown, or near the Convoy supply centre on the city baseball diamond in Overbrook) were telepathically trying to bait Justin Trudeau to "just say it … say it … say 'Just watch me'!" After weeks of the Convoy occupation of Ottawa, as well as occupations of a few border crossings, with F*** Trudeau,

Confederate, and Gadsden flags flying high, many wanted the prime minister to invoke emergency powers. On February 14, 2022, the government did so (although without any quotable quotes). The Emergencies Act gave the federal government the right to seize the assets of some Convoy participants, tow trucks that had been blocking bridges and clogging Ottawa's downtown, declare a certain area a securitized zone, and call in other levels of police to forcibly remove the protesters. By February 18, the everyday yawn of Ottawa had been restored.

In the requisite post-emergency inquiry in February 2023, after months of interviews and public testimonies, Justice Paul Rouleau declared that, yes, the government had been justified. Jocelyn Stacey and Nomi Lazar summarized the five-volume report: "But beneath Rouleau's unruffled tone roils a current of chastisement, complicating headlines vindicating the federal government. The rule of law in an emergency is everybody's job and Rouleau found that, in February 2022, nearly everyone fell short." In his report, he criticized the federal government for characterizing all of the protestors as violent, disregarding their legitimate rights to protest; however, the protestors overstepped these legitimate rights by engaging in violence and bringing weapons to their protest. The Ottawa police failed by not policing the situation at all, and CSIS was negligent in its role in predicting and managing the situation (Stacey and Lazar 2023). The Convoy, lack of policing, Emergencies Act, protest dispersion, commission, and ongoing legal cases of the Convoy leaders present in stark relief the messiness of maintaining a social contract in a large, diverse nation.

COURTS

The legal system — access to a lawyer, and a fair trial — are all crucial in a liberal democracy. Here again, the balance of powers is negotiated. Police have state-given powers to arrest citizens, but citizens, regardless of the severity of their crimes, have the right to a fair trial. Once someone is arrested, there is a period where the Crown decides whether to actually pursue the case, dismiss the case, or work toward an agreement or plea deal (for less serious crimes). If the charge is to stick and the matter is to be tried, then there may be months or years of back and forth between the Crown and the accused, where the Crown has to disclose all of its information and an investigation to strengthen the charges may continue. This process is also mired in structures of social inequality shaping all of life in Ottawa. Access to defence lawyers is based on one's material resources; Crown decisions on which cases and defendants to try are shaped by colonial, and patriarchal understandings of crime (sexually assaulting one's wife was not illegal until 1983); juries and what constitutes "one's peers" also reflect dominant power dynamics. In 2018, protesters took to Parliament Hill, affixing placards to the fence. One read "all white jury, all white supremacy," after the all-white jury's acquittal of Gerald Stanley for murdering twenty-two-year-old Cree man Colten Boushie in Saskatchewan.

After officials tired of making the trek to Perth to have cases heard, Bytowners built a courthouse at Daly Avenue and Nicholas Street in 1842. This courthouse was rebuilt in 1871 after a fire (Duhamel 1961) and is now a part of Ottawa Arts Court (you can still visit a prison cell en route to an art show). In 1868, when Patrick Whelan was arrested for murdering Thomas D'Arcy McGee, it was at the original courthouse here that he was tried. In the trial, John A. Macdonald, who was both prime minister and a good friend of the deceased, sat beside the judge, glaring at Whelan throughout the trial. The jury banned Catholics and was most likely stacked with anti-Irish Protestants eager to convict the Catholic (and presumed Fenian) Whelan (Canadiana 2019).

In 2022, Pat King, Tamara Lich, and other Convoy agitators were brought to 161 Elgin Street, to a courthouse built in 1980. While there are other courts in town, here you'll find the Ontario Superior Court as well as small claims, criminal, and family courts. The courthouse bears witness to people defending their efforts to overthrow the government, but also parents fighting for child support, neighbours suing each other over the placement of a fence, multinational corporations fighting over the terms of contracts, people trying to avoid paying speeding tickets, and almost everything in between. This modern building is adorned on its exterior with a sculptural work by artist collective General Idea titled *Canadian Shield* (1986), installed in 1990: an abstract piece featuring large boulders jutting out of the building, it is open to interpretation, much like the law.

The Federal Court hears cases in the Thomas D'Arcy McGee Building at 90 Sparks Street. The Tax Court of Canada occupies a similar glass high-rise at 200 Kent Street. Disaffected defendants or plaintiffs can appeal the rulings from these courts by taking their case to the Federal Court of Appeal, also in the McGee Building. If, after an appeal to the Federal Court of Appeal (or Ontario Court of Appeal, for matters originally heard at 161 Elgin), you remain dissatisfied with your case outcome, you'll have to seek permission (or "leave") to travel west on Wellington Street to have your case heard by the Supreme Court of Canada.

The Supreme Court of Canada was established in 1875, but the final court of appeal for Canadians was the British Privy Council until 1933 (criminal cases) and 1949 (civil cases). In 1875, the court occupied a room in Centre Block before moving to a modest two-storey building on Bank Street in 1882 (Government of Canada 2017). It was here, where, in 1928, Emily Murphy, Nellie McLung, Henrietta Muir Edwards, Irene Parly, and Louise McKinney argued that women were indeed "persons" and should thus be eligible to be appointed to the Senate. They lost initially, but won when their case (the "Persons case," officially *Edwards v. Canada*), was heard by the British Privy Council (de Bruin and McIntosh 2006). The success of the case meant both that women were to be considered "persons" under Canadian law and, significantly, that the Constitution should be understood as a "a living tree capable of growth and expansion within its natural limits" and not interpreted through its strict original positions. This has become known as the "living tree doctrine," an understanding of law as something that must grow and adjust with an evolving society (Taylor 2019).

In 1936 the federal government began construction of a purpose-built building for the Supreme Court of Canada, which was to be the "crowning structure in the new government complex" (Gournay and Vanlaethem 2000, 198), at a Wellington Street location chosen by Gréber. Architect Ernest Cormier drew on the chateau style already present in Ottawa with the Château Laurier, as well as classicism, which "symbolized the authority and effectiveness of political institutions." Deliberate use of natural light expressed an "ideal of a transparent judicial system" and included grillwork, stained glass, and entrances that were "reminiscent of windows in houses designed by Frank Lloyd Wright, whose work Cormier greatly admired." The Supreme Court of Canada moved into this building in 1946 (Gournay and Vanlaethem 2000, 205, 207–8).

Harold Munro, whose farm at Innes and Blair was expropriated by the NCC for the creation of the Greenbelt, challenged the expropriation, but lost at the Supreme Court in 1966 (Supreme Court of Canada n.d.). In 2013, the SCC issued its ruling in the *Bedford* case, which decried that three laws (not being able to keep a bawdy house, living off of the avails of prostitution, and communicating in public for the purposes of prostitution) were all unconstitutional, and were struck down (*Canada (Attorney General) v. Bedford* 2013). The legal architecture underpinning all Canadians' rights and freedoms — as well as reinforcing the access of the bourgeoisie and the state to land and labour — is interpreted, challenged, and reinforced here.

CUSTODY AND INCARCERATION

Incarceration, holding people against their will, and controlling nearly all aspects of their lives — when and where to sleep, what to eat, when to wake — is the ultimate expression of state power. Here, too, criminologists and activists have detailed the ways in which the state oversteps its power. In Ottawa, those awaiting trial and those serving less than two years are held at the Ottawa-Carleton Detention Centre (OCDC). Those convicted of crimes with sentences of longer than two years to serve are sent to prisons outside of Ottawa.

On a Thursday evening in May 2024, I strolled over to the Atelier — a community space at St. Paul's University — for a chili cook-off fundraiser to support the Coalition Against the Proposed Prison (CAPP). In 2017 the Ontario government announced that they were going to respond to problems of overcrowding and disrepair at the OCDC by replacing the 585-bed prison with a new 725-bed facility. The proposed new prison was designed to be a $1 billion public-private partnership built on the land of the former Kemptville Agricultural College in Kemptville, 60 kilometres south of Ottawa. In response, the Criminalization and Punishment Education Project (CPEP) launched their NOPE: No to Prison Expansion campaign and CAPP was formed, made of locals from Kemptville opposed to the destruction of farmland alongside activists and criminologists in Ottawa opposed to the expansion of the prison-industrial complex.

In Bytown's early days, people were held in a military jail on Barrack's Hill, then a jail in the basement of the town's 1842 courthouse. In 1862 the Carleton County Gaol was built on Nicholas Street. For over a century it held convicted criminals in tiny cells without heat, plumbing, or adequate ventilation (Heritage Ottawa n.d.b). In 1972 the province of Ontario built the Ottawa-Carleton Detention Centre to replace the Nicholas Street jail. At its opening, the detention centre was praised for a "country-club setting, colour coordinated dormitories, lounges and library ... [It] will be the kind of place prisoners won't mind calling home" (Doyle, Piché, and Sutton 2022, 3).

Black American feminist Angela Davis uses the term "prison-industrial complex" to refer to the structures of policing and detention that enrich many industries while disproportionately incarcerating Black, Indigenous, and poor people (Davis 2003, 64). The prison-industrial complex materially benefits prison, construction, and food services industries while maintaining status quo classed, racialized, and gendered power dynamics. As of 2022, Black people, who make up 3.5 percent of the population in Canada, are overrepresented in prisons, as 9.2 percent of those incarcerated (CBC News 2022). The Indigenous population in federal prisons in 2018 was 28 percent, a gross overrepresentation of their 4.1 percent of the population in Canada (Clark 2019). When the Ontario government proposed a shiny new detention centre in Kemptville, many were quick to argue that this would not help inmates or public safety. Criminologist Justin Piché argued that expanding restorative justice opportunities, expanding pre-charge and post-charge diversion programs, reviewing mandatory minimum sentences, extending "temporary absences" so that inmates could access their lawyers, employment, and health care (resources that would allow them to return to society) would all address issues of incarceration and public safety more effectively than building a new detention centre (CPEP Group 2016b). At the chili cook-off, activists were fundraising to pay for legal fees to appeal the provincial court's earlier dismissal of CAPP's judicial review application in 2022.

Critical criminologists at Carleton University and the University of Ottawa established the CPEP as a research and advocacy hub that brings together activists, academics, and community members to address the many issues of incarceration. Today, the majority (two-thirds) of those in OCDC are there in remand, meaning they are awaiting trial and have not been convicted of any crime (Doyle, Piché, and Sutton 2022, 3). Because OCDC was not designed for long-term stays, it does not offer rehabilitation programs or services like AA meetings or adequate medical, psychiatric, or dental care. Former inmates detail conditions of overcrowding and a lack of time outside, sometimes going months at a time without fresh air. These conditions lead to the release of people back into the population who have exacerbated social and health problems (CPEP Group 2015). Nearly 25 percent of people in OCDC have health issues, schizophrenia, or bipolar disorder. Inmates have described conditions where three inmates were kept in a cell, with people sleeping on floors, being peed on, tripped on, and fed insufficient food. One former inmate described getting yard time three times in the span of two months (CPEP Group 2016b). In 2011 Christina Jahn, a woman with mental health issues and cancer, was in solitary confinement for two hundred days. In 2012, Julia Bilotta gave birth while in segregation; her baby later died of respiratory problems acquired in the OCDC (Doyle, Piché, and Sutton 2022, 4).

What industries benefit from the abhorrent conditions at OCDC? One of CPEP's campaigns focused on how Bell Canada was for many years the beneficiary of this incarceration system. While Bell is celebrated for its "Let's

Talk" campaign to address the stigma of mental illness, beginning in 2013 Bell charged OCDC inmates exorbitant rates and only allowed phone calls to pre-approved numbers on regular landlines. A twenty-minute call to a lawyer cost inmates nearly $30. CPEP members argued that Bell's practices were predatory, contributed to alienation, and created barriers to proper legal and social supports (Benslimane et al. 2019). By 2024, a new company had been given the contract for phone services; inmates can now buy pre-paid cards, and the cost of long-distance calls has been substantially reduced (Jones 2024).

In the 1990s the OCDC closed its on-site kitchen and now serves food provided by Compass Group that is cooked off-site and reheated at OCDC. The food is often soggy, spoiled, and 65–90 percent of the food is left uneaten. Hunger is a problem in OCDC. CPEP explains that the institution (i.e., the state) pays millions of dollars for this contract with Compass Group. CPEP advocated for the reopening of an on-site kitchen, a solution that would provide job training, improve food, and save money (CPEP Group 2016a). In her ethnography on life inside OCDC, sociologist Laura McKendy detailed that issues with poor quality food were a dominant concern of inmates. One of her interviewees stated, "When I was there, there was a snail in my peas.... A snail. And there was one other girl, she had glass in her food." Another reported that "sometimes the meals would come freezing ... sometimes it would be raw or not even cooked" (McKendy 2018, 107). The only winners in this arrangement are the owners of the British multinational food services company Compass Group.

COMMUNITIES, COPS, TOWN, AND CROWN

In the liberal democracy that is Canada, safety and security are managed through a balancing of individual rights and collective needs. It is a balance that is negotiated (or ignored) by government spies working out of Ogilvie Road, considered (or not) when police respond to calls about men acting strange at the Bridgehead coffee shop. It is also a balance understood by the CAMS organizers protesting expanded ByWard Market security cameras and is a priority for judges in the courthouse on Elgin Street deciding if and for how long someone should be incarcerated. The RCMP and CSIS are tasked with balancing the interests of the nation with the rights of citizens to varied ends, a balance carefully considered by Justice Rouleau in his findings about the use of the Emergencies Act in 2022. Critical criminologists, including members of CPEP, detail how racialized and poor people are overpoliced, overincarcerated, and face police violence at higher rates. Here, there is no balance — the police instead uphold the dominant power relations that disadvantage people who are racialized, poor, and women. Many people argue that security and safety can be maintained with smaller police budgets if there are also more robust investments in public housing, health care, schools, community spaces, and clean and vibrant green spaces. These can be the next steps in the ongoing negotiations between state, citizenry, individual rights, and collective security. Charges of vagrancy lessen when everyone is housed or welcomed in public spaces. Public mischief can be mitigated when people live within communities of people watching out for them, and the "acting strange" is made intelligible by friends and neighbours.

At the Centretown Community Association booth at a visit to the Elgin Street farmers' market, I picked up a brochure for Anchor: Alternative Neighbourhood Crisis Response. The brochure read, "If you are experiencing or witnessing a mental health or substance-related crisis, 24/7/365 community-based response in our area," and then, "Call 2-1-1" with a map of the catchment area for this program (Ottawa River to Highway 17, the Rideau Canal to Preston Street). This project — the work of a coalition of community health centres and the City of Ottawa — is a concerted move against the overpolicing and overincarceration of people with addictions and mental health conditions. The energizing of other community spaces — libraries, community arenas, playgrounds — and through equitable access to education all nourish a society with less crime and less punishment.

Chapter 10

MARKETS AND MALLS

THE RICHMOND DEPOT BUILT IN 1818 on the Jock River, and the Lanark depot on the Clyde River, small buildings stocked with food and basic wares, were the region's first stores (Vance 2012); other shops in the ByWard Market soon followed. Today Ottawa has a retail landscape typical of North American cities; it is a mixture of street shopping, quietly dying mid-sized malls, shiny renovated malls, big box complexes, farmers' markets, and the nostalgic memories of mid-twentieth-century department stores.

Sharon Zukin explains that markets that were tied to particular places and offered sites to trade and acquire goods existed in feudal times, and "the denseness of interactions and the goods that were exchanged offered local communities the material and cultural means for their social reproduction — that is, their survival as communities" (Zukin 1991, 6). Industrialization, with its increased division of labour and the rise of factory work, transformed the meaning of the market: the concept of "market no longer internalized place. Instead, in a long and painful process that lasted through most of the nineteenth century, place began to internalize market culture" (Zukin 1991, 7). Within three hundred years, markets transformed from being specific, significant culture-building places to spaces co-opted by the alienating logic of an abstract capitalist market. Market squares create place; the market-driven logic of capitalism creates what anthropologist Marc Augé calls "non-places," those contemporary spaces marked by homogeneity and fleeting interactions (Augé 1995). In this chapter I argue that following trends in other cities shaped by advanced capitalism, markets in Ottawa have shifted from being inextricably tied to place (e.g., the ByWard Market) to becoming tied to an abstract market and acting as non-places in the form of big box stores and Amazon distribution centres. Second, consumer shopping spaces have been and continue to be important third places for women, teenagers, and various diasporic communities.

EARLY OTTAWA MARKETS

In the heart of the ByWard Market neighbourhood, a two-storey 1926 brick classical revival market building is surrounded every spring and summer by lavender, flowers, vegetables, and maple products for sale. Inside the building, there are places to buy bagel sandwiches, gourmet candy apples and Lebanese, Japanese, and Mexican food. There is the bakery that has, since 2009, capitalized on the fact that President Obama ate one of their cookies and it has since sold "Obama cookies." There are clothing shops, local soap producers, souvenirs for sale, and Adaawewigamig, a shop supporting A7G: Assembly of Seven Generations, an Indigenous youth organization. There is a BeaverTails kiosk which tried to replicate that Obama cookie magic with a specially designed BeaverTail for the visiting Prince Charles and Camilla in 2022 (they did not eat any, at least publicly). In front of the building, a plaza's seating references historic shipping crates in its form. The market is old, new, and new-old, in the heart of the city but embracing the area's rurality. It is local, tied to a specific history, and a site for regional farmers to sell their goods directly to customers. It is also a people place, for meeting, shopping, sitting.

Colonel By first surveyed and divided lots for the ByWard Market neighbourhood in 1826, the year work began on the Rideau Canal. The next year, the first market building was constructed, with subsequent replacements built on the same site in 1848, 1864, 1871, and last in 1926. The ByWard Market (both the market itself and the neighbourhood to which it lends its name) has embodied Zukin's description of feudal markets as sites of intense social interaction and as liminal spaces of social, economic, and political exchange (including the Stoney Monday riots of 1849).

Early on, the market became an important place for the city's small Jewish population. In the late nineteenth century, Jewish people emigrated from Europe to Canada, pushed by anti-Semitic "Pale of Settlement" bans in many regions of Europe (Lo 1999, 239–40). There is a long tradition, dating to the Middle Ages, of Jewish people working as peddlers; the mobility of the profession allowed Jews to avoid labour discrimination, it required minimal start-up capital, and self-employment allowed Jews to practise their faith easily. By 1881, there were twenty Jewish people living in Ottawa, out of a population of 21,545. The Jews that originally settled in Ottawa were Ashkenazi Orthodox, mostly coming from shtetls in Russia and Lithuania. Typically, men came, settled in the ByWard Market, grew their businesses, then sent for their wives and children to join them. The noted first Jew in Ottawa was Moses Bilsky. Bilsky, born in Lithuania, moved to Montreal in 1845, then to New York, where he fought for the Union Army in the American Civil War, before settling in Ottawa in 1865 with his wife Pauline and opening a jewelry and pawn shop on Rideau Street. "Bilsky and Son Limited" became one of the largest jewellery firms in Eastern Canada. Jewish settlers also worked as tailors and furriers. Louis Shapiro would meet lumberjacks at the train station who had been in the bush for months, bring them to his men's clothing store, give them food and drinks and sell them clothes — an impeccable service that led to lasting relationships (Lo 1999).

The Jewish community grew in Ottawa in part because the peddler licensing fees in Ottawa cost ten cents, much lower than the $25 fees in Montreal. Land was also plentiful and cheap, allowing peddlers to expand from selling wares from a pushcart to opening a shop. By 1900, there were two synagogues in Lowertown, and by 1901, there were 398 Jews living in Ottawa, the majority of whom were living in the ByWard neighbourhood (Lo 1999). Some of these early Jewish peddlers would make their mark on the changing retail landscape as they expanded and sold their wares in the newly emerging department stores. The neighbourhood was developing as a place of ethnic and linguistic intermingling. Italians were also peddlers in the neighbourhood; they worshipped at St. Elizabeth's chapel on Murray Street (Pantalone 2013).

DEPARTMENT STORES

Early nineteenth-century department stores were local, independently owned businesses. They used a one-price system (no more bargaining with salespeople), relied on departmental organization of goods, had rapid stock turnover, occupied multi-floor buildings, and included amenities like seating, public washrooms, and lunch counters (Howard 2015).

Caspar Caplan opened Caplan's Department Store on Rideau Street in 1897, four years after immigrating from Lithuania. Eventually the store encompassed two blocks (Heritage Ottawa n.d.a). Archibald Jacob Freiman, a Jewish immigrant also from Lithuania, opened the Canadian House Furnishing Co. at 223 Rideau in 1899 with Moses Cramer when he was nineteen years old. The businesses expanded and moved to a location at 73 Rideau Street in 1903 (the location that would become the Bay). Eventually Freiman became the sole proprietor and it became known as Freiman's. Freiman's was the first place in Ottawa with an escalator (Powell 2019a). It also had a lunch counter in the basement that served popular malted milkshakes. Charles Ogilvy moved from Edinburgh, Scotland, to Ottawa as a toddler in 1863. In 1887, he opened a dry goods store on Rideau Street. In 1907, Ogilvy's opened in a building designed by locally renowned architect Werner Ernst Noffke at 126 Rideau Street as one of Ottawa's first steel and concrete buildings. The store was famous for packaging customers' purchases in tartan boxes. By 1934, Ogilvy's was Ottawa's largest department store (Cook 2012).

Department store owners' investments in creating welcoming, often architecturally stunning and technologically intriguing buildings, created shopping spaces that encouraged browsing and hanging out, creating a new type of third place, especially for women. In a newspaper story, Mildred Beechy offered this memory from her childhood, describing what she and her sisters did when they got some allowance:

> Our favourite excursion was to take the bus downtown to Freiman's Department Store on Rideau Street. Bus fare was four for 25 cents. Once there, we would race to the basement and order a 10-cent chocolate malted milk. Absolutely delicious. With the rest of our dollar, we would walk across to Woolworths to buy a jewellery trinket, hairbands, or Ben Hur perfume for 42 cents. We would think we were the richest girls in Ottawa. Sometimes we would pay 50 cents to swim at the Château Laurier. Lying on the chaise lounges, we would fantasize that we were princesses living in a castle. (Deachman 2017)

In a lifelong learning class on Ottawa that I teach, students shared special memories of these department stores: the lunch hour at Ogilvy's cafeteria being opened with a bagpiper, getting glimpses of Mr. Freiman checking in on his store, a special change chute and the malt milkshakes at Freiman's. It's not surprising that with the decline of independent department stores beginning in the 1970s, people began to experience department store nostalgia.

In the heyday of the department stores, shopping offered a novel way for women to experience some urban freedom in the face of otherwise misogynist urban environments. Today shopping continues to be imagined as female. Feminist scholars offer twinned critiques of this imagining, both of which suggest that, rather than leisure, much of the shopping women do is labour. Women shop for groceries, to keep their children clothed, for birthdays and holidays, and presents for teachers and mothers-in-law. This aspect of feminized shopping was codified in the early history of department stores. Donica Belisle explains, "In the interwar period, Vancouver department stores sponsored cooking competitions for secondary schools. Domestic science teachers also brought students to department stores to attend fashion shows" (Belisle 2007, 69). Department stores facilitated women's unpaid labour of social reproduction.

Second, much of women's shopping is a gendered form of what sociologist Heidi Bickis calls "appearance work." Patriarchal norms dictating that women are more valued for their bodies than their full subjectivities put demands on women to shop in order to produce appropriately feminine bodies through acquiring proper clothing and engaging in expensive and time-consuming grooming (Bickis 2020). This type of labour is masked as leisure, a patriarchal gloss perfected by department stores. Department stores developed amenities that would later become taken for granted in malls: "complimentary lavatories, restrooms, and writing rooms offered semiprivate spaces where female customers relieved themselves and enjoyed repose" (Belisle 2007, 67). The presence of the so-called "man chair" — chairs near fitting rooms, mostly occupied by the male companions of female shoppers — reflect presumptions of gendered shopping: men patiently wait while women labour to align with gendered expectations.

Department stores were sites of consumption, but they were also workplaces. In the 1940s, Eaton's, The Bay, and Simpson's "offered among the best workplace benefits in the Dominion," including medical insurance, vacation days, sports teams, summer camps, and arts and leisure clubs (Belisle 2007, 64). Charles Ogilvy gave his employees shares in the company. Caplan's store was the first in the city to institute a five-day work week. It also had an employee bowling league and recreation association (Powell 2022). Department stores also, however, were sites of gendered and racial pay inequities: "prior to World War II, department stores were famous for their refusals to hire non-Anglo-Celtics" (Belisle 2007, 64). Department stores paid male employees more than their female counterparts, an issue that galvanized female employees in the 1940s to support (largely unsuccessful) unionization campaigns (Belisle 2007).

In July 1984, Caplan's closed its doors. In 1995, the Canril Corporation bought the building and in 2003, after a small fire, the city allowed for the building to be demolished, as long as a replica of the Caplan's façade be part of the new site development (Heritage Ottawa, n.d.a). The designers of the "90 George Street Project," a nineteen-storey condo built in 2009, used photogrammetric records to guide them in creating a reconstruction of the Caplan's façade for the front of the building (currently the store Urban Outfitters). In 2013, the flagship Ogilvy's store on Rideau Street was torn down, "brick-by-brick, panel-by-panel, window-by-window" (Padolsky quoted in Cook 2012). The corner of the renovated Rideau Centre, facing the newly named Ogilvy Square, sits behind a restored 1907 façade made from recovered cornices and the original ornamental brickwork of Ogilvy's. Ogilvy's, and the nostalgic memories of the tartan boxes and quality wares, is honoured here.

COMMERCIAL STREETS

Despite valiant efforts by city planners and business improvement associations throughout the city's history, Ottawa does not have a Rodeo Drive, Fifth Avenue, or La Rambla. High-end consumption is limited to the upper floors of some malls, a few shops on Sussex Drive and Sparks Street, and an under-two-hour drive to ... Montreal! Ottawa's failure to sustain a high-end shopping street can be summed up in the story of one of Ottawa's oldest, most promising and then most disappointing shopping districts: Sparks Street.

Nicholas Sparks, a one-time employee of Philemon Wright, bought two hundred acres on the south side of the Ottawa River in 1821. Sparks subdivided his land and began selling lots along "Sparks Street" in 1847. Sales were slow, and the "street" remained largely rural and residential until Ottawa was named the capital city in 1855 (Gordon 2015). By the 1870s, a post office and city hall were built in Uppertown and Sparks Street had become home to "lumber brokers, insurance companies, booksellers, and other corporate offices" and "had surpassed Sussex as the prime shopping street" (Gordon 2015, 96, 101). In the 1880s, the federal government began renting office space on the upper floors of buildings on Sparks Street. The vibrancy of the street benefited from streetcars being installed on it in 1891 (Gordon 2015).

Gréber suggested redeveloping Sparks Street as a pedestrian mall, an idea that gained traction after the removal of the streetcar lines in 1959. Led by the Sparks Street Development Association, redevelopment began in 1960, when traffic was closed to pilot a summer pedestrian mall (Gordon 2015). A pedestrian-only street in the 1960s, when other cities were planning for cars and destroying heritage Victorian buildings, was a bold experiment (Taylor 1986). To create a pedestrian mall, "the asphalt was painted in bold stripes to imitate the paving in European squares; benches were brought in; the NCC loaned some trees from its nursery, which were placed in concrete planters," and four blocks became a permanent pedestrian space in June 1967 (Gordon 2015, 235). While initially "successful beyond expectation" (Taylor 1986, 174), Sparks Street Mall was threatened by the growing number of suburban shopping centres and increasing dominance of federal government office buildings on the street. By the 1980s, the federal government owned the entire north side of Sparks Street (Taylor 1986), zapping its commercial and social energy.

The commercial shopping streets in Ottawa, while not necessarily prized by fashionistas, have been and continue to be (except perhaps contemporary Sparks Street) meaningful sites of work, commerce, urban vibrancy, community building, and the circulation of goods. A distinct counter-image to the upscale shopping streets in other North American cities is found on Clarence Street in the ByWard Market. In the nineteenth century, Clarence contained warehouses, blacksmiths and carriagemakers, and secondhand dealers. The directories of Clarence Street households in 1900 showed a Francophone dominance, but there were also German, Italian, Jewish, and Chinese last names. In line with the tradition of peddling, Jewish people in Ottawa heavily participated in the secondhand trade, drawing on their experiences with the credit system, in tailoring, and because the secondhand clothing market could easily be a husband-and-wife enterprise, with men collecting goods and women selling them (Tunbridge 1986). Urban historian John Tunbridge argues that from the nineteenth century to the 1980s, Clarence Street was a "zone of discard," which he defined as a neighbourhood (or street) with a concentration of dilapidated buildings, rooming houses, warehouses, "low-grade stores" and parking lots (Tunbridge 1986, 247).

Disparaging Clarence Street as a "zone of discard" reflects a commitment to a capitalist logic of endless consumption. However, thrifting and repairing, rather than being exclusively the activities of the poor or frugal, are increasingly being understood as a crucial challenge to the endless waste produced in a consumer society. Thrifting also ties us more specifically to other places and other people, quite literally through the circulation of storied garments. Vintage ties, shoes, and kilts offer a contrast to the anonymity of mass-produced fast fashion. I recently engaged in some local textile circulation: I dropped off a bag of used clothes at St. Vincent de Paul thrift store on Wellington Street, and then I stopped by next door at Flock — a store featuring locally designed and produced clothing — and bought myself a dress. Old and new, both forms of the very local circulation of clothing. Many thrift stores are ongoing extensions of nineteenth-century charitable organizations: St. Vincent de Paul's, the May Court Club, the Mission, Salvation Army. There are also corporate and American-owned thrift shops: Value Village and Goodwill. Workers at the charity-run thrift shops argue that the American, corporate thrift shops take resources — both clothes and income — out of the city where it would otherwise support local charities and a local economy. In 1999, with the arrival of US-owned Value Village to Ottawa, St. Vincent de Paul's immediately saw a drop in donations. James Strate, executive director of St. Vincent de Paul's in 1999 explained that "we support over 600 people each month with clothing and furniture, free of charge. Anyone who has fallen on hard times or been put on the street through abuse has access to our service. We give $50,000 a year to the school breakfast program … yet we are a business. We receive no governmental aid" (Geisterfer 1999). In this moment, the commerce of thrift meets the local histories of religious charitable organizations and transnational trade in used clothing. Another form of thrift is on spectacular display every May during the "Great Glebe Garage Sale" (and the many other neighbourhood-organized garage sale festivals in the city). Here thrift is the driver of a seasonal collective effervescence, as neighbours buy neighbours' little seedlings, vintage clothes, and rickety furniture, and the kids of the Glebe price-gouge locals by selling $3 lemonades in Dixie cups. Thrifting exists at both a deeply local and historic market-based level, as well as in transnational, corporate extraction of value. Two blocks south of Clarence, at 98 George Street is the original Giant Tiger, a discount retailer that arrived on the retail scene in the 1940s (Laucius 2006). The retail contributions of Ottawa are resolutely for the people.

Ottawa streets past and present have been and continue to be anchored by neighbourhood grocery stores and have served communities through the presence of laundromats and drycleaners. Boushey's Market, Loeb, and Hartman's were all locally owned grocery stores. After arriving from Cincinnati and settling off of Somerset Street West in 1912, Moses Loeb and his wife Rose created a small grocery store on LeBreton Flats. Loeb also began a small wholesale business, selling candy and cigarettes from his horse-drawn cart to other grocery stores. Decades later, in 1952, his son Bertram bought thirty-four locations of regional grocery chain Independent Grocers Alliance (IGA). When the chain (now Loeb) was bought by Metro-Richelieu in 1999, there were forty-one Loeb grocery stores in Ottawa. Like markets and department stores, locally owned grocery stores are attuned to the places they inhabit. Bertram Loeb was committed to his local community; he gave large donations to Carleton University (bestowing the Loeb building its name), the National Arts Centre (NAC), and the Ottawa Civic Hospital (Loeb Research Institute).

Grocery stores are crucial for the cultural resilience of diasporic communities. For the small Chinese community in the 1920s, the Yick Lung grocery store at 201 Albert Street was an important community space because of the charm of Mrs. Wong: "The grocery, which had no set hours, became a place where the few wives in the community could meet to chat. Sue's sociable wife, known for her sympathetic ear and wise counsel, lined the vestibule with chairs so that men, too, could sit, smoke a water pipe, and enjoy the family atmosphere" (Chong 2012). In Overbrook, DuMouchel Meat and Deli has anchored a corner in the residential neighbourhood at Donald and Lola Streets since 1948 (or so the building's mural declares). On my recent visit, picking up some sausages, a customer asked the butcher for oxtail, a meat commonly used in Jamaican cuisine but not found in most Canadian grocery stores, and the clerks procured the desired cut. On nearby Montreal Road, Moussa's Market offers a broad selection of Arabic sweets, spices, labneh. Similar small, ethnic retail grocery stores (SERGs) cater to their proximate clientele across the city. Since the 1930s, Preston Street has been home to a number of Italian grocery stores. A study on the SERGs in Toronto's Regent Park found that the small groceries provide much more than groceries: customers appreciated the comfort of shopping in their first language, buying from owners who had knowledge of their grocery needs, the abundance of halal food, and that many shops extended shop credit without fuss or stigma (Komakech and Jackson 2016, 419), like the secondhand shops of historic Clarence Street. The SERGs in Regent Park were being threatened by the ongoing gentrification of the neighbourhood, and their value was not accounted for in developer and politicians' descriptions of the neighbourhood (Komakech and Jackson 2016).

While the aforementioned grocery stores all had male owners, grocery shopping continues to be gendered labour. In a study of Canadian heterosexual couples with children in 2020, women did the grocery shopping in 62.6 percent of the families, down from 70 percent before the pandemic. In the early months of the pandemic, when leaving the house was imagined as risky, grocery shopping suddenly seemed risky and the gendered nature of the task temporarily shifted slightly. One domestic task that stayed resolutely gendered female was doing laundry (Shafer, Scheibling, and Milkie 2020, 535). Doing the laundry has also historically been imagined as soul-cleansing labour, as characterized by the Home for Friendless Women in the nineteenth century. Ottawa laundries have also been a site of racialized labour.

Today a stretch of Somerset Street West, with numerous Chinese, Vietnamese, and Laotian restaurants and grocery stores, is known as Chinatown. This neighbourhood grew in the 1980s after the city welcomed thousands of Indochinese refugees between 1978 and 1980. This was not Ottawa's first Chinatown, though — that was a strip of businesses along Bank and Albert Streets, including the Yick Lung grocery. The earliest Chinese inhabitant in Ottawa was a man named Mr. Tam, who arrived to the city in the late 1880s. Unlike the Irish, Scottish, and other Europeans who were courted to the region with assisted emigration schemes, the Chinese were met with a head tax in 1885 and a total ban on Chinese immigration from 1923 to 1947. In the face of these restrictions, the Chinese population grew slowly. By 1909, there was a population 168 Chinese people in Ottawa, a few Chinese cafes, and twelve Chinese-owned laundries (Yee 2005, 91). Sue Wong came to Ottawa at the age of thirteen in 1902, after paying a $100 head tax, and began working at his uncle's laundry (Workers History Museum 2018b). These earliest businesses were not warmly received. In 1895 the Ottawa Labour Council encouraged its members to boycott Chinese laundromats, suggesting that the Chinese in Ottawa were a "curse to the city." In 1897, Chinese laundromats were made to pay a $10 annual municipal "water use" tax, which other laundromats were not required to pay (Powell n.d.b).

After immigrating to Canada from Jamaica in the 1930s, Herbert Brown established Brown's Cleaners and Tailors on Bank Street in 1957. Herbert and his wife Estelle became leaders in the Caribbean diasporic community in Ottawa. By the late 1950s, Herbert had been given the nickname "Pops." He walked seven women down the aisle as their stand-in father. Estelle Brown was a renowned seamstress who made the wedding dresses of many Caribbean women who immigrated to Ottawa through the West Indian Domestic Scheme (Bowden 2017).

If Sparks Street is understood to be a failure, one need only look closer at Montreal Road or Somerset Street West to see a richness of commercial street life. Here, the circulated goods at thrift shops, the Middle Eastern, Asian, and Caribbean spices in SERGs, are tied to specific places. Ottawa's shopping streets are layered with histories of migration and suggest that these areas are more than mere sites of commercial transaction — they are where people do the labour of social reproduction (grocery shopping, laundry) and where shopkeepers and patrons maintain diasporic communities and uphold individuals and families: extending credit, stitching wedding dresses, and sharing the news on the street.

MALLS

Malls are pretty good hangouts. Teenagers love them. New parents needing to walk with their babies but wanting to avoid Ottawa's wintery sidewalks find cozy refuge. Even the most generic malls offer important social opportunities. Carlingwood mall in the city's west end, referred to affectionately by locals as "Crawlingwood," is routinely occupied by parents with strollers and seniors as a place for casual strolling. The University of Ottawa Heart Institute celebrates on their website that there are heart-friendly mall-walking groups at seven Ottawa malls.

In North America, malls emerged alongside auto-burbs and an invigorated postwar consumer culture. Ottawa's first mall — the Westgate — opened in the city's west end in May 1953, built by real estate developer Harold Shenkman. The mall's opening included the presentation of a "futuristic radioactive gamma ray device designed by Canadian Aviation Electronics" and a grocery store with equally futuristic conveyor belt checkouts, wide aisles for browsing, and notably pleasant music. Early businesses included "Reitman's, Kresge's, Kiddytown, Royal Bank, Milk Bar, Throop Pharmacy, Handy-Andy, Chery's Flowers, Tip Top Tailors, Paul's Service Centre" (Allston 2015b). Freiman's — locally well-known from its Rideau Street location — opened a second location as one of the Westgate's early anchor stores.

On March 16, 1983, Ottawans marked the opening of the city's newest destination downtown mall, the Rideau Centre. To facilitate its construction, a block of stores had been demolished, a move protested by locals concerned that the new mall would worsen traffic and take business away from existing stores. Fortunately, the mall drew people to downtown, and local ByWard Market stores benefited from the "halo effect" produced by the mall (Tunbridge 1986, 254). Unlike independently owned shops and the early department stores, malls are consumer spaces with many owners. Cadillac Fairview, the company that owns the Rideau Centre (among many Canadian malls), is entirely owned by the Ontario Teachers' Pension Fund. Many other malls (the Westgate, St. Laurent, Merivale) are owned by real estate investment trust RioCan. Ownership of consumer spaces has become, as Zukin details, abstracted. Owners note their mall ownership as figures on investment statements.

Between the 1950s and the birth of the big box store in the early 2000s, malls developed their own complete ecosystems. Like department stores, malls encourage browsing, getting lost in commodities; some feature impressive architectural features; they are mostly equipped with escalators, elevators, and are visited every December by Santa Claus. The Rideau Centre was a later addition to earlier malls that bookended the city: the Bayshore Shopping Centre in west Ottawa, built in 1973, and St. Laurent Shopping Centre, built in 1967; all three feature European-style arched-glass arcades, adopted to encourage bedazzlement by a deluge of shiny new commodities.

Rob Shields argues that many people miss the "non-economic activities of people" and the "passive resistance and non-compliance with the indexes and norms urging consumption" at malls (Shields 1994, 210). The large size, long opening hours, and diversity of attractions in malls offer themselves as highly flexible third places; no interest in a specific sport or a particular beverage is required to warrant hanging out at a mall. The thoughtful ambiance of malls (seating, public washrooms, water features, even cake vending machines) contributes to their appeal. Ottawa artist and nostalgic Andrew King mused about the utility and character of the now-almost-extinct but once ubiquitous mall fountain:

> The water fountain and accompanying greenery of a mall was to create an "oasis" for the shopper, a place to relax and enjoy the shopping experience, like going on a vacation. Under the calming sounds of burbling water amidst lush tropical plants, you could buy your slacks and some MMMMMMuffins to snack on. The fountain was where parents would tell kids to meet if they got separated, a rendezvous place, and a spot for kids to toss coins into the depths of the crystal clear waters in hopes that a special wish came true. (King 2019)

While mall fountains have been disappearing, malls continue to offer great places for convivial hanging around. To those savvy to the escalator–stair–glass elevator labyrinth of the Rideau Centre, a rooftop terrace gives visitors (and rabbits) opportunities to lounge among cedar hedges, mature spruce trees, and flower beds.

FROM THE POWER CENTRE TO THE DISTRIBUTION CENTRE

If malls were seen as a threat to shopping streets, they would soon face their own threat: big box stores. The stalwart store at the front of this retail landscape offensive: Walmart. Walmart arrived in Canada in 1994, when it bought 122 Woolco stores; by 2002, it had become Canada's number one retailer (Government of Canada 2005). In Ottawa, power centres (commercial centres featuring big box stores located on the urban fringes) popped up in the late 1990s. Ottawa's South Keys Shopping Centre was built in 1996. Ninety-four acres of industrial land became transformed into the Ottawa Train Yards shopping district near Ottawa's train station in 2003. Power centres cater to automobility, leading to what Statistics Canada refers to as the "donut effect" — cities having population growth and activity along the edges, but struggling downtowns (Beaujot 2003, 18). Four power centres in Ottawa — South Keys, Baseline Road, Orléans, Kanata — are owned by the SmartCentres REIT.

Something is arguably lost in the sea of homogeneity offered by power centres. Anthropologist Marc Augé defines non-places: "if a place can be defined as relational, historical, and concerned with identity, then a space which cannot be defined as relational, or historical, or concerned with identity will be a non-place" (Augé 1995, 78). Power centres are "non-places" — they make few references to the cities they inhabit. Ottawa's South Keys and Edmonton's South Edmonton Commons are interchangeable. Instead of encouraging connections to places and other people notable in market spaces, non-places rely on "solitary contractuality" (Augé 1995, 94). Customers are discouraged from interacting on a personal level with retail workers, feeling at home, or lingering in these spaces. Drive-through Starbucks have replaced the milkshake counters at Freiman's. Parking lots have replaced the vibrant street life of 1960s Clarence Street. There are no fountains here.

Walmarts can and are being threatened by an even larger economic force: Amazon and online shopping. Despite their ongoing Twitter selfies with local businesses, local politicians in Ottawa and Gatineau collaborated to submit a proposal for a competition to house the second headquarters for Amazon in 2018. Invest Ottawa spent $100,000 working on their bid (Willing 2018). Mayor Jim Watson pitched to Amazon that they occupy a site on LeBreton Flats for Amazon's second headquarters. In a promotional video, the narrator states, "Amazon can step in on the ground floor of this generational city-building undertaking to establish a comparable eight-million-square-foot HQ2 right on the edge of nature" (Lofaro 2017). Despite municipal politicians' jockeying, Ottawa lost its bid to Arlington, Virginia.

Amazon did build a distribution centre in Ottawa's east end in 2018, though. The developer, Broccolini, proposed that the city waive a $800,000 interest charge on development fees for this one-million-square-foot facility. The city agreed (CBC News 2018a). Unfortunately, Amazon does nothing for urban life and is a horrible employer. Rachel Westley quit her job at the distribution centre after experiencing bullying, sexual harassment, and a repetitive strain injury. Absences are responded to sternly, with "points" deducted for employees who punch in as little as three minutes late (Helmer 2020). Amazon encourages workers to leave after a few years to keep labour costs low — raises end after three years, and there is an annual worker rollover of 150 percent on the warehouse floors (Kelly 2021). In 2020, at 2.6 million square feet, Ottawa's newest and largest building was opened, a new Amazon distribution centre in Barrhaven (Fleming 2022).

LOVE LOCAL

From Bytown's early days, owners, employees, and shoppers in these consumer spaces have had experiences mediated by ethnicity, gender, race, and class. The earliest shopping spaces — peddler's carts — were the labour and result of Jewish immigrants taking up historically Jewish employment in the face of discrimination from other occupations. Department stores were designed with predominantly female customers and primarily white female employees in mind. Meanwhile, other consumer spaces — the many SERGs, Chinatown laundries, Brown's laundry — offered important work and community spaces for diasporic communities often in the face of broader societal discrimination. Shopping and consumer spaces do much more than maintain consumer society.

With the opening of Amazon distribution centres, the shift from the locally specific, dynamic, and populated marketplace of the ByWard Market to a global, largely invisible, abstract place of global commerce seems complete. Yet that shift is not absolute. The pandemic brought great threats to and concern over the viability of stores and malls, a threat that was accentuated when the 2022 Convoy led to a month-long closure of the Rideau Centre. Online shopping soared during the pandemic. Yet local shops pivoted and created their own delivery systems. Black Squirrel Books assembled "mystery boxes" of books curated according to customers' stated interests. Small produce, meat, and cheese shops in the ByWard Market collaborated to create a one-stop shop local grocery delivery service and, to undercut American-owned Uber Eats, restaurants created a local restaurant-delivery app, Love Local. Customers responded, wanting to support local shops and restaurants, knowing that if they wanted there to be a city to return to after the pandemic, these stores needed to survive. One day in May 2021, I walked down to Elgin Street and saw from afar the windows of Perfect Books covered in brown paper. My heart sank, worried that my neighbourhood bookstore would be a pandemic casualty. Yet when I got closer, I read the sign saying that the store was temporarily closed because it was renovating and expanding! Local grocery shops, bookstores — like the always community-minded Octopus Books in the Glebe — music stores that double as music schools, cafés with bulletin boards advertising all manner of community events (and photo collages of the neighbourhood dogs), and pizza shops that sponsor local kids' sports teams have all been community builders and do significant work in maintaining society.

Chapter 11

GOODNIGHT OTTAWA

OTTAWA PUTS ITSELF TO BED and spends some restless minutes tossing and turning, thinking, "Am I safe? Am I fun? Am I romantic? Am I alive…?" Nighttime is a time of intense scrutiny for Ottawa, a city imagined to roll up its sidewalks at 5 p.m.

If we define nighttime as when the sun sets, at 45.42 degrees latitude, Ottawa has more access to nighttime than many cities. On the shortest day of the year, December 21, in Ottawa the sun sets at 4:23 p.m. — thirty-seven minutes before the end of the typical nine-to-five workday. Socially, though, nighttime does not begin when the sun sets — our understandings of night refer not just to time, but to a set of social practices and ideas. Will Straw refers to the "nocturnalization" of modern life as "the movement of more and more social and symbolic practices out of the day and into the night, from the seventeenth century onward" (Straw 2014, 187). Night is socially produced along what sociologists call "clock time" or "social time." Clock time emerged in nineteenth-century Europe with industrialization and urbanization, and it involved broad adoption of clocks, timetables, and discrete and universal measurements of time. It is distinct from understanding time in relation to the natural world, which is known as cyclical or agrarian time (Machum 2020, 197). A universally standard "social time" was also, incidentally, invented by an Ottawan. Sir Sandford Fleming, who wintered at his family home, Winterholme, at 230 Chapel Street in Sandy Hill, proposed international time zones and a standardized reading of time in his 1876 book, *Terrestrial Time*, which was first accepted by railway executives and eventually adopted by Canada and other countries (Regehr 2008).

Today, experiences of the night are marked by a tension between order — lighting policy, policing, nightlife planning — and enchantment — celebratory lights, an ecosystem of nocturnal critters, sitting in the dark with strangers at the movies, dancing with friends in dimly lit clubs. Night Ottawa is the collective achievement of historic forces (electric lighting innovations with Thomas Ahearn) and ongoing planning (the newly appointed "night mayor," officially the city's "Nightlife Commissioner"). Throughout this exploration of nighttime Ottawa, this chapter addresses fundamental questions of this book: Who is Ottawa for? Is Ottawa a city for lovers? For women? Is it for the moths and migratory birds? Is Ottawa for working-class men and women who want cheap beer and soothing live folk music on a Tuesday? Or is Ottawa for tourists interested in taking in the world's latest rendition of *Les Miserables*? This chapter is also about time: shifts from day to night to dawn, as well as questions about historic time, mortality, and afterlife. To explore these themes, I begin with a history Ottawa's street lighting, then offer an Ottawology of walking the night streets, nightlife, romantic Ottawa (waterfalls, romantic comedies), going to the theatre and movies, death, and afterlife.

ILLUMINATING OTTAWA

We will begin this nocturnal sojourn with a visit to the moon — Ottawa's moon. In 2010, renovations to the Museum of Nature were completed and the visiting Queen Elizabeth II cut the ribbon "unveiling" the new glass tower of the museum, named the "Queen's Lantern" in her honour. This glass tower has been used for hanging dramatic showpieces, like the moon, a colossal sculpture by British artist Luke Jerram. In the beginning, the moon would have been the dominant light fixture in Ottawa's night sky.

Beginning in the seventeenth century, street lighting enabled people to adopt the evening stroll and other entertainment activities as pleasant journeys into the night; dinner hour in France moved later by three hours between 1690 and 1740 (Straw 2014). A source of much of this enchantment is found on the second floor of the Museum of Nature, where you will find the museum's largest artifact — a blue whale skeleton — the remains of the world's largest mammal and a relative of the city's earliest source of light: the sperm and right whales. Whale blubber fuelled the lamps that hung over Bytown's wells circa 1850. The city's lamps were also lit by coal and naphtha (Cook 2023).

The nocturnalization of Ottawa was encouraged by business owners in the interest of expanding the workday. Electric lighting first illuminated Ottawa's factories: E.B. Eddy installed arc lights in his woodenware works by Chaudière Falls in 1881, painting the interior walls white to reflect the weak incandescence. The Parliament buildings were outfitted in Edison's sixteen-candlepower lights by 1883 (Cook 2023). Electric lighting facilitated the capitalist, rational, order of the Ottawa night.

Despite the claims of Hydro Ottawa, Ottawa was not the first electrically lit city in Canada: Peterborough had some electric street lighting in May 1884, and in December that same year, Pembroke was the first city to be fully lit by electric street lighting. Ottawa's Ahearn and Soper were subcontractors for the latter. In Ottawa, Royal Electric, which became Ottawa Electric Light Company, was responsible for 165 arc lamps to be kept on "dark to daylight, excepting when the moon shines bright and clear, and the sky is unclouded." Ottawa was officially electrified on May 1, 1885 (Cook 2023, 16, 19). But even then, lighting was coordinated with the city's natural light source, the moon.

There are few neon signs in Ottawa. Gréber found them to be a challenge to the "dignity and stateliness" of the city (quoted in Miguelez 2015, 295), preferring, one can presume, more order. Lighting did improve the orderly circulation of traffic. Since 1928, when the first traffic light was installed on Sparks Street, intersections have benefited from traffic lights (Hydro Ottawa n.d.). Lighting is also frequently used to enchant, for neighbourhood branding, and community bonding: a little block on Somerset Street, from Bank to O'Connor, wraps its trees in lights during the winter, and neighbourhoods feature distinctive streetlights. In 1895 the Ottawa Winter Carnival included the lighting of an ice castle, the Parliament buildings, and Sparks and Bank Streets (Tepperman 2009). In 1900, a 1,050-foot pier at Britannia Park was electrically lit, illuminating a dramatic evening stroll (Cook 2023). Since the 1980s there has been a "Sound and Light" show on Parliament Hill that has included a dynamic telling of Canadian history through light projections onto the Centre Block. Trees in nearby Confederation Park feature holiday lights from November to February. They are outdone, however, by the residents of Taffy Lane in Orléans, who turn the street into an attraction every winter with their exuberant display of lights.

Lighting has facilitated nighttime production, urban celebrations, orderly road traffic, and public safety. But is something lost with all of this artificial night lighting? Since 2016, Hydro Ottawa has converted 58,000 of the 76,000 street lightbulbs on public property to light-emitting diode (LED) lights, reducing the city's lighting energy consumption by 66 percent (Hydro Ottawa 2023). LED lights illuminate differently than the high-pressure sodium (HPS) lights they replaced. I live downtown, in the brightest part of the city; no matter the season, or weather, it's never fully dark here. There are streetlights, and bright (and loud) fireworks in the summer, city crews with their bright and loud trucks, and many office towers with their lights always on. According to the Ottawa Light Pollution map, on the Bortle scale — the agreed-upon measure of light pollution — downtown Ottawa is an 8, which is the second brightest ranking on the scale. What do the relatives of the taxidermied bats and racoons at the Museum of Nature make of this illuminated city? Are the nocturnal stick-bugs and moths confused? While LEDs use less energy, they shine brighter and whiter. Light pollution has increased 6 percent per year in recent years, and 30 percent of streetlights shine upwards, illuminating the sky (a phenomenon known as "sky glow"). Illumination impacts the growth and flowering of plants; moths and all manner of insects are confused; and disoriented birds collide into buildings (250,000 birds die annually in Ottawa from such collisions) (Roy 2017). On a walk through the bird exhibit at the Museum of Nature, our ornithologist tour guide excitedly showed my class his favourite bird, the whippoorwill. How, I asked, was this cuddly little brown bird impacted by night lighting? He explained that night lights attract and then kill all sorts of insects, the food of the whippoorwill (and many other birds). In 2017, the NCC committed to creating "dark zones" near the green spaces it oversees, like along the Rideau Canal and Greenbelt spaces, in the interest of wildlife (Roy 2017).

For much of the twentieth century, from 1904 to 1970, Ottawans had unique access to the night sky at the Dominion Observatory, an Ewart-designed sandstone building on the grounds of the Central Experimental Farm. Until its closing, Ottawans fuelled by curiosity about the trajectory of Haley's Comet and questions about satellites came to stargaze. Yet access to the brilliant starry night was gendered by design. The building was built without a women's washroom, and for many decades only one woman — Miriam Burland — worked at the observatory (Hinchcliff and Jasen 2021).

This is not the only way in which the access to night has been gendered. Women's safety is often used as a justification for more night lighting. However, it's not necessarily true that brighter night streets are safer for women. In fact, a group of Australian design scholars found that "high illuminance" did not correspond with women feeling safer — lighting that created "floodlit" effects was experienced as less safe. These researchers concluded that more lighting is not better, but better lighting — lighting attuned to human perception and the ability to distinguish shapes and colours — was most helpful for perceptions of safety (Kalms 2019). And disrupting structures of patriarchy is even more helpful.

IS OTTAWA SAFE?

Night Ottawa is enchanting, but unfortunately, strolling freely in the night has never been universally enjoyed. Night strolling is the purview of men; the flâneur can be a "gentleman stroller," while historically the walking woman has been seen as already deviant, and people deemed gender nonbinary or queer, or homeless, are also more vulnerable to street harassment and violence. In 1989, there was a spree of homophobic violence against men read as gay. In August 1989, Château Laurier employee Alain Brosseau was followed and dragged onto the Alexandria Bridge; his assailants apparently said, "nice shoes, faggot" before throwing him to his death in the river. This was a tragic tipping point in a summer where seven people were pushed off the cliff of Major's Hill Park; two died. As the gay community insisted that these were hate-motivated homophobic attacks, the police slowly began to take seriously the patterned nature of this violence (Village Legacy Project n.d.).

Whole swaths of urban night entertainment are designed exclusively for (heterosexual) men, including in men's-only social clubs like Ottawa's Laurentian Club and Rideau Club (which did not welcome women until 1950). Remnants of gender-segregated leisure remain. At 1084 Wellington, the Elmdale Tavern still shows a "Ladies and Escorts" sign on the west side of the building. "Gentlemen's clubs," designed for male customers with female performers, also offer up the urban night as a time and place for male pleasure. The "Rib Room" at the Riverside Hotel in Vanier in the 1960s offered steaks served up by one of the restaurant's "bunnies"; it was the closest Ottawa came to having a Playboy Club (King 2015). Bars and nightclubs are not officially gender segregated today, but cursory peering into any sports bar may suggest that gendered nighttime leisure patterns hold steady.

Why can't women — cis and trans — stroll freely or occupy any public nighttime space? Sociologist Erving Goffman, whose research focused on small-scale interactions, developed some theories to explain the ways in which people experience public space differently. Goffman defined people acting outside of a "normal" social role (e.g., being drunk or in costume), people who are visibly marked by their power (in uniform — e.g., police officers), and people routinely denied power (children, women, trans and nonbinary people, racialized people, poor people) as all occupying an "exposed position." Those in such a position are denied what Goffman termed "civil inattention": the acknowledgement of another's presence without making any overtures toward more interaction. It is civil to acknowledge that someone else is there, but also civil to leave them alone (Goffman 1972, 385). People feel that it is appropriate to initiate conversation, or in more violent intrusions, to yell, catcall, or touch those in exposed positions. In 2018, 61 percent of Canadian women ages fifteen to twenty-four experienced some sort of unwanted sexual advance in a public place, and trans people were more than twice as likely to experience unwanted sexual advances in public than cisgender people

(Canada, Women and Gender Equality 2024). While those with power are exposed by virtue of their chosen occupation and have the power to rebuke such intrusions, those exposed by their lack of power are vulnerable in public places, and more so under the cover of darkness.

Experiences and fear of violence and harassment curtail opportunities for women, trans, queer, and racialized people to stroll, explore, and frequent nightlife attractions, especially alone. While Goffman and many etiquette books suggest saying thanks in the face of certain sexualized comments directed frequently towards women, Carol Gardner's ethnographic research on catcalling showed that this strategy often led to an escalation of the situation, where the men then proceeded to continue with "double entendres, abusive commentary or prolonged and detailed assessments" (Gardner 1995, 357).

In Ottawa and elsewhere, women have collectively been responding to the limitations on their nighttime freedom created by street harassment and violence. Take Back the Night marches — loud, public resistance to the gendering of night mobilities as a male prerogative — have taken place every September in Ottawa since the 1970s. Every December 6 (the anniversary of the Montreal Massacre), Enclave: The Women's Monument in Minto Park, is the site of vigils to mourn women murdered in Ottawa and beyond. The Ottawa Coalition to End Violence Against Women and the Sexual Assault Network developed "Project SoundCheck" as a program for festival and event organizers and bars that includes bystander sexual violence prevention training, safety audits, and educational resources (OCTEVAW 2018). November 20, Trans Day of Remembrance, offers an opportunity every year for community members to gather at the Canadian Tribute to Human Rights to mourn lost lives and speak out against transphobic violence.

While many women do not feel safe to roam night Ottawa, the limitations of women's right to the urban night is especially acute for sex workers. Since the 1800s, sex workers in Ottawa have been met with efforts toward moralizing and criminalization. Colonel By ordered the destruction of a shanty by the canal that was occupied by a "group of 'loose' women" playing "havoc with the morals of the Sappers and Miners" (Andrews 1998, 147). The "Home for Friendless Women" likewise offered such imagined moral reform. A moralizing agenda is at the foundation of policing and legal systems that see the criminalization of sex work as a means of helping vulnerable victims. Former Ottawa police chief Vern White suggested that the hyper-policing of sex work in Ottawa was justified because "there are bigger issues involved with prostitution than just prostitution.… A lot of them have either addictions or medical issues- mental health or other. Our job is ... to try to get them some help" (quoted in Bruckert and Hannem 2013, 299).

In Canada, sex work has never been illegal; however, living off sex work, operating a bawdy house, or advertising sex work have all been illegal. In the 1880s, new laws in Ontario dictated that keepers of brothels of Indigenous sex workers would receive harsher penalties. However, there were few guidelines to determine what a brothel was, other than readings of the "character of the premises." In effect, places where Indigenous women (or those understood to be Indigenous) gathered were, regardless of activity, interpreted as brothels. These laws worked to effectively criminalize sex work but also to criminalize being an Indigenous woman in the city (Backhouse 1991, 241).

The criminalization around sex work is felt profoundly by women engaged in street-level sex work in Ottawa. A study by POWER (Prostitutes of Ottawa, Work, Educate, Resist) found that one of the main challenges faced by sex workers in Ottawa today is violence at the hands of the police. One study respondent (Brooke, a street-based worker) sums it up: "the police and the violence. Put the two together and this is my biggest concern" (POWER 2010, 46). Sex workers are routinely arrested for solicitation, jaywalking, trespassing, and public nuisance, and they experience verbal abuse, callouts, public shaming, public strip searches, and physical and sexual violence by police. Faye explains the police practice of "starlight tours":

> Cops drive you far away and then they beat us up. They drive us to Orléans at two or three in the morning and they make us walk back. There are no buses. They make you walk back from the woods. The next day, you see the same cops and they don't say anything. If you say something, they arrest you for obstruction. (Bruckert and Hannem 2013, 307)

These types of interactions with the police lead to a number of avoidance strategies by street-level sex workers that make them less safe, including working alone, jumping into cars, and changing their personal appearance frequently (Bruckert and Chabot 2014).

POWER offers a third understanding of sex work by arguing that sex work should be treated not as an individual moral failure, nor as a crime, but as work. Sex workers should be afforded workplace protections, including the ability to work without threat of violence from clients or the state. So, is Ottawa safe? The safety of the night is structured by entrenched patriarchy underpinning violence against women, homophobia, and transphobia. The institution tasked with maintaining public safety day and night — the police — has proven to be indifferent to some (during the homophobic spree of hate crimes in 1989) and the source of danger for others (sex workers).

IS OTTAWA FUN?

In his autobiography, My Way, Ottawa-born crooner Paul Anka describes his childhood impression of his hometown: "Ottawa was a small government town, somewhat conservative, but beautiful, even idyllic, from the fairy-tale tower of the House of Commons building to the dappled, leafy streets with the whir of kids on bikes and the ice-cream truck. It was a wonderful place to grow up. Life was pleasant, uneventful, and predictable, which is why I eventually left" (Anka 2013, 11). Anka describes a warm childhood growing up on Bayswater Avenue in Hintonburg, surrounded by his extended Lebanese family, helping his father with his restaurant, the Locanda, attending Fisher Park High School, pining over an older woman named Diana Ayoub at his church. At thirteen years old, Anka stole his mom's car and drove across the Champlain Bridge to the bright nights and good times on offer in Hull. The bus/cab/Uber ride from Carleton University and the University of Ottawa to the seediest Hull drinking holes continues to be a rite of passage unique to Ottawa university students too young to legally consume alcohol in Ontario.

Trotting over to Hull for a drink became especially popular during the decade when Ottawa was legally a dry city. In September 1916, the Ontario Temperance Act went into effect, limiting bars to selling watery 1.4 percent beer and weak spirits. In December 1917, a federal law made the importation of alcohol into "dry" areas illegal, meaning a ban on bringing booze from Quebec into Ontario. This law was passed in the Museum of Nature, which was the temporary House of Commons after Parliament burned down in 1916. Both laws shifted boozy partying to Hull (and a speakeasy scene in Ottawa). Prohibition laws in Ontario loosened in 1924, when the government allowed 2.5 percent beer and 4.4 proof spirits, and then in 1927, the government established the existing Liquor Control Act. Ottawans couldn't legally drink alcohol in bars again until 1934 (Powell 2019b).

Despite this history of migrating to Hull for libations, Ottawa has its own history of bars. At a bar in the ByWard Market, the city's oldest neon sign reads "Château Lafayette House" (Ramsay-Borg 2015). The Château Lafayette was thus named in 1936, although its history as a hotel originates in the early nineteenth century. By the 1950s, the Laff had embodied all the characteristics of a "dive bar." When it took a hit in the early 2000s with the passing of provincial non-smoking laws, the bar bought a Quiznos franchise for half of the space; the owners credit the Quiznos for allowing the bar to continue to support live music. While the Quiznos has since shut, the Laff continues to be a venue for live music (including Saturday afternoon performances by local legend Lucky Ron). It is a quintessential accessible third place; the Wi-Fi password on my last visit was "Labatt50" and the walls are covered in photographs, including memorial tributes to regular customers and staff. The bar market has a history of fulfilling all manner of idiosyncratic nightlife needs. The sticky-floored Great Canadian Cabin, the Honest Lawyer with its single bowling alley, the house music on offer at Atomic, and the *Hitchhiker's Guide to the Galaxy*-inspired cocktails at Zaphod's all might inspire nostalgia, in a generation that came of age in the late 1990s, as places for fleeting pleasures. Ottawans that were young adults in the 1960s might wax nostalgic for Café Le Hibou, a coffeehouse that moved from Rideau Street to Bank Street to its final Sussex Drive location between 1960 and 1975. The café didn't serve alcohol but was a smoky 1960s coffeehouse that circulated coffee and other non-alcohol stimulants. It hosted poetry nights (Irving Layton, Gwendolyn MacEwen) and folk, country, and blues performers (Gordon Lightfoot, Joni Mitchell, Ian Tyson, Bruce Cockburn), with customers seated at tables with red-checked tablecloths and Chianti bottles as candle holders. Its final location was facilitated in part by the NCC, which was, at the time, developing Sussex Drive as a ceremonial "Mile of History." The NCC imagined the café, with its vibrant culture and youthful energy, worthy of Sussex Drive (Rockburn 2015).

In Centretown, the marquee of the Gilmour reads "an average Canadian pub." There are average Canadian pubs across this expansive, amalgamated urban-suburban-rural city. People are playing trivia, darts, competing in monthly pinball competitions, playing pool or Scrabble, having awkward dates and good dates, befriending bartenders, debuting autobiographical ballads at open-mic nights, toasting departed friends, and escaping their troubles at these establishments. Bars are doing quite a lot of the heavy lifting of making Ottawa a sociable and livable city. They are sites of low-stakes frivolity, but they are also sites of surveillance and entrenched and resisted gendered, ableist, heteronormative, and age-based social segregation. Because of its importance to our collective well-being, urban scholars, activists, and business owners were already concerned about the decline of urban nightlife before the pandemic. Straw and Reia pointed to gentrification, changing demographics of urban tourism brought on by cheaper flying, higher rents in tourist neighbourhoods, and conflicts over noise and "public disorder" as threats to the vitality of urban nightlife (Straw and Reia 2021, 12). Here, nighttime order and enchantment are at odds. Patterns documented in European and other North American cities are echoed in Ottawa.

Gentrification has pushed many dive bars out of Ottawa's historic and tiny gay village. Pro-gentrification urbanist Richard Florida argued that knowledge economy workers, engineers, artists, designers, and gay men were the "creative class," brought cultural revitalization in cities, and, as such, should be welcomed by city builders. Many critics note that Florida's understandings of culture are rooted in a narrow understanding of culture creators as artists that produce things people can buy, and his vision of gentrification is one in which middle-class culture displaces other alternative, working-class, punk, and queer cultures (Granzow and Dean 2007, 91; Gelbard 2023). In Ottawa, gay men were not welcomed as gentrifiers; rather, spaces for gay social life have been, over time, shuttered and replaced by the official naming of a few blocks as Ottawa's gay village.

Given the closeting effect of the gay purge of the 1950s through to the 1990s, Ottawa has not had a significant concentration of queer people living and playing in a specific neighbourhood. Yet, throughout the twentieth century, gay men and women have occupied many downtown public spaces. Historian Patrizia Gentile describes a gay Ottawa of the mid-twentieth century that was hidden, dispersed, and right under the nose of the country's seat of political power. The Lord Elgin's basement bar and a steam room in the Château Laurier were sites of gay male congregation. Major's Hill Park, Strathcona Park, and Remic Rapids were all cruising areas for gay men. Gay women had fewer public spaces, relying more on social networks and house parties for socializing. Gentile notes two significant sites: the Townhouse Motel on Rideau Street, which held weekly lesbian dances, and the Coral Reef, a bar on Nicholas Street that hosted lesbian nights on Thursdays and Fridays (Gentile 2010). While in many cases the presence of the government is the convenient alibi for Ottawa's stodgy reputation, when it comes to the absence of a prominent gay village, it actually is a legitimate explanation. Gentile explains that of the sites she mentions, "The legacy of the security campaigns against queers and of the fear that these surveillance strategies created continues to be felt in Ottawa's queer community" (Gentile 2010, 209). Gentile notes a small concentration of gay-oriented businesses on a few blocks of Bank and Somerset Streets (what is now marked as The Village/Le Village) — however, of the spots she mentions (Centretown Pub, Wilde's, and After Stonewall) only Centretown Pub still exists. Nathaniel Lewis argues that today, Ottawa gay men largely consume gay culture in Montreal and Toronto, and the dominant expression of queer sexualities in Ottawa is one of "homonormativity," a queerness that echoes middle-class heteronormative understandings of family, private homeownership, citizenship (Lewis 2012, 298, 304), and suburbanism.

Gentrification, which leads to establishments catering to middle-class cultural tastes, threatens the vitality of everyday dive bars like the Laff and the Gilmour. Sarah Gelbard argues that bureaucratic measures focused on nighttime economies can limit opportunities for finding inclusive spaces within a city, despite positing "inclusivity" and "safety" as their stated goals. In the city's 2017 Ottawa Music Strategy (OMS), the plan suggests that the city should imagine music as key to the city's "brand" and work to increase "participation among youth and women" (Gelbard 2023, 180). Yet bureaucratic understandings of music and nightlife defer to the preferences of the most mainstream middle-class common denominator, and other types of culture are often disparaged. For example, the OMS doesn't understand punk spaces, which "have become a stand-in for unsafe space and a launching pad for strategic rebranding and targeted for revitalization" (Gelbard 2023, 182). But punk spaces, festivals, and venues like the House of TARG in Old Ottawa South pursue their own paths toward safety and inclusivity. House of TARG's public safety statement reads: "the heartbeat of TARG is to serve our community and we will always be committed to that … we strive to do what we can to make our limited resources available to friends, organizations & initiatives we believe in" (Gelbard 2023, 183).

Many of the priorities identified in the OMS are to connect the music industry "with business, entrepreneurship and the larger creative economy" (quoted in Gelbard 2023, 180). For Gelbard, the bureaucrats involved in supporting the city's nightlife do not see the value of places that do not align with a tourist-friendly brand for the city. A focus on tourists' interests also disregards the significance of third places. For a place to be a second home to some, it must, by definition, not be home-like for everyone. There is a measure of exclusivity in these home-like leisure spaces that need not be interpreted as oppressive. In fact, some tourists precisely seek out these gems. The couple from Louisiana seated beside me at the bar at the Laff on my last visit were truly delighted by their experience. Everyone can come to the Laff, not everyone will find it home-like, and that's precisely why it *is* home-like to the regulars, who know exactly when to throw a cigarette at Lucky Ron during his singing of "Tillsonburg." A welcoming and inclusive city would have planning policies that allowed for the flourishing of many flavours of belonging: punk bars, seniors' centres, YMCAs, boxing clubs, cricket pitches, pinball arcades, hip-hop festivals, Legions, bingo halls. The city's nightlife commissioner, Matthieu Grondin, is the bureaucratic bridge between order and enchantment and has, in his early tenure, been working on issues regarding the overticketing of delivery trucks and noise bylaws that require festivals to shut everything down (even if a thunderstorm has devastatingly delayed a Snoop Dogg concert!) (White-Crummey 2025). In 2024 the NCC bought the building that until recently was a Chapters bookstore on Rideau Street. The plan is for that building to become a mid-size live music venue, a hopeful sign of further bureaucratic facilitation of some nighttime enchantment.

Gentrification has led to the shuttering of nightlife venues — as seen in the closing of James Street Feed Company for a condominium — but also the creation of new opportunities for nighttime and mid-morning leisure. Some of the new offerings on LeBreton Flats trade in a common gentrifiers' strategy: replacing the culture of the working-class with a nostalgic and elevated simulacrum of working-class culture. Gelbard recalls taking a cab to the Orange Monkey, a bar in City Centre. Upon arrival, her cab driver resisted dropping her off: "'Is this the place?' he says with concern. 'I can't let you out here, miss. I don't think it's safe'" (Gelbard 2023, 182). Until recently City Centre was a series of largely abandoned city warehouses, perfectly co-opted for all manner of creative pursuits (including playing loud music).

Now, the complex includes a microbrewery, a CrossFit gym, an art gallery, and Art Is In, a bakery with a wildly popular weekend brunch. Urban commentator Shawn Micaleff wrote an entire book on the cultural politics of brunch, arguing that shelling out a lot of money on some variety of eggs, toast, juice, and coffee is an example par excellence of conspicuous consumption. Micaleff employs the concept developed by early twentieth century economist/sociologist Thorstein Veblen, who coined the term "conspicuous consumption" to refer to consumption that highlights two things: one's access to money and one's distance from labour to earn that money (i.e., how "old money" someone was). Brunch is also an exemplar of conspicuous leisure, as those unburdened by work can show off this freedom by breakfasting later in the day. Brunch is distinct from diner breakfasts, cheaper fare that you can get "all day!" in many establishments. One of the first Ottawa establishments designed precisely for eating breakfast-ish foods (an eating house, as they were known before restaurants were common) was a "beanery" run by the apparently eternally old and cranky George Bulger, who served up steak, eggs, and beans late into the night for politicians at his diner on Metcalfe Street between Queen and Albert starting in 1890 (Deachman 2022, 6). Micaleff details how many Toronto brunch spots employ an aesthetic of the labouring lumberjack, served alongside expensive mimosas, as an example of an ironic conspicuous consumption. Brunchers demonstrate their distance from labour by consuming brunch in an environment with all of the markings of working-class labour (Micaleff 2014). This is true in the warehouse-turned-bougie brunch spot Art Is In, with its $31 French toast stack, and this phenomenon is also on display on LeBreton Flats.

Between 1852 and 1945, the Flats were dominated by lumber mills, paper mills, hydroelectric generating stations, some manufacturing, and breweries. These were mostly cleared out with the expropriation, but in 1974, motivated by heritage conservation groups, the NCC catalogued the existing heritage buildings and retrofitted "some of them into active spaces of consumption" (Mathews and Picton 2014a, 347). Ottawa's oldest stone mill, the Thompson-Perkins and Bronson pulp mill, built in 1842, became the Mill Street Brew Pub in 2012. Matthews and Picton explain that the rehabilitation of this building was done to offer tourists and locals imagined "authentic" and unique interactions with the city's industrial past. However, the industrial chic of the Mill Street Brew Pub is firmly ironic, because city zoning stipulations do not allow for actual brewing on site — such manufacturing has been deemed to negatively impact the character of the land use there (Mathews and Picton 2014b, 351).

Ottawans make their own fun, treasure their "average Canadian pubs," punk bars, pool halls, dance clubs. Ottawans' fun, like the fun on offer in many cities, must negotiate forces of gentrification that challenge the survival of these everyday spaces and give birth to new forms of conspicuous leisure. Fun in Ottawa is also structured by its proximity to Quebec, with its lower drinking age, and its function as the capital city, impacted by the "gay purge" and with a compulsion to cater to tourists' needs.

IS OTTAWA ROMANTIC?

In 2006 Ottawa got a new pedestrian bridge: the Corktown Bridge, spanning the Rideau Canal at Somerset Street. Ottawans quickly appropriated the bridge as a place to express their undying romantic love via etched locks, throwing keys into the canal. How romantic! How Parisian! William Lyon Mackenzie King, who liked to envision Ottawa as Parisian in design and mood, would have been pleased! But of course, no act of whimsy or spontaneity can be left alone, and after a Paris bridge collapsed under the weight of similar "love locks," structural engineers at the University of Ottawa studied whether the Corktown Bridge could sustain the weight of Ottawa's collective romance. The researchers determined that it's near impossible for Ottawa to be too romantic for this particular bridge. Furthermore, biologists declared that the dramatically tossed keys pose little threat to the aquatic life of the canal (Smith 2014). In any case, many of the love locks are combination locks, so … *amusez-vous bien*, Ottawa lovers.

In the nineteenth century, the romantic era of the celebrated picturesque, Ottawans popularized another site as the venue for romance: a pathway behind the Parliament buildings. It was either Dominion architect Thomas Seaton Scott or minister of public works William Macdougall who orchestrated the grooming of a gentle path to be strolled along, which became known as Lover's Walk by 1873 (Powell n.d.a). Despite Lover's Walk and the Corktown Bridge, romantic is not a "place myth" (Shields 1991) for Ottawa. In fact, in a now-debunked story, Ottawa was at one time known as a city with a higher-than-average subscription to the adultery website Ashley Madison.

Ottawa should be more romantic. Like North America's capital of romance, Niagara Falls, Ottawa is also blessed with dramatic waterfalls. According to B.J. Hudson, waterfalls combine elements of the picturesque — partial concealment, rough textures — with the "delightful horror" of the sublime (Hudson 2000, 75). Waterfalls are like romance itself — mysterious, dramatic, beautiful. Before they were dammed, Chaudière Falls was seen as second only to Niagara Falls for its splendor. In Orléans, just off of busy St. Laurent Boulevard, is Princess Louise Falls: tall, narrow, less known, and almost visible from the Starbucks across the street. Artificially created during the Rideau Canal construction, Hog's Back Falls are near sublime, offering much biological, physical, and mental well-being from its spray. These waterfalls also hold a mythic quality — it is rumoured that "Devil's Hole," a feature of the falls, is occupied by a sea monster (Gray 2018, 69). In recent years, the NCC has opened bistros at a number of picturesque locations — Patterson Creek, Remic Rapids Park, Confederation Park — and has collaborated with businesses to create seasonal taverns, like the Tavern on the Island (Bate Island Park), Tavern on the Hill (at Major's Hill Park), and Tavern by the Falls (Rideau Falls). The Rideau Falls Tavern, perched right at the top of the falls (at the juncture of the Ottawa and Rideau rivers), with stunning views, roaring waterfall acoustics, and sensorial mist to accompany pina coladas and tacos, suggests that order (a bureaucratically run Crown corporation) and enchantment (waterfalls) can work in concert to make Ottawa not just romantic, but broadly delightful.

Romance is, in part, trickery: projections, revelations, surprises, like those veiled by the mist of waterfalls, and so, in a fashion, Ottawa is quite romantic since the city often slyly stands in for New York, Chicago, and all manner of Smalltown, USA, portrayals in many romantic Lifetime and Hallmark movies. Sparks Street is often decked out in Christmas decorations and fake snow in the spring and fall. The charming cobble streets in the ByWard Market, Confederation Park with its tree lights aglow, the Rink of Dreams, or the Rideau Canal all provide the perfect romantic backdrop. Manotick provided the perfect set for *Candy Cane Christmas* (2020). Flapjack's Diner on Preston Street and Bramasole on Bank Street feature in the film *Rock 'n' Roll Christmas* (2019), the Sens Rink of Dreams offers a romantic set in the 2020 film *Christmas Unwrapped*, and the Glebe Community Centre features in the 2019 film *Christmas Jars*. While on screen Ottawa is a silent, disingenuous background for very contrived, if cozy, winter romances, going to the theatre and the movies have offered opportunities for real-life romances and unremarkable but still meaningful quiet intimacy with strangers.

IS OTTAWA DRAMATIC?

Since 2011, the Carleton Engineering Musical has been delighting audiences in the Kailash Mital Theatre of Carleton University with comedic classics: WD-40, Duct Tape, and Walt Engie. While a relatively recent addition to the city's amateur theatre scene, the C-Eng Musical has picked up on the city's oldest theatre tradition. The very first theatrical performance in Bytown was The Village Lawyer in February 1837, also a production of engineers — those of the Bytown Fifteenth Regiment — in their time off (Miguelez 2004). From this early beginning, theatre has offered a playful outlet for amateur actors. At back stages across the city, professional and amateur creatives find themselves in front of magical hat racks, boas, and corsets, in the company of other visionaries ready and eager to transform a modest or opulent theatre space into other worlds to share with a dozen or a few hundred strangers. Live theatre has been an opportunity to entertain but also to stimulate, nourish cultural distinctness, and forward social progress. At the city's earliest theatre, the Union Hall Theatre, Ottawans were offered Uncle Tom's Cabin — a play about slavery in the United States that was a departure from the typically "Victorian puritanical standards" and cultural tastes of the local community (Miguelez 2004, 24).

An auditorium in Bytown's city hall (then at Confederation Square) was appropriated as a theatre in 1850. Here, poet and bureaucrat William Pittman Lett organized the staging of plays by travelling theatre troupes. Other Ottawa theatres were likewise born and died in the nineteenth century, like Her Majesty's Theatre at 112 Wellington, the first purpose-built theatre constructed in 1856. The Grand Opera House was an upscale venue that received Lord and Lady Dufferin on its opening night in 1875, charged $3 admission, and welcomed opera singers from abroad to entertain Ottawa's culturally hungry audiences. In 1906, the Monument Nationale opened in Lowertown, at 113 George Street. This grand, four-storey building with a tower (now the site of Giant Tiger) was the heart of Francophone culture in Ottawa, offering a location for theatrical performances, reading rooms, a bowling alley, and political assemblies, including many addresses by Wilfrid Laurier (Miguelez 2004).

Located at Sparks and Queen Streets (now Confederation Square) and attached to the Russell House Hotel, the Russell Theatre, Ottawa's premiere cultural centre between 1897 and 1928 was the most opulent theatre Ottawa had seen, with a mosaic foyer floor, plush red carpets, box chairs, and curved staircases that led to the standing room gallery (Miguelez 2004). Its destruction (by both fire and federal expropriation of the land) marked the end of an era of theatres, ushering in a new crop of venues to shape Ottawa's current theatrical landscape.

Just a few months before the Russell Theatre staged its last production, a group of theatre enthusiasts from the Ottawa Drama League (a group created by the Ottawa Women's University Club), had appropriated a Methodist church on King Edward Avenue and refashioned it as the Little Theatre. The Ottawa Little Theatre staged its first play, *Anthony and Anna,* on January 4, 1928 (Miguelez 2004), and today, it is one of Canada's longest running community theatres. Despite this performing space, the city still lacked what the Russell Theatre provided — an opulent venue that Ottawa could proudly offer to travelling opera singers, foreign ballets, and theatre troupes. This absence was keenly felt by Hamilton Southam, who, for six years, dedicated his life to creating a national performing arts space. The result, the National Arts Centre (NAC) on Elgin Street, opened its doors on June 2, 1969, with an opening night performance of an avant-garde ballet, *Kraanerg*. In the opening weeks there were also performances of the ballets *Swan Lake* and *Romeo and Juliet,* Canadian playwright George Ryga's *The Ecstasy of Rita Joe,* and performances by the Montreal and Toronto symphony orchestras (Jennings 2019). The opening lineup demonstrated the goals of the centre: to showcase both international and national performing arts. Since then, the brutalist building, a design of Fred Lebensold, noted for its affliction of "hexagonitis" in the motif on the ceilings, floors, outdoor planters, and the very shape of the columns (Jennings 2019, 36), received a major glass-clad renovation by Diamond Schmitt Architects in 2017, adding considerable public space for free indoor concerts, children's programming, and enjoying the views of the canal or Elgin Street. In 2019, the fiftieth season of the NAC, the theatre added a dedicated Indigenous programming to join the English and French programs.

In August 1975, a new theatre joined Ottawa's scene: the Great Canadian Theatre Company (GCTC). From 1982 until 2008, this company, established by Carleton professors and students with a mandate of producing exclusively Canadian plays, operated out of a renovated truck garage on Gladstone at Preston. It now occupies a purpose-built theatre in Hintonburg. The Gladstone Theatre — which has been, since 2008, an independent performing arts space — took over the theatre space at Gladstone and Preston.

While Ottawa's live theatre scene is strong, the magic of telling stories met technological magic with the rise of moving pictures in the 1890s, leading to a moviegoing tradition that enchants, stimulates, and offers opportunities for real life romance.

Analyze That, a 2002 Robert DeNiro and Billy Crystal movie gets 23 percent on Rotten Tomatoes. It is an entirely unexceptional movie — but for my friend Jon and his wife, Jennifer, seeing that film at the Mayfair in 2003 allowed them to continue a first date neither wanted to end after wandering through Winterlude attractions and having dinner at Von's Bistro in the Glebe. The Mayfair, for Jen and Jon — as for, I am sure, countless couples — holds a central place in their biography as a couple. For many, a Halloween viewing of *Rocky Horror Picture Show* or a singalong viewing of *The Sound of Music* at the Mayfair have offered quirky moments of nighttime collective effervescence with friends and strangers.

Outside of three remaining and precious urban movie theatres — the 1930s Mayfair in Old Ottawa South, the 1940s Bytowne Cinema on Rideau Street, and the Cineplex Odeon at Lansdowne Park — downtown Ottawa has become a bit of a movie theatre desert. Yet there is a considerable ghost landscape of movie theatres. The parking lot beside the Staples on Bank Street (the Rialto), the Strand restaurant (formerly Tim Horton's) in Old Ottawa South (the Strand Theatre), the Harvey's/Starbucks/Johnny Farina's on Elgin Street (the Elgin Theatre and the Elgin Little Theatre), the Home Hardware in the Glebe (the Avalon Theatre) are all haunted with memories of a more popcorned era. The theatre that Ottawa singer Alanis Morrisette sang about in "You Oughta Know" has likely been shuttered (was it the World Exchange cinema? The Rideau Centre theatre? The Somerset Theatre?). The loss of movie theatres is more than lost access to stars and stories (Hollywood stories are more accessible than ever); in the Depression-era 1930s, the proprietor of the Rialto Theatre, Mr. Levinson, said, "I'm not selling movies, I'm selling a heated sheltered park bench for a dime" (quoted in Miguelez 2004, 135). The Nelson Theatre (the precursor to the Bytowne Theatre) boldly stated, "It's COOL inside" under its marquee in the 1950s (Miguelez 2004, 277). Movie theatres also historically provided the setting of fairly innocent childhood deviance (for petty theft, sneaking into double features, and hiding out while skipping school). In-theatre clocks (like the one still on display at the Mayfair), allowed obedient children to make it home by curfew (Miguelez 2004). My neighbour remembers the Strand as having a reputation of being frequented by the so-called Yohawks and Squirrels, youth "gangs" in the 1960s.

Before moviegoing was the public viewing pleasure it is today, going to the movies meant standing for a few minutes to look through a viewfinder — the kinetoscope. Ottawa's first kinetoscope viewing took place in a storefront at 55 Sparks Street on November 3, 1894. To enjoy the kinetoscope, viewers looked through a peep hole into a box to witness the short moving images within; for a dime you could enjoy three minutes of entertainment (Tepperman 2009). The kinetoscope — a device that embodied the excitement of the age of electrification — was embraced in a way that typifies Ottawa's orientation toward the night. The arrival of "movies" in this form was met with excitement and skepticism. Movies were the earliest form of the "commodification of entertainment" (Tepperman 2009, 7), marking a transition from folk to mass culture, and they were met with suspicion as the films themselves showed practices otherwise frowned upon (drinking, fighting, being a scantily clad woman). However, the scientific nature of the technology provided a cover for respectable Ottawa to watch films showing women dancing at a time when burlesque performances were outlawed (Tepperman 2009). The arrival of the vitascope in Ottawa on July 18, 1896, allowed for crowds of people to watch moving pictures together. As part of the opening of the West End Park, a park developed by the OLA, the vitascope projected moving images onto a larger screen for collective viewing. Up to eight hundred people were at the park on that July evening to watch a short film featuring people walking around Prospect Park, Brooklyn (Allston 2016). This early film projection was advertised to the masses, but one journalist described the first movie audience as "comprising the elite of the city" (quoted in Tepperman 2009, 15).

The 1910s to the 1930s saw an explosion of theatres, many of which were architecturally elegant and experimental with new technologies. The Flower Theatre, built in 1914 at 128 Sparks Street, boasted air conditioning and a retractable roof (Miguelez 2004)! The Imperial Theatre, built in 1914, was dubbed Canada's "most gorgeous" theatre, with its beaux-arts classical design, lion heads on each side of the central window, "discreetly rich and elegant décor" (Miguelez 2004, 113), and a prominent and impressive pipe organ. The Imperial was predominantly a movie theatre until 1955. It reopened as a nightclub in 1970, known best as Pandora's Box, a strip club, before it became reimagined in 1977 as Barrymore's, a prominent live music club, until its closure in 2020 (Miguelez 2004).

By the 1970s, new movie theatres had become increasingly low-brow and offered collective and individual opportunities to push collective sexual mores. Associations with poverty contributed to a sense of moviegoing as of ill-repute and low cultural value. But in the dark, access to this leisure opportunity expanded. Movie theatres, even more than libraries, allow people to hide, in public. The Rialto Theatre offered seedy movies Mondays to Wednesdays, and from Thursdays to Sundays, more family-friendly fare. Rialto — which was known by the nickname "the Rat Hole" — was also a known gay male cruising area (Village Legacy Project n.d.).

From the 1960s to the 1990s, many theatres were built in strip malls and then in mega-plexes in Kanata and Barrhaven. Yet theatres began shuttering at the beginning of the new millennium. In 2013 the World Exchange cinema closed; that same year Empire Theatres closed its theatre in the Rideau Centre. Then, in 2020, the pandemic hit, and movie theatres risked becoming some of the pandemic's first casualties. The Mayfair offered anxious Ottawa cinephiles an opportunity to sponsor a seat for $150, a revenue generator to help the theatre manage the shutdown. The seats sold out so quickly that the venue offered sponsorship plaques for the popcorn machines, projectors, and other fixtures. They reopened at limited capacity in June 2020 with a kind of on-the-nose showing of *Return of the Living Dead*.

IS OTTAWA ALIVE?

Before the city opens its eyes and stretches to face a new Ottawa day, it considers a final existential woe: what happens when we don't wake? A sociological approach toward death allows us to ask questions about the rise of multinational funeral companies (the profits on our future deaths are part of others' prospective stock portfolios), the efficacy of alternatives like those offered by the Funeral Co-operative of Ottawa, and the necessity and work of the city's overtaxed shelters to provide palliative health care. Sociologists also, extending the logic of the social determinants of health (that access to health is impacted by class, gender, race, sexuality), analyze the social determinants of access to a "good death": a peaceful, secure, old-age death. Sociologists pay attention to the differential ways in which lives lost are mourned, something I have done in my research on Ottawa monuments — some deaths are meant to have given birth to the nation (soldiers mourned at the National War Memorial), while other deaths (the unsolved, everyday murders of women largely by their male partners, the unsolved murders of Indigenous women) are not treated with such profound solemnity (Davidson 2024). A thanatological study of Ottawa might begin at one of the sixteen cemeteries in Ottawa. The oldest existing cemeteries are the Catholic Notre-Dame Cemetery of Ottawa (established in 1872) — the eternal home of Wilfrid Laurier, Élisabeth Bruyère, and Yousuf Karsh — and the Beechwood Cemetery, an Anglo-Protestant cemetery established in 1873 that is the resting place of Robert Borden, J.R. Booth, Sandford Fleming, and Tommy Douglas, along with the cemeteries of the national military and RCMP. An Ottawologist of death might turn their attention to the collections of the Bytown Museum, which include memorial hair wreaths from the 1860s, Victorian mourning clothes, and memorial ribbons, buttons, and stationary.

Death is situated at the crux of the very personal, intimate, and private, and the social and collective — it is a phenomenon that brings us back to the root of sociological inquiry — to see the relationship between private troubles and public issues. Every death is the extinguishment of someone so unique, and yet death is the most ultimate of unavoidable, universal experiences. This shared reality was most evident in 2017, when LRT construction crews struck the remains of seventy-nine Bytowners (Schnurr 2017).

The presence of these Bytown burial sites was for many not a surprise. The first settler civilian cemetery in the city, built in the 1820s, was bordered by what are now Wellington and Metcalfe Streets to the north and south, and Elgin and Queen Streets to the east and west. Many of these early Bytowners were relocated to Beechwood Cemetery as the city grew. One of the concerns was that, in the era of natural burial, an urban cemetery posed problems — mainly smell. Cemeteries both contained *and* inspired anxieties about mysterious contagious diseases. Through analyzing one of the skeletons, Museum of

History archeologist Janet Young determined that one of the people, a man, had died in his late thirties, had survived a bout of tuberculosis, and had a fish-rich diet, all indicators that he was solidly middle class. Yet he was buried in the company of working-class people. An analysis of a white, slimy substance in the coffin led to the identification of lime — and the conclusion that this man had died of cholera. The unknown origin of cholera inspired new burial practices; victims had to be buried within three hours of their death, in coffins filled with lime, buried four feet underground, with a burial procession taking place on the river (Young 2023a). Here, the lime residue is evidence of a private trouble — an individual death — experienced collectively as a threat to public health.

These findings confirm other demographers' understandings of mortality and life expectancy in the early nineteenth century. Young's further work tells of a woman who died in her twenties who had bad teeth, worn-out joints, and was malnourished. Young determined that due to wear on her teeth (indication that they were used as a "third hand" in the work of hat-making) and ACL injuries (potentially indicating she constantly held a head form between knees), this woman was likely a milliner — a hat maker. One of the most telling indicators was this skeleton's preserved brain and hair tissue. Milliners used mercury to toughen animal fibres when making hats. With constant exposure, mercury can preserve tissues after death — and cause neurological issues in life, driving some hatters (perhaps this Bytowner) mad (Young 2023b).

Burial returns our attention to our collective human relationship with the rest of the natural world, symbolically, spiritually, and materially. In her study of coffins, Young determined that these caskets were made of bark — some of the abundant waste wood produced in the lumber city. Trees offered material for the final resting places of these settlers and for many today. In the 1830s, it was not the emerald ash borer that bothered trees, but the pine sawyer beetle. They chewed up trees at night so loudly they were nicknamed the "Ottawa cow" beetle. The Ottawa cow lays its eggs under bark, and the emerging larvae leave tracks in trees but also, Young found, in the bones of the deceased (Young 2023c). We are reminded here that throughout our lives we have multidirectional relationships with the natural world. But is death and burial the end of the story for *Ottawology*?

William Lyon Mackenzie King clearly did not imagine death to be the end. In the house he inherited from Laurier, now known as the Parks Canada historic site Laurier House, Mackenzie King gathered with friends, including Dominion archivist Arthur Doughty, to conjure the departed through table rapping (McMullin 2000). Mackenzie King did not conjure spirits to guide him in making political decisions but rather for comfort; biographer Blair Neatby wrote that Mackenzie King "found the reassurance he needed in the almost daily signs of the presence of loving spirits" (McMullin 2000, 219). Mackenzie King's spiritualism operated within a broader culture in which the occult was popular. This was also the period of electrification and embracing scientific and technological advancements. The ghost conjuring of the early twentieth century worked with science. Maurice Ackroyd, son of famed spiritualist Samuel Augustus Ackroyd and grandfather of Dan Ackroyd, the writer and actor in the 1984 movie *Ghostbusters*, worked as an engineer for Bell and made serious inquiries about "the possibility of constructing a high-vibration crystal radio as a mechanical method for contacting the spiritual world" (Ackroyd 2009, x). At Laurier House, visitors can view one of Mackenzie King's many crystal balls (Gzovski 2024) as well as the house's elevator, sophisticated technology for its day. Communicating with the afterlife was not incompatible with the rational, scientific world, but rather just the next frontier — rationality and enchantment together.

We conclude this long Ottawa night back where we began, at the Museum of Nature. It's well-known that the Museum of Nature is haunted. Local lore posits that it is perhaps the museum's architect, David Ewart, or even Wilfrid Laurier — whose body laid in state in the building during his wake — that are unsettling museum staff, making the figure of a man appear in mirrors and move through people's bodies. Ghosthunters have identified many sites in the city as haunted: the Château Laurier, the Bytown Museum, Grant House (current home of Beckta restaurant), the Colonel By memorial fountain in Confederation Park, the Heritage building (formerly Normal School) on Elgin Street, Lisgar Collegiate, the old jail/Ottawa youth hostel, and many abandoned houses and barns in rural Ottawa. Usually, hauntings inspire an unsettled feeling, some apparitions in mirrors, and flickering lights, and at the Bytown Museum the ghost of Colonel By has been accused of playing with the computer (Leslie 2016). I wouldn't argue that Ottawa is exceptionally haunted, although with the neo-Gothic buildings and bridges, an atmospherically lit canal, and many barns in ruin, there are material conditions in place that ghosts seem to enjoy.

DAWN

Ottawa, like all cities, is a palimpsest of human and non-human uses and histories. Fast food chains paper over the memories of theatres, suburban malls bury the farms of half a century ago, hospitals are built where century-old trees once stood, wetlands threaten to haunt suburban homes from below as spring flooding. Layers upon layers. It's inevitable that remains will haunt us, and it's also fine and fair that we cannot, even with all of our disciplinary tools — of sociology, thanatology, demography, archeology — understand everything that goes on, and has gone on, in the Ottawa night.

The sun is rising over Ottawa. The cooks at the all-night Elgin Street Diner are preparing for their morning shifts; the bakers at Kettlemans are furiously rolling out batches of bagel dough to satisfy the breakfast rush, ER nurses, security guards, and other shift workers are going home, the racoons are scampering off to go to sleep. This hopeful time of day is embodied in a sculpture by Anishinaabe artist Rebecca Belmore titled *Dawn*, commissioned for and on permanent display in the NAC. The sculpture features a ten-metre-high tree fabricated from various woods, smoothed to appear sun-bleached, leaning against the wall. The tree is topped with the head of an eagle, and large copper cones, reminiscent of the jingles of a jingle dress, offer a large tail. Belmore named the sculpture for "a beautiful time of day, full of hope after rest and dreams, a better day ahead of us" (Belmore quoted in Martin 2022). The promise for a more joyful, inclusive, sustainable Ottawa begins at dawn.

REFERENCES

Abdulle, Mohamoud. 2000. *Somali Immigrants in Ottawa: The Causes of Their Migration and the Challenges of Resettling in Canada*. Ottawa: University of Ottawa.

Ackroyd, Dan. 2009. "Foreword." In *A History of Ghosts: The True Story of Seances, Mediums, Ghosts, and Ghostbusters*. New York: Rodale.

Addie, Jean-Paul D., Robert S. Fielder, and Roger Keil. 2015. "Cities on the Edge: Emerging Suburban Constellations in Canada." In *Canadian Cities in Transition: Perspectives for an Urban Age, 5th ed.*, edited by Pierre Filion, Marcus Moos, and Tara Vinodrai. Don Mills: Oxford University Press.

Al-Dubikhi, Sami, and Paul Mees. 2010. "Bus Rapid Transit in Ottawa, 1978 to 2008: Assessing the Results." *Town Planning Review* 81 (4): 407–24.

Alhmidi, Maan. 2025. "Number of Homeless People in Ottawa Has Grown to 3,000, Local Charity Says." *Global News*, April 9. <globalnews.ca/news/11123296/ont-ottawa-homeless/>.

Alkon, Alison Hope, and Christie Grace McCullen. 2011. "Whiteness and Farmers Markets: Performances, Perpetuations … Contestations?" *Antipode* 43 (4): 937–59.

Allston, Dave. 2015a. "Making Way for the Highway: How the Queensway Came to Kitchissippi." *Kitchissippi Times*, June 11. <kitchissippi.com/2015/06/11/ottawa-history-queensway-416/>.

——. 2015b. "Did You Know That Ottawa's First Mall Was Built in Kitchissippi?" *Kitchissippi Times*, May 20. <kitchissippi.com/2015/05/20/westgate-shopping-centre/>.

——. 2016. "The Kitchissippi Museum: West Ottawa's Early Holland Avenue Streetcar Resort: West End Park." *The Kitchissippi Museum* (blog), August 3. <kitchissippimuseum.blogspot.com/2016/08/west-ottawas-early-holland-avenue.html>.

Alta Vista Community Association. 2024. "History of Alta Vista – Avca." <avca.ca/history-of-alta-vista/>.

Anand, Avanthika. 2023. "Police Board OKs $15.2M Budget Increase, New Public Feedback Rule." CBC News, February 28. <cbc.ca/news/canada/ottawa/ottawa-police-2023-budget-increase-public-rule-1.6762432>.

Anderson, Peter Grant. 2016. "Comparing Nineteenth and Twenty-First Century Ecological Imaginaries at Ottawa's Central Experimental Farm." *Canadian Journal of Urban Research* 25 (1): 38–49.

Andrew, Caroline, and Angela Franovic. 2020. "Reaching Suburbia: Towards a Socially Just Transit System for Ottawa." In *The Life of North American Suburbs*, edited by Jan Nijman. Toronto: University of Toronto Press.

Andrews, Mark E. 1998. *For King and Country: Lieutenant Colonel John By, R.E., Indefatigable Civil-Military Engineer*. Merrickville: Heritage Merrickville Foundation.

Anka, Paul. 2013. *My Way: An Autobiography*. New York: St. Martin's Publishing Group.

Aptekar, Sofya. 2019. "The Public Library as Resistive Space in the Neoliberal City." *City & Community* 18 (4): 1203–19. <doi.org/10.1111/cico.12417>.

Augé, Marc. 1995. *Non-Places: Introduction to an Anthropology of Supermodernity*. London: Verso.

Backhouse, Constance. 1991. *Petticoats and Prejudice: Women and Law in Nineteenth Century Canada*. Toronto: Women's Press.
Bagnall, James. 2016. "Bagnall: The Trouble with Job Numbers in Tech." *Ottawa Citizen*, March 29. <ottawacitizen.com/business/local-business/bagnall-the-trouble-with-job-numbers-in-tech>.
———. 2020. "Inside the Slow-Rolling Disaster of Ottawa's $9-Billion LRT Project." *Ottawa Citizen*, March 4. <ottawacitizen.com/news/local-news/blood-on-the-tracks-why-ottawas-flagship-project-crashed>.
Bain, Alison. 2015. "Re-Imaging, Re-Elevating, and Re-Placing the Urban: The Cultural Transformation of Canadian Inner Cities." In *Canadian Cities in Transition: Perspectives for an Urban Age, 5th ed.*, edited by Pierre Filion, Marcus Moos, Tara Vinodrai, and Ryan Walker. Don Mills: Oxford University Press.
Ballingall, Alex. 2017. "Teepee Erected on Parliament Hill Highlights Pain of Canada 150, Activists Say." *Toronto Star*, June 29. <thestar.com/news/canada/teepee-erected-on-parliament-hill-highlights-pain-of-canada-150-activists-say/article_10bd4e3c-5940-58cc-ab68-533074a4b58f.html>.
Beaujot, Roderic. 2003. "Projecting the Future of Canada's Population: Assumptions, Implications, and Policy." *Canadian Studies in Population* 30 (1): 1–28.
Belisle, Donica. 2007. "Negotiating Paternalism: Women and Canada's Largest Department Stores, 1890–1960." *Journal of Women's History* 19 (1): 58–81.
Bellamy, Rhoda. 2001. "The Architecture of Government." In *Ottawa*, edited by Jeff Keshen and Nicole St-Onge. Ottawa: University of Ottawa Press.
Belliveau, Richard, Carolyn Quinn, and Susan Ross, eds. 2017. *From Walk-Up to High-Rise: Ottawa's Historic Apartment Buildings*. Ottawa: Heritage Ottawa.
Benslimane, Souheil, Justin Piché, Sarah Speight, Lydia Dobson, and Aaron Doyle. 2019. "Will You Accept the Charges?: The Case for the Government of Ontario to Move Away from the Prohibitive, Predatory, and Outdated Telephone System in Its Provincial Jails and Towards Accessible, Free Calling That Promotes Connections Essential to Community Well-Being and Safety." Criminalization and Punishment Education Project (CPEP). <cp-ep.org/wp-content/uploads/2019/10/jailhotline-oct2019reportfrontpage.png>.
Bickis, Heidi. 2020. "A Long Weekend of Rest and Labour: Thanksgiving, Holiday Body Work, and the Holiday Body." In *Seasonal Sociology*, edited by Tonya K. Davidson and Ondine Park. Toronto: University of Toronto Press.
Bider, Emma Ruth. 2024. "Imagining Tree Futures of Ottawa: Climate Change, Activism and Politics in the Urban Forest." PhD thesis, Carleton University.
Biglieri, Samantha, Maxwell Hartt, and Natalie St. Channer. 2021. "Aging in Urban Canada." In *Aging People, Aging Places: Experiences, Opportunities and Challenges of Growing Older in Canada*, edited by Maxwell Hartt, Samantha Biglieri, Mark Rosenberg, and Sarah Nelson. Bristol: Bristol University Press.
Blank, Joshua C. 2016. *Creating Kashubia: History, Memory, and Identity in Canada's First Polish Community, 1st ed.* McGill-Queen's Studies in Ethnic History, Series Two 38. Montreal: McGill-Queen's University Press.
Boswell, Randy. 2016. "River of Sawdust: A Polluted Ottawa River Offended Even Oscar Wilde in the 19th Century." *Ottawa Citizen*, August 21. <ottawacitizen.com/news/local-news/river-of-sawdust-a-polluted-ottawa-river-offended-even-oscar-wilde-in-the-19th-century>.
Bothwell, Robert. 2011. "Lester B. Pearson." *Canadian Encyclopedia*, July 6. <thecanadianencyclopedia.ca/en/article/lester-bowles-pearson>.

Bowden, Olivia. 2017. "The Capital Builders: How 'Pops' and Estelle Brown Started a Dry Cleaner and Supported a New Community." *Ottawa Citizen*, February 19. <ottawacitizen.com/opinion/columnists/the-capital-builders-how-pops-and-estelle-brown-supported-a-new-community>.

Bowler, Diana E., Lisette Buyung-Ali, Teri M. Knight, and Andrew S. Pullin. 2010. "Urban Greening to Cool Towns and Cities: A Systematic Review of the Empirical Evidence." *Landscape and Urban Planning* 97 (3): 147–55. <doi.org/10.1016/j.landurbplan.2010.05.006>.

Breton, Ryamond. 1998. "Ethnicity and Race in Social Organization: Recent Developments in Canadian Society." In *The Vertical Mosaic Revisited*. University of Toronto Press.

Breton, Yves, and Lucie Lecomte. 2007. *Vanier-on-the-Ottawa: Today for Tomorrow*. Ottawa: Muséoparc Vanier Museopark.

Britannica. 2025. "Oblates of Mary Immaculate: Missionary, Charismatic, Congregation." March 26. <britannica.com/topic/Oblates-of-Mary-Immaculate>.

Bruckert, Chris, and Frédérique Chabot. 2014. *Challenges: Ottawa Area Sex Workers Speak Out*. Ottawa: POWER – Prostitutes of Ottawa-Gatineau Work Educate and Resist.

Bruckert, Chris, and Stacey Hannem. 2013. "To Serve and Protect? Structural Stigma, Social Profiling, and The Abuse of Police Power in Ottawa." In *Selling Sex : Experience, Advocacy, and Research on Sex Work in Canada*, edited by Emily van der Meulen, Elya M. Durisin, and Victoria Love. Sexuality Studies Series. Vancouver: UBC Press.

Buckley, Brian. 2008. *Gift of Freedom: How Ottawa Welcomed the Vietnamese, Cambodian, and Laotian Refugees*. Renfrew: General Store Publishing House.

Buffam, Bonar. 2020. "Rites of Spring: Multiculturalism and the Celebration of Vaisakhi in Vancouver." In *Seasonal Sociology*, edited by Tonya K. Davidson and Ondine Park. Toronto: University of Toronto Press.

Bulmer, Ben. 2017. "150 Years of History in the Hills." Gatineau Valley Historical Society, June 28. <gvhs.ca/>.

Bulthuis, Mike. 2011. "Underpass Memories Should Not Be Extinguished." *Spacing Ottawa* (blog). August 2, 2011. https://spacing.ca/ottawa/2011/08/02/underpass-memories-should-not-be-extinguished/.

Bunch, Adam. 2013. "Toronto's First Truly Terrible Leader — the Slave-Owning Gambling Addict Peter Russell." *Spacing Toronto* (blog), May 28. <spacing.ca/toronto/2013/05/28/torontos-first-truly-terrible-leader-the-slave-owning-gambling-addict-peter-russell/>.

Burton, Jim. 2022. "Sketches of My Overbrook." *Connexions*, Summer 2022.

Butler, Colin. 2021. "Ontario Loses 175 Acres of Farmland to Urban Development a Day, Says Farmers Group." CBC News, May 31. <cbc.ca/news/canada/london/urban-development-disappearing-farmland-ontario-1.6044620>.

Cairns, James. 2017. *The Myth of the Age of Entitlement: Millennials, Austerity, and Hope*, 1st ed. Toronto: University of Toronto Press.

Canada (Attorney General) v. Bedford. 2013. SCC 72, [2013] 3 S.C.R. 1101. <decisions.scc-csc.ca/scc-csc/scc-csc/en/item/13389/index.do>.

Canada, Bureau of Management Consulting. 1977. *The Ottawa Bus-Pass System: An Examination of Effects, Advanced Copy Prepared for the Urban Transportation Research Branch*. Montreal: Transport Canada, Urban Transportation Research Branch.

Canada, Women and Gender Equality. 2024. "Facts, Stats and WAGE's Impact: Gender-Based Violence." October 25. <canada.ca/en/women-gender-equality/gender-based-violence/facts-stats.html>.

Canadiana. 2019. *The Assassination of D'Arcy McGee*. <youtube.com/watch?v=ueTqBHfngPY>.

Capillé, Cauê. 2018. "Political Interiors: The Case of Public Libraries." *Space and Culture* 21 (4): 408–23. <doi.org/10.1177/1206331217739825>.
CapitalGems.ca. 2013. "Pink Lake Mica Mine." <capitalgems.ca/pink-lake-mica-mine.html>.
Cartwright, D.G. 1977. "Institutions on the Frontier: French-Canadian Settlement in Eastern Ontario in the Nineteenth Century." *Canadian Geographer* 21 (1): 1–21. <doi.org/10.1111/j.1541-0064.1977.tb00983.x>.
Catling, P.M., and B. Kostiuk. 2010. "Successful Re-establishment of a Native Savannah Flora and Fauna on the Site of a Former Pine Plantation at Constance Bay, Ottawa, Ontario." *Canadian Field-Naturalist* 124 (2): 169–78. <doi.org/10.22621/cfn.v124i2.1056>.
Cave, Diana. 2022. "Safety in Cameras? An Exploratory Study of the Ottawa Public Surveillance (CCTV) Project." Ottawa: Carleton University.
CBC News. 2015. "Study Debunks Benefits of Mike Harris-Era Amalgamation in Ontario." May 26. <cbc.ca/news/canada/toronto/study-debunks-benefits-of-mike-harris-era-amalgamation-in-ontario-1.3087959>.
____. 2016. "Nearly Half of Ottawa's Public Washrooms Closed, Study Finds." May 5. <cbc.ca/news/canada/ottawa/public-washroom-study-ottawa-1.3567159>.
____. 2018a. "Amazon Announces New Warehouse in Ottawa's East End." July 10. <cbc.ca/news/canada/ottawa/amazon-warehouse-official-announcement-orleans-1.4740392>.
____. 2018b. "Architects behind NAC Revamp to Design New Library." November 15. <cbc.ca/news/canada/ottawa/ottawa-central-library-design-chosen-1.4906898>.
____. 2018c. "Sandy Hill Residents Make Rooming Houses a Municipal Election Issue." September 3. <cbc.ca/news/canada/ottawa/sandy-hill-residents-frustrated-with-rooming-houses-1.4808630>.
____. 2018d. "Should Ottawa Adopt Sweden's Gender-Balanced Snow-Clearing Policies?" January 24. <cbc.ca/news/canada/ottawa/sweden-snow-clearing-gender-ottawa-1.4500636>.
____. 2019. "Ottawa's Rooming Houses Dwindling, Report Finds." August 22. <cbc.ca/news/canada/ottawa/rooming-house-decline-ottawa-1.5254825>.
____. 2022. "Canada Failing Black, Indigenous Prisoners as Overrepresentation Persists: Report." November 1. <cbc.ca/news/politics/canada-black-indigenous-prisoners-overrepresentation-1.6636962>.
____. 2023a. "Indigenous Group, Church Aim to Create 'Little Village' of Affordable Housing." June 12. <cbc.ca/news/canada/ottawa/affordable-housing-indigenous-people-ottawa-1.6872537>.
____. 2023b. "Ottawa Police Report Sharp Drop in No-Knock Raids." August 8. <cbc.ca/news/canada/ottawa/dynamic-entries-ottawa-police-service-use-of-force-1.6929673>.
CBC/Radio-Canada. 2021a. "Exposed: Sexism Within Ottawa Police." *The Fifth Estate*. <tvmaze.com/episodes/2034995/the-fifth-estate-46x07-exposed-sexism-within-ottawa-police-fatal-care>.
____. 2021b. "When Police Don't Knock. " *The Fifth Estate*. <curio.ca/en/catalog/b954b206-0161-43f8-bb1d-a116e76e4b0c>.
Centre de recherche en civilisation canadienne-française. 2017a. "Bytown and its First French Canadians." *Vie française dans la capitale*, February 11. <viefrancaisecapitale.ca/espace/bytown_and_its_first_french_canadians-eng>.
____. 2017b. "Lowertown's Golden Age." *Vie française dans la capitale*, June 30. <viefrancaisecapitale.ca/espace/lowertowns_golden_age-eng>.

Chianello, Joanne. 2017. "Councillor Wields New Power to Put 'Bunkhouse' Developers on the Spot." CBC News, July 6. <cbc.ca/news/canada/ottawa/sandy-hill-development-ottawa-1.4190966>.

Chong, Denise. 2012. "Sue Wong." *Lives of the Family* (blog), April 26. <livesofthefamilies.wordpress.com/sue-wong/>.

Church, Kelly. 2016. "Sustaining Black Ash Traditions." *First American Art Magazine* (blog), May 18. <firstamericanartmagazine.com/black-ash/>.

Circle of All Nations. n.d. "William Commanda." <circleofallnations.ca/new/william-commanda/>.

City of Ottawa, Community and Social. 2024. "Indigenous Relations." City of Ottawa. October 7. ottawa.ca/en/city-hall/creating-equal-inclusive-and-diverse-city/indigenous-relations>.

City of Ottawa, Strategic Initiatives. 2024. "Diverse Economy." July 17. <ottawa.ca/en/business/why-bring-your-business-ottawa/diverse-economy>.

City of Toronto. 2021. "Canopy TO." <toronto.ca/legdocs/mmis/2021/ie/bgrd/backgroundfile-173552.pdf>.

Clark, Scott. 2019. "Overrepresentation of Indigenous People in the Canadian Criminal Justice System: Causes and Responses." Ottawa: Department of Justice Canada. <justice.gc.ca/eng/rp-pr/jr/oip-cjs/oip-cjs-en.pdf>.

Clavette, Ken. 2001. "The 'Rag Tag and Bobtail': The Rise and Fall of Ottawa's Early Working Class, 1860–1880." In *Ottawa: Making a Capital*, edited by Jeff Keshen and Nicole St-Onge. Ottawa: University of Ottawa Press.

Clement, Wallace. 1975. *The Canadian Corporate Elite: An Analysis of Economic Power*. Toronto: McClelland and Stewart.

Clifford, Jim, and Stéphane Castonguay. 2022. "British Ghost Acres and Environmental Changes in the Laurentian Forest during the Nineteenth Century." *Journal of Historical Geography* 78 (October): 126–38. <doi.org/10.1016/j.jhg.2022.05.002>.

Cole, Desmond. 2022. *The Skin We're in: A Year of Black Resistance and Power*, 1st ed. Toronto: Anchor Canada.

Cole-Harris, Bertha. 1892. *Lights and Shades of Mission Work, or, Leaves from a Worker's Note Book: Being Reminiscences of Seven Years Service at the Capital, 1885–1892*. Ottawa: Free Press.

Cook, Bryan. 2023. *Ahearn and Soper — The Electrification of Ottawa*. Ottawa: Historical Society of Ottawa.

Cook, Maria. 2012. "On the Eve of Demolition, the History of Ogilvy's Shines." Ottawa Citizen, December 15. <ottawacitizen.com/news/ottawa%20&%20area/on-the-eve-of-demolition-the-history-of-ogilvys-shines>.

CPEP Group. 2015. *Life Inside Ottawa's Jail*. <youtube.com/watch?v=KSyBuSsejNU>.

———. 2016a. *End Food Privatization at Ottawa's Jail*. <youtube.com/watch?v=kE1bS51JOBM>.

———. 2016b. *Strategies to Reduce Crowding at the Ottawa-Carleton Detention Centre*. <youtube.com/watch?v=XTGV6QUyY8Q>.

Craske, Peter. 1992. *Law and Order in the Early Days of Bytown/Ottawa*. Bytown Pamphlet Series 41. Ottawa: Historical Society of Ottawa.

Crawford, Blair. 2023. "Para Transpo Riders Frustrated by What's Offered to Them Compared to New on-Demand Bus Service." *Ottawa Citizen*, September 14. <ottawacitizen.com/news/local-news/para-transpo-riders-frustrated-by-whats-offered-to-them-compared-to-new-on-demand-bus-service>.

Crosby, Andrew. 2020. "Financialized Gentrification, Demoviction, and Landlord Tactics to

Demobilize Tenant Organizing." *Geoforum* 108: 184–93. <doi.org/10.1016/ j.geoforum.2019.09.011>.
Crosby, Andrew C., and Jeffrey Monaghan. 2018. *Policing Indigenous Movements: Dissent and the Security State*. Winnipeg: Fernwood Publishing.
Cruikshank, Ainslie. 2017. "More Women Commute by Public Transit than Men, Census Data Shows." Toronto Star, November 29. <thestar.com/news/gta/more-women-commute-by-public-transit-than-men-census-data-shows/article_eb65e23e-3731-5a2c-a0d9-c3e1d88f9738.html>.
Curtis, Bruce. 2019. *The Politics of Population: State Formation, Statistics, and the Census of Canada, 1840–1875*. Toronto: University of Toronto Press.
Dance, Anne. 2014. "Negotiating Public Space on Canada's Parliament Hill: Security, Protests, Parliamentary Privilege, and Public Access." *Journal of Canadian Studies* 48 (2): 169–97.
Davidson, Tonya. 2024. *Tours Inside the Snow Globe: Monuments and National Belonging in Ottawa*. Waterloo: Wilfrid Laurier University Press.
Davis, Angela Y. 2003. *Are Prisons Obsolete?* New York: Seven Stories Press.
Davis, Donald. 1999. "A Capital Crime? The Long Death of Ottawa's Electric Railway." In *Ottawa: Making a Capital*, edited by Jeff Keshen and Nicole St-Onge. Ottawa: Ottawa University Press.
Davis, Kingsley, and Wilbert E. Moore. 1945. "Some Principles of Stratification." *American Sociological Review* 10 (2): 242–49. <doi.org/10.2307/2085643>.
Deachman, Bruce. 2017. "Capital Voices: 'It Was Hard for Us to Lie to Our Mother.'" *Ottawa Citizen*, June 7. <ottawacitizen.com/news/local-news/capital-voices-it-was-hard-for-us-to-lie-to-our-mother>.
——. 2019. "Moe Boushey: 1937–2018: 'He Always Said, "I'll Take Care of You, " and He Always Did.'" *Ottawa Citizen*, February 16. <ottawacitizen.com/news/local-news/moe-boushey-1937-2018-he-always-said-ill-take-care-of-you-and-he-always-did>.
——. 2022. *Front Page Ottawa: Stories from the Ottawa Citizen 1865 to Present*. Ottawa: Ottawa Press and Publishing.
Dean, Joanna. 2005. "'Said Tree Is a Veritable Nuisance': Ottawa's Street Trees 1869–1939." *Urban History Review* 34 (1): 46–57. <doi.org/10.7202/1016046ar>.
de Bruin, Tabitha, and Andrew McIntosh. 2006. "Persons Case." *Canadian Encyclopedia*, February 7. <thecanadianencyclopedia.ca/en/article/persons-case>.
Dej, Erin. 2020. *A Complex Exile: Homelessness and Social Exclusion in Canada*. Vancouver: UBC Press.
Delamont. 2019. "How the Fight for This Immigrant Neighbourhood Became a Fight for All Immigrant Neighbourhoods." *TVO Today*, August 29. <tvo.org/article/how-the-fight-for-this-immigrant-neighbourhood-became-a-fight-for-all-immigrant-neighbourhoods>.
Delaney, Jill. 1991. "The Garden Suburb of Lindenlea, Ottawa: A Model Project for the First Federal Housing Policy, 1918–24." *Urban History Review* 19 (3): 151–65.
Dib, Kamal. 2022. *Beyond Bytown: The History of the Lebanese Community in Ottawa*. Musée Bytown Museum. <youtube.com/watch?v=1k-lpC6lZ6c>.
Dick, Melissa, Trevor J. Porter, Michael F.J. Pisaric, Eve Wertheimer, Peter deMontigny, Joelle T. Perreault, and Kerry-Lynn Robillard. 2014. "A Multi-Century Eastern White Pine Tree-Ring Chronology Developed from Salvaged River Logs and Its Utility for Dating Heritage Structures in Canada's National Capital Region." *Dendrochronologia* 32 (2): 120–26.
Dickson, Courtney. 2017. "Is Ottawa's Proposed Mega-Shelter the Right Way to Tackle Homelessness?" *THIS*, November 30. <this.org/2017/11/30/is-ottawas-proposed-mega-shelter-the-right-way-to-tackle-homelessness/>.

Dorries, Heather, Robert Henry, David Hugill, Tyler McCreary, and Julie Tomiak. 2019. *Settler City Limits : Indigenous Resurgence and Colonial Violence in the Urban Prairie West.* Winnipeg: University of Manitoba Press.

Doyle, Aaron, Justin Piché, and Kelsey Sutton. 2022. "The Struggle over the Ottawa-Carleton Detention Centre: Challenging Neutralization Techniques, Fighting State Inertia." In *Contesting Carceral Logic*, edited by Michael J. Coyle and Mechthild Nagel. London: Routledge.

Duhamel, Roger. 1961. *City on the Ottawa.* Ottawa: Queen's Printer and Controller of Stationary.

Durkheim, Émile. 2001. *The Elementary Forms of Religious Life.* Oxford: Oxford University Press.

Eade, Ron. 1997. "Victoria Island to Become Native Cultural Centre: Elders Plan to Transform Run-Down Property into Spiritual Haven." *The Ottawa Citizen*, August 17, 1997.

Edmond, Martha. 1993. *Rockcliffe Park: A History of the Village.* Ottawa: The Friends of the Village of Rockcliffe Park.

Egan, Elisabeth, and Erica Ackerberg. 2023. "A Love Letter to Libraries, Long Overdue." *New York Times*, February 14. <nytimes.com/2023/02/14/books/review/library-public-local.html>.

Egan, Kelly. 2020. "Social Justice Activist's Wit a 'Superpower': Life in Public Housing Inspired the Stories in Dorothy O'Connell's Book *Chiclet Gomez*." *Ottawa Citizen*, June 9.

El-Geneidy, Ahmed, Zachary Patterson, and Evelyne St-Louis. 2015. "Transport and Land-Use Interactions in Cities: Getting Closer to Opportunities." In *Canadian Cities in Transition: Perspectives for an Urban Age, 5th ed.*, edited by Pierre Filion, Marcus Moos, Tara Vinodrai, and Ryan Walker. Don Mills: Oxford University Press.

Elliott, Bruce S. 1991. *The City Beyond: A History of Nepean, Birthplace of Canada's Capital, 1792–1990.* Nepean: City of Nepean.

———. 2004. *Irish Migrants in the Canadas: A New Approach.* Montreal: McGill-Queen's University Press.

Evelyn, Charelle. 2020. "'It's a Lot of Lip Service': Black Federal Public Servants Hope 'Floyd Effect' Will Finally Drive Change as Anti-Racism Movement Grips Canada." *The Hill Times*, June 15. <hilltimes.com/story/2020/06/15/its-a-lot-of-lip-service-black-public-servants-in-the-hunt-for-data-change-as-anti-racism-movement-grips-canada/228498/>.

Fagan, Laurie. 2017. "Federal Public Service Ranks in Capital Grow to Highest Level in 7 Years." CBC News, January 10. <cbc.ca/news/canada/ottawa/federal-public-servants-in-ottawa-on-rise-1.3927997>.

Fleming, Tyler. 2022. "Amazon's New Fulfillment Centre Is Ottawa's Largest Building." *CTV News Ottawa*, October 20. <ottawa.ctvnews.ca/amazon-s-new-fulfillment-centre-is-ottawa-s-largest-building-1.6118540>.

Foster, Cecil. 2019. *They Call Me George: The Untold Story of The Black Train Porters.* Windsor: Biblioasis.

Frizzell, Sara. 2022. "Township of Russell, Ont., Now Named after 'all Russells,' Not Slave Owner." CBC News, May 20. <cbc.ca/news/canada/ottawa/russell-township-ontario-name-change-rededication-1.6459830>.

Gaffield, Chad. 1997. *History of the Outouais.* Laval: Les Presses de L'Universite Laval.

Gardner, Carol. 1995. *Gardner: Passing By: Gender and Public Harassment.* University of California Press.

Garreau, Joel. 1991. *Edge City: Life on the New Frontier, 1st ed.* New York ; Doubleday.

Garrett, Mary. 1990. "Poet Laureate of the Poor: Dorothy O'Connell." *Canadian Woman Studies* 11 (2): 36–37.

Geisterfer, Michael. 1999. "Rag War Rages between US Empire and Tiny Charity Fortune in Used Goods; St. Vincent de Paul's Coffers Drop since Value Village Came on the Scene": *National Post*, April 3.

Gelbard, Sarah. 2015. "UrbSanity: Brutal Heritage." *Spacing Ottawa* (blog), January 16. <spacing.ca/ottawa/2015/01/16/auto-draft/>.

———. 2023. "Radical Solidarities in Punk and Queer Refusals of Safety and Inclusion Narratives in Planning." *Urban Planning* 8 (2): 177–86.

Gentile, Patricia. 2000. "Government Girls and 'Ottawa Men': Cold War Management of Gender Relations in the Civil Service." In *Whose National Security? Canadian State Surveillance and the Creation of Enemies*, edited by Gary Kinsman, Dieter Buse, and Mercedes Steedman. Toronto: Between the Lines Press.

———. 2010. "Capital Queers: Social Memory and Queer Place(s) in Cold War Ottawa." In *Placing Memory and Remembering Place in Canada*, edited by Opp James and Walsh John. Vancouver: University of British Columbia Press.

Gerster, Jane. 2021. "The Dark Side of the RCMP." *The Walrus*, October 20. <thewalrus.ca/can-the-rcmp-be-saved/>.

Giddens, Anthony. 1984. *The Constitution of Society: Outline of the Theory of Structuration.* Cambridge: Polity Press.

Gillis, Megan. 2017. "Capital Facts: Ottawa Was Almost the Crabapple Capital." *Ottawa Citizen*, March 3. <ottawacitizen.com/news/local-news/capital-facts-ottawa-was-almost-the-crabapple-capital>.

Gillis, Peter R. 1986. "Rivers of Sawdust: The Battle over Industrial Pollution in Canada, 1865–1903." *Journal of Canadian Studies* 211: 84–103.

Gismondi, Melissa. 2024. "The Untold Story of the Hudson's Bay Company." *Canadian Geographic*, June 21. <canadiangeographic.ca/articles/the-untold-story-of-the-hudsons-bay-company/>.

Glowacki, Laura. 2023. "Ottawa Aims to Close Cycling 'Missing Links' in New Transportation Plan." CBC News, April 18. <cbc.ca/news/canada/ottawa/ottawa-cycling-travel-drive-walk-transportation-plan-2046-1.6813592>.

Goffman, Erving. 1972. *Relations in Public: Microstudies of the Public Order, 1st Harper Colophon ed.* New York: Harper & Row.

Gordon, David L.A. 2015. *Town and Crown: An Illustrated History of Canada's Capital.* Ottawa: Invenire.

———. 2002a. "Ottawa-Hull and Canberra: Implementation of Capital City Plans." *Canadian Journal of Urban Research* 11 (2): 179–212.

———. 2002b. "William Lyon Mackenzie King, Planning Advocate." *Planning Perspectives* 17 (2): 97–122.

Gournay, Isabelle, and France Vanlaethem. 2000. "The Supreme Court of Canada Building." In *The Supreme Court of Canada and Its Justices, 1875–2000*. Ottawa: Dundurn Press.

Government of Canada. 2005. "Consumer Trends Report — Chapter 2: Consumers and Changing Retail Markets." Statistical Reports: Innovation, Science and Economic Development Canada, July 20. <ised-isde.canada.ca/site/office-consumer-affairs/en/consumer-trends-report-chapter-2-consumers-and-changing-retail-markets>.

Government of Canada. 2017. "The Supreme Court of Canada." <publications.gc.ca/collections/collection_2017/csc-scc/JU5-27-2013-eng.pdf>.

Grabowski, Jan. 2001. "Polish Immigrants in Northern Ontario and the Ottawa Valley

during the Early Twentieth Century." In *Ottawa: Making a Capital*, edited by Jeff Keshen and Nicole St-Onge. Ottawa: University of Ottawa Press.
Graeber, David. 2015. *The Utopia of Rules: On Technology, Stupidity, and the Secret Joys of Bureaucracy*. Brooklyn: Melville House.
Graham, Joseph W. 2021. *Insatiable Hunger: Colonial Encounters in Context*. Montreal: Black Rose Books.
Granatstein, J. L. 1998. *The Ottawa Men: The Civil Service Mandarins, 1935–1957*. Toronto: University of Toronto Press.
Granzow, Kara, and Amber Dean. 2007. "Revanchism in the Canadian West: Gentrification and Resettlement in a Prairie City." *TOPIA* 18 (September): 89–106.
Gravel, Jean-Yves. 1976. "Besserer, Louis-Théodore." *Dictionary of Canadian Biography*. <biographi.ca/en/bio/4297>.
Gray, Casey James. 2018. "Sites of Grave Meaning: The Heritage of Human Remains on the Rideau Canal." Ottawa: Carleton University.
Gzovski, Mick. 2024. "Speaker Startled by Sparkling Sphere — Canada's History." *Canada's History*, May 7. <canadashistory.ca/explore/religion-spirituality/speaker-startled-by-sparkling-sphere>.
Hamilton-Hobbs, Emma. 2014. "From Friendless Women to Fancy Dress Balls: William James Topley's Photographic Portraits." Ottawa: Carleton University.
Harcourt, Bernard. 2001. *Illusion of Order: The False Promise of Broken Windows Policing*. Cambridge: Harvard University Press.
Harris, Richard. 2004. *Creeping Conformity: How Canada Became Suburban, 1900–1960*. Toronto: University of Toronto Press.
Hassan, Shereen, and Dan Lett. 2023. "6. Biological Influences on Criminal Behaviour." In *Introduction to Criminology*. Surrey: Kwantlen Polytechnic University. <kpu.pressbooks.pub/introcrim/part/6-biological-influences-on-criminal-behaviour/>.
Hayden, Dolores. 2003. *Building Suburbia: Green Fields and Urban Growth, 1820–2000, 1st ed*. New York: Pantheon Books.
Hazelview. n.d. "Portfolio Summary." Accessed August 27, 2024. <hazelview.com/investment-solutions/for-advisors/investment-solutions/hazelview-global-real-estate-fund/portfolio-summary>.
Henderson, Rick. 2023. "London Oxford — The First Black Settler in the Ottawa Valley." *Capital Chronicles*, February 17.<capitalchronicles.ca/post/london-oxford-the-first-black-settler-in-the-ottawa-valley>.
Hendricks, David, and Paul Philpott. 1985. *Ottawa Transportation — From Horses to Buses*. Ottawa: Ottawa Historical Society.
Hercules Stevenson, Angella Misty. 2013. "Uptown East Proposal for the Redevelopment of Manor Park Ottawa." Ottawa: M.Arch thesis, Carleton University.
Heritage Ottawa. 2017. "1. Union Station. Government Conference Centre." Heritage Ottawa, January 12. <heritageottawa.org/50years/union-station>.
———. n.d.a. "28. Caplan's Department Store." Accessed October 14, 2024. <heritageottawa.org/50years/caplans-department-store>.
———. n.d.b. "Carleton County Gaol." Accessed November 3, 2024. <heritageottawa.org/50years/carleton-county-gaol>.
Herongate Tenant Coalition. 2018. "The Battle for Heron Gate." *Briarpatch*, August 23. <briarpatchmagazine.com/articles/view/the-battle-for-heron-gate>.
Hewitt, Steve. 2002. *Spying 101: The RCMP's Secret Activities at Canadian Universities, 1917–1997, 1st ed*. Toronto: University of Toronto Press.
———. 2019. "'Happy-Go-Lucky Fellow': Lone-Actor Terrorism, Masculinity, and the 1966

Bombing on Parliament Hill in Ottawa." *Canadian Historical Review* 100 (1): 46–67.
Hilmer, Norman. 2015. "Library of Parliament." *Canadian Encyclopedia*, June 5. <thecanadianencyclopedia.ca/en/article/library-of-parliament>.
Hinchcliff, Richard, and Patricia Jasen. 2021. *Building Canada's Farm: An Illustrated Guide to the Buildings at the Central Experimental Farm.* Ottawa: Friends of the Experimental Farm.
Hinchcliff, Richard, and Roman Popadiouk. 2007. *For the Love of Trees: A Guide to the Trees of Ottawa's Central Experimental Farm Arboretum.* Renfrew: General Store Pub. House.
Hirsch, R. Forbes. 1992. *The Bytown Mechnics' Institute.* Ottawa: Historical Society of Ottawa.
Historical Society of Ottawa. 2023. "Lowertown East: Urban Renewal and Aftermath." December 29. <historicalsocietyottawa.ca/publications/ottawa-stories/changes-in-the-city-s-landscape/tag/Lowertown>.
Hitsman, Eric. 2024. "Aspirational Homeownership in a Time of Crisis: An Ethnography of New Homeowners in an Ottawa Suburb." Ottawa: Carleton University.
Holthuis, Annemieke E. 1991. "The Emergencies Act, the Canadian Charter of Rights and Freedoms, and International Law: The Protection of Human Rights in States of Emergency." Montreal: McGill University. <proquest.com/docview/303983338/abstract/3A597A4FE6414104PQ/1>.
Home Children Canada. 2025. "St. George's Home — Ottawa." British Home Children in Canada. <canadianbritishhomechildren.weebly.com/st-georges-home---ottawa.html>.
Horral, Andrew. 2016. "The 'Foreigners' from Broad Street: The Ukrainian Sojourners from Ottawa Who Fought for Canada in the First World War." *Social History* 49: 73–103.
Hourigan, William. 2022. "Report of the Ottawa Light Rail Transit Public Inquiry." <archives.gov.on.ca/en/e_records/olrtpi/files/documents/Report-of-the-Ottawa-Light-Rail-Transit-Public-Inquiry.pdf>.
Howard, Ebenezer. 2003. "Garden Cities Of To-Morrow." *Organization & Environment* 16 (1): 98–107.
Howard, Vicki. 2015. *From Main Street to Mall: The Rise and Fall of the American Department Store.* Philadelphia: University of Pennsylvania Press.
Hoytema, Jacob. 2019. "James Street Pub to Close Permanently This Fall." *Ottawa Citizen*, July 5. <ottawacitizen.com/news/local-news/james-street-pub-to-close-permanently-this-fall>.
Hudson, B.J. 2000. "The Experience of Waterfalls." *Australian Geographical Studies* 38 (1): 71–84.
Hum, Peter. 2023. "The Desi-Fication of Merivale Road." Ottawa Citizen, November 9. <ottawacitizen.com/feature/the-desi-fication-of-merivale-road>.
Hutt, James. 2022. "The Battle of Billings Bridge." *The Breach*, February 16. <breachmedia.ca/the-battle-of-billings-bridge/>.
Hydro Ottawa. 2023. "Lighting up Our City for Energy Efficiency." Hydro Ottawa, March 21. <hydroottawa.com/en/blog/lighting-our-city-energy-efficiency>.
——. n.d. "Our History." Accessed October 19, 2024. <hydroottawa.com/en/about-us/our-company/our-history>.
Ibbitson, John. 2016. "Everett Klippert Case." *Canadian Encyclopedia*, July 15. <thecanadianencyclopedia.ca/en/article/everett-klippert-case>.
Imeri, Monika, Sneha Sumanth, and David Hugill. 2022. "West Centretown Is Changing: Who Is It Changing For?" Ottawa: Carleton University, Department of Geography and Environmental Studies and Somerset West Community Health Centre.
Indeed.com. 2024. "Childcare Provider Salary in Ottawa, ON." <ca.indeed.com/career/childcare-provider/salaries/Ottawa--ON>.

IPM Council of Canada. 2024. Home page. <public.ipmcouncilcanada.org/index.aspx>.
Ireton, Julie. 2021. "'Far from Bankrupt': Catholic Order That Ran 48 Residential Schools Faces Criticism." CBC News, November 24. <cbc.ca/news/canada/ottawa/oblates-complex-corporate-structure-protect-money-from-liabilities-residential-school-1.6259013>.
____. 2024. "'Blue Wall of Silence' Protects Police Officers Accused of Gender-Based Violence, Victims Say." CBC News, April 24. <cbc.ca/news/canada/ottawa/paid-to-stay-home-one-third-officers-accused-gender-based-violence-1.7181385>.
Jeffords, Shawn. 2019. "Funding for Library Services Slashed by Half in Ontario Budget." Global News, April 18. <globalnews.ca/news/5181564/library-services-funding-slashed-by-half-ontario-budget/>.
Jenkins, Phil. 2020. *An Acre of Time, 3rd ed*. Ottawa: Ottawa Press and Publishing.
Jenkyns, Michael. 2010. "Ottawa District Then and Now: Freemasonry in Ontario, 1855–." Gryphon Jenkyns Enterprises.
Jennings, Sarah. 2019. *Art and Politics, 2nd ed*. Montreal: McGill-Queen's University Press.
Jhally, Sut. 1990. *The Codes of Advertising: Fetishism and the Political Economy of Meaning in the Consumer Society*. New York: Routledge.
Johnstone, Hillary. 2020. "Library's New Door Policy Leaving Homeless out in the Cold, Councillor Says." CBC News, February 5. <cbc.ca/news/canada/ottawa/catherine-mckenney-ottawa-public-library-metcalfe-locking-doors-1.5451755>.
Jones, Allison. 2024. "Bell Made $64 Million by Charging Jail Inmates' Families 'exorbitant' Rates for Phone Calls, Says Lawsuit." *Financial Post*, August 9. <financialpost.com/news/bell-made-64-million-on-jail-phone-calls-lawsuit>.
Jones, Danielle. 2017. "39. The Daly Building." Heritage Ottawa, November 22. <heritageottawa.org/50years/daly-building>.
Kalms, Nicole. 2019. "More Lighting Alone Does Not Create Safer Cities. Look at What Research with Young Women Tells Us." *The Conversation*, May 28. <theconversation.com/more-lighting-alone-does-not-create-safer-cities-look-at-what-research-with-young-women-tells-us-113359>.
Kavchak, Andrew. 2004. *Remembering Gouzenko: The Struggle to Honour a Cold War Hero*. Toronto: The Mackenzie Institute.
Kelly, Jack. 2021. "Amazon Prime Day Offers Great Sales — Here's What Workers Suffer Through To Make This Happen." *Forbes*, June 17. <forbes.com/sites/jackkelly/2021/06/17/amazon-prime-day-offers-great-sales-heres-what-workers-suffer-through-to-make-this-happen/>.
Kennelly, Jacqueline. 2020. "Urban Masculinity, Contested Spaces, and Classed Subcultures: Young Homeless Men Navigating Downtown Ottawa, Canada." *Gender, Place & Culture: A Journal of Feminist Geography* 27 (2): 281–300. <doi.org/10.1080/0966369X.2019.1650724>.
Kelling, George and James Wilson. "The police and neighborhood safety: Broken windows" *Atlantic Monthly*, 127 (2) (1982), pp. 29-38
Kent, Dave. 2024. "How Immigration Has Shaped Ottawa's Cultural Mosaic — Part III." Historical Society of Ottawa, May 1. <historicalsocietyottawa.ca/publications/past-presentations/tag/immigration>.
Kern, Leslie. 2010. "Selling the 'Scary City': Gendering Freedom, Fear and Condominium Development in the Neoliberal City." *Social & Cultural Geography* 11 (3): 209–30.
____. 2021. *Feminist City: Claiming Space in a Man-Made World*. London: Verso.
Kerr, Susan A. 2004. "The Schizoid Presentation of Self in Everyday Life: A Phenomenological Analysis of Dundonald Park." MA thesis — Carleton University.
Kestler-D'Amours, Jillian. 2018. "Hundreds Face Mass Eviction in Canada's Capital."

Al Jazeera, August 21. <aljazeera.com/features/2018/8/21/heron-gate-mass-eviction-we-never-expected-this-in-canada>.

King, Andrew. 2015. "Ottawa's Bunny Club." *OTTAWA REWIND* (blog), April 2. <ottawarewind.com/2015/04/02/ottawas-bunny-club/>.

———. 2019. "Fountains Of Our Youth: The Lost Shopping Mall Fountain." *OTTAWA REWIND* (blog), January 30. <ottawarewind.com/2019/01/29/fountains-of-our-youth-the-lost-shopping-mall-fountain/>.

Kinsman, Gary. 1995. "'Character Weaknesses' and 'Fruit Machines': Towards an Analysis of the Anti-Homosexual Security Campaign in the Canadian Civil Service." *Labour / Le Travail* 35: 133–61.

Kitchen, Kevin, Laurent Messier, and Jane Sadler. 1996. *Braddish Billings, Esq: Early Ottawa Entrepreneur*. Ottawa: Ottawa Historical Society.

Klinenberg, Eric. 2019. *Palaces for the People: How Social Infrastructure Can Help Fight Inequality, Polarization, and the Decline of Civic Life*. New York: Broadway Books.

Klodawsky, Fran, Susan Farrell, and Tim D'Aubry. 2002. "Images of Homelessness in Ottawa: Implications for Local Politics." *Canadian Geographer* 2: 126–43.

Komakech, Morris D.C., and Suzanne F. Jackson. 2016. "A Study of the Role of Small Ethnic Retail Grocery Stores in Urban Renewal in a Social Housing Project, Toronto, Canada." *Journal of Urban Health* 93 (3): 414–24. <doi.org/10.1007/s11524-016-0041-1>.

Lachance, Claude. 2024. "Letter: Move This Dangerous Inter-City Bus Terminus – Centretown BUZZ." *Centretown BUZZ*, April 17.<centretownbuzz.ca/2024/04/letter-move-this-dangerous-inter-city-bus-terminus/>.

Lambert, Jessica. 2018. "Transportation Equity: Community Conversations." Ottawa: Healthy Transportation Coalition, City for All Women Initiative.

Landry, Pierrette. 2001. "The Library of Parliament Today." August. <citeseerx.ist.psu.edu/document?repid=rep1&type=pdf&doi=a325dca8f8f72e904bd1a5609e5ffe71829e61be>.

Landsman, Gail H. 2009. *Reconstructing Motherhood and Disability in the Age of "Perfect" Babies*. New York: Routledge.

Laucius, Joanne. 2006. "The Quiet Roar: How Ottawa's Giant Tiger Is Stealthily Creeping across the Country." *Ottawa Citizen*, June 10.

———. 2018. "Bill Teron, 1932–2018: 'Father of Kanata' Left His Mark around the World." *Ottawa Citizen*, March 12. <ottawacitizen.com/news/local-news/bill-teron-1932-2018-the-story-father-of-kanata-was-a-rags-to-riches-saga-with-ripples-felt-around-the-world>.

———. 2020. "Take a First Peek at What Ottawa's New 'super Library' Will Look Like." *Ottawa Citizen*, January 23. <ottawacitizen.com/news/local-news/take-a-first-peek-at-what-ottawas-new-super-library-will-look-like>.

Lawrence, Bonita. 2012. *Fractured Homeland: Federal Recognition and Algonquin Identity in Ontario*. Vancouver: UBC Press.

Lazar, Nomi Claire. 2009. *States of Emergency in Liberal Democracies*. Cambridge: Cambridge University Press.

Leaning, John. 2003. *Hintonburg & Mechanicsville: A Narrative History*. Ottawa: Hintonburg Community Association.

Lee, David. 2006. *Lumber Kings and Shantymen: Logging, Lumber and Timber in the Ottawa Valley*. Toronto: James Lorimer & Co.

Leslie, Mark. 2016. *Creepy Capital : Ghost Stories of Ottawa and the National Capital Region*. Toronto: Dundurn Press.

Lewis, Nathaniel M. 2012. "Gay in a 'Government Town': The Settlement and Regulation of Gay-Identified Men in Ottawa, Canada." *Gender, Place & Culture: A Journal of Feminist Geography* 19 (3): 291–312. <doi.org/10.1080/0966369X.2011.624590>.

Lim, Jolson. 2017. "The Capital Builders: The Horse Whisperer Who Charmed the Wealthy Too." *Ottawa Citizen*, February 27. <ottawacitizen.com/opinion/columnists/the-capital-builders-paul-barber-trained-horses-and-charmed-wealthy-ottawans>.

Liodakis, Nikolaos. 2012. "Race and Ethnic Relations." In *Sociology: A Canadian Perspective, 3rd ed.*, edited by Lorne Tepperman, Patrizia Albanese and Jim Curtis. Don Mills: Oxford University Press.

Lo, Laurelle. 1999. "The Path from Peddling: Jewish Economic Activity in Ottawa Prior to 1939." In *Ottawa: Making a Capital*, edited by Jeff Keshen and Nicole St-Onge. Ottawa: University of Ottawa Press.

Lofaro, Joe. 2017. "Invest Ottawa's Amazon Bid Focuses on LeBreton Flats Project — Which Isn't Approved Yet." CBC News, October 23. <cbc.ca/news/canada/ottawa/lebreton-flats-ottawa-amazon-bid-video-1.4366701>.

Lost Ottawa. 2019. "Teenage Pay in the 1970s and '80s — Pic of the Week." November 4. <lostottawa.ca/2831-2/>.

Lowe, Lezlie. 2018. *No Place to Go: How Public Toilets Fail Our Private Needs, 1st ed.* Toronto: Coach House Books.

Lythall, Ryan. 2023. "Trust in Our Public Transit System Remains Stormy." *Ottawa Life*, April 10. <ottawalife.com/article/trust-in-our-public-transit-system-remains-stormy/>.

Macdougall, Greg. 2015. "Nine Algonquin Chiefs, AFNQL Oppose 'Zibi' Condos and Resolve to Protect Sacred Area in Ottawa/Gatineau." *EquitableEducation.ca* (blog), November 25. <EquitableEducation.ca/2015/algonquin-chiefs-afnql-oppose-zibi>.

MacEwen, Angella, and Cole Eisen. 2017. "Yes, Mr. Weston, You Can Afford a Living Wage." *Hamilton Spectator*, August 14. <thespec.com/opinion/contributors/yes-mr-weston-you-can-afford-a-living-wage/article_80a3e1bc-2e5d-54ab-9f8d-5187380eb0ef.html>.

Machum, Susan. 2020. "Spring Sowing for Fall Harvest: An Exploration in Time in Farmers' Food Production and Marketing." In *Seasonal Sociology, 1st ed.*, edited by Tonya K. Davidson and Ondine Park. Toronto: University of Toronto Press.

MacKinnon, Bobbi-Jean. 2018. "Briefcase Found in Attic Holds Clues to Secret Society of Francophones." CBC News, January 19. <cbc.ca/news/canada/new-brunswick/secret-order-jacques-cartier-francophone-acadian-documents-1.4493106>.

MacLaughlin, Tieja. 2021. "About — TCU Development Corporation." August 21. <tcudevcorp.com/about/>.

MacLeod, Ian. 1978. "Environmentalists Are Shouting No, No, On." *Ottawa Citizen*, May 4.

Marsh, James. 2012. "The Parliament Hill Fire of 1916." *Canadian Encyclopedia*, February 2. <thecanadianencyclopedia.ca/en/article/fire-on-the-hill-feature>.

Martin, Carl. 2022. "A New Dawn at the NAC." National Arts Centre, July 6. <nac-cna.ca/en/stories/story/dawn-has-risen-at-the-nac>.

Martin, Carole. 2002. "Isabella Preston: Canada's Horticultural Heroes." *Canadian Gardening* 13 (6).

Martin, Gary. 2013. "Manufacturing 'Home': Sustainability Discourses in Suburban Ottawa." PhD thesis, Carleton University.

Martin, Gary, and Patricia Ballamingie. 2016. "Faith Missions and Church Redevelopment in Ottawa, Ontario." *Canadian Journal of Urban Research* 25 (1): 80–88.

Masoumi, Azar. 2023. *Refugees Are (Not) Welcome Here : The Paradox of Protection in Canada.* Vancouver: University of British Columbia Press.

Mathews, Vanessa, and Roger M. Picton. 2014a. "Intoxifying Gentrification: Brew Pubs and the Geography of Post-Industrial Heritage." *Urban Geography* 35 (3): 337–56. <doi.org/10.1080/02723638.2014.887298>.

———. 2014b. "Intoxifying Gentrification: Brew Pubs and the Geography of Post-Industrial Heritage." *Urban Geography* 35 (3): 337–56. <doi.org/10.1080/02723638.2014.887298>.

McCallum, Conrad J. 2015. "The Allumettières in Sites of Collective Remembering." *Active History* (blog), February 12. <activehistory.ca/blog/2015/02/12/the-allumettieres-in-sites-of-collective-remembering/>.

McCrostie, James. 1997. *Being Poor in Ottawa in the Winter of 1891*. Bytown Pamphlet Series. Ottawa: Historical Society of Ottawa.

McDonald, Danielle. 2019. "Report to / Rapport Au: Ottawa Public Library Board." Ottawa: Ottawa Public Library. <pub-ottawa.escribemeetings.com/filestream.ashx?documentid=45008>.

McGrath, John Michael. 2024. "OPINION: The Encampment-Clearing Bill Is What Happens When Doug Ford Takes the Courts Seriously." TVO Today, December 17. <tvo.org/article/opinion-the-encampment-clearing-bill-is-what-happens-when-doug-ford-takes-the-courts-seriously>.

McIntosh, Alice, and Celine Cooper. 2013. "October Crisis." *Canadian Encyclopedia*, August 13. <thecanadianencyclopedia.ca/en/article/october-crisis>.

McKay, Jackie. 2024a. "Disturbing Audio Played in Court during Wet'suwet'en' Hearing." CBC News, September 4. <cbc.ca/news/indigenous/wet-suwet-en-coastalgaslink-court-1.7312342>.

———. 2024b. "RCMP Officers Mocked People Being Arrested at Wet'suwet'en Blockade as 'Orcs' and 'Ogre.'" CBC News, January 18. <cbc.ca/news/indigenous/rcmp-audio-wetsuweten-coastal-gaslink-1.7086861>.

McKay, Samantha. 2015. "Despite Concerns, Zibi Name Will Stay." *Centretown News* (blog), March 14. <capitalcurrent.ca/archive/centretownnews/1997-2016/2015/03/14/despite-concerns-zibi-name-will-stay/>.

McKendy, Laura. 2018. *The Pains of Jail Imprisonment: Experiences at The Ottawa-Carleton Detention Centre*. PhD thesis, Ottawa: Carleton University.

McMullin, Stanley Edward. 2000. *Anatomy of a Seance: A History of Spirit Communication in Central Canada, 1850-1950*. Montreal: McGill-Queen's University Press.

McSheffrey. 2023. "Man Stabbed to Death Outside Shelter in Vancouver's Fairview Neighbourhood." Global News, January 9. <globalnews.ca/news/9397285/man-stabbed-to-death-vancouver-shelter/>.

Media Co-Op. 2012. "Community Confronts Condo Developers in Centretown, Ottawa." July 11. <mediacoop.ca/story/community-confronts-condo-developers-centretown-ottawa/11667>.

Mercer, Caroline. 2017. "The History of the ByWard Market Lives on at Cundell Stables." *Apartment613*, October 24. <apt613.ca/the-history-of-the-byward-market-lives-on-at-cundell-stables/>.

Micaleff, Shawn. 2014. *The Trouble with Brunch: Work, Class and the Pursuit of Leisure*. Toronto: Coach House Books.

Mickiewicz, Paulina. 2016. "Access and Its Limits: The Contemporary Library as a Public Space." *Space and Culture* 19 (3): 237–50. <doi.org/10.1177/1206331215596478>.

Miguelez, Alain. 2004. *A Theatre Near You: 150 Years of Going to the Show in Ottawa-Gatineau*. Manotick: Penumbra Press.

———. 2015. *Transforming Ottawa: Canada's Capital in the Eyes of Jacques Greber*. Ottawa: Old Ottawa Press.

Mika, Nick, and Helma Mika. 1982. *Bytown, the Early Days of Ottawa*. Belleville: Mika Pub.
Miller, Jacquie. 2017. "Archbishop Defends Artistic Use of Giant Spider on the Cathedral as Part of La Machine." Ottawa Citizen, August 2. <ottawacitizen.com/news/local-news/archbishop-defends-artistic-use-of-giant-spider-on-the-cathedral-as-part-of-la-machine>.
Mills, C. Wright. 1959. *The Sociological Imagination*. New York: Oxford University Press.
Mills, Desmond. 2023. "You Said It: Broken Windows." *Ottawa Sun*, July 8. <ottawasun.com/opinion/letters/you-said-it-broken-windows>.
Mills, Stu. 2024. "Protections for Bank Street Widening Decades Too Late, Says Naturalist." CBC News, May 10. <cbc.ca/news/canada/ottawa/findlay-creek-bank-street-widening-ecosystem-1.7199118>.
Moffatt, Margarete. 1986. *Dr. Edward Van Cortlandt Surgeon 1805–1875*. Ottawa Historical Society.
Motluk, James E., Terry Steyn, John Kenneth Galbraith, Jack Layton. 2000. *Life under Mike*. Toronto: Guerrilla Films, Inc.
Mulligan, Sloane, Andrew Crosby, and Josh Hawley. 2023. "Renoviction and the Right to Stay Put: Informality, Tenant Organizing, and the Landlord-Municipal Relationship." *Annual Review of Interdisciplinary Justice Research* 12: 179–204.
Naiman, Joanne. 2012. *How Societies Work: Class, Power, and Change*, 5th ed. Halifax: Fernwood Publishing.
Nanos. 2015. "City of Ottawa Residents' Impressions of a New Central Library." Ottawa.
National Capital Commission. 1998. *A Capital for Future Generations: Vision for the Core Area of Canada's Capital Region*. Ottawa: National Capital Commission.
———. 2019. "Tree Canopy Assessment." City of Ottawa, Ville de Gatineau. <ncc-website-2.s3.amazonaws.com/documents/FINAL_Tree_Canopy_Assessment_EN.pdf?mtime=20190923125127>.
National Film Board of Canada. 1979. *Paperland: The Bureaucrat Observed*. <nfb.ca/film/paperland/>.
National Gallery Archives. 1987. "C., Fit-up and Move, C.3.c, Landscaping Interior and Exterior: NBO, Box 2b, Press Release from the National Gallery."
National Research Council. 2019. "Achievements." March 19. <nrc.canada.ca/en/corporate/history/achievements>.
Neatby, H. Blair, and Donald C. McEown. 2002. *Creating Carleton: The Shaping of a University*, 1st ed. Montreal: McGill-Queen's University Press.
Neuhaus, Jessamyn. 1999. "The Way to a Man's Heart: Gender Roles, Domestic Ideology, and Cookbooks in the 1950s." *Journal of Social History* 32 (3): 529–55.
Newell, Christina. 1995. *Hintonburgh: A Working Class Streetcar Suburb at the Turn of the Century*. Bytown Pamphlet Series. Ottawa: Historical Society of Ottawa.
Ng, Andrew. 2008. "Panhandlers Want Direct Access to Meter Donations." *Centretown News* (blog), February 13. <capitalcurrent.ca/archive/centretown-news/1997-2016/2008/02/13/panhandlers-want-direct-access-to-meter-donations/>.
Noppen, Luc. 1988. *In the National Gallery of Canada: "One of the Most Beautiful Chapels in the World."* Ottawa: National Gallery of Canada.
Novakowski, Nick. 2010. "Ottawa: The Knowledge City and a Labyrinth of Obstacles." *GeoJournal* 75 (6): 553–65.
OCASI: Ontario Council of Agencies Serving Immigrants. 2016. "Somali Refugee Resettlement in Canada Paper Presented at the 18th National Metropolis Conference in Toronto on Getting Results: Migration, Opportunities and Good Governance." <ocasi.org/sites/default/files/OCASI_Presentation_Somali_Resettlement_Metropolis_2016.pdf>.

Office of the Auditor General of Canada. 2017. "Report 1 — Phoenix Pay Problems." November 21. <oag-bvg.gc.ca/internet/English/parl_oag_201711_01_e_42666.html>.
Oke, T.R. 1987. *Boundary Layer Climates, 2nd ed.* Oxford: Routledge.
O'Regan, Brian. 1994. *Pioneer Trips to Some Ottawa Valley Stopping Places.* Bytown Pamphlet Series. Ottawa: Historical Society of Ottawa.
Ottawa Citizen. 1991. "Oil Fouls City Creek," May 12.
———. 2013. "Library and Archives Canada — By the Numbers." May 27. <web.archive.org/web/20130527011049/http://www.ottawacitizen.com/news/Library+Archives+Canada+numbers/8335604/story.html>.
Ottawa Coalition to End Violence Against Women (OCTEVAW). 2018. "Project SoundCheck." <projectsoundcheck.ca/>.
Ottawa Neighbourhood Study. n.d. Accessed May 24, 2025. <neighbourhoodstudy.ca/>.
Ottawa Public Library. 2023. "2023 Annual Report." <biblioottawalibrary.ca/sites/default/files/annualreport-2023-en.pdf>.
OttawaStart.com. 2019. "LINKED: The $100-Million Strandherd Drive Widening Boondoggle." October 11. <ottawastart.com/linked-the-100-million-strandherd-drive-widening-boondoggle/>.
Paine, Elizabeth. 2015. "A User's Guide to the Islands, the Falls, Zibi and the Windmill Development." *Ottawa Citizen*, August 24. <ottawacitizen.com/news/local-news/a-users-guide-to-the-the-islands-the-falls-zibi-and-the-windmill-development>.
Palmer, Jean. 2000. "Recent Heritage." In *Ottawa: A Guide to Heritage Structures.* Ottawa: City of Ottawa.
Pampel, Fred. 2007. *Sociological Lives and Ideas: An Introduction to the Classical Theorists, 2nd ed.* New York: Worth Publishers.
Panico, Giacomo. 2021. "Ottawa's 'Indigicity': Vanier's Rise as an Urban Home for Indigenous People." CBC News, October 22. <cbc.ca/news/canada/ottawa/vanier-indigenous-home-1.6217811>.
Pantalone, Salvatore. 2013. *Growing Up in "La Colonia."* Bytown Pamphlet Series. Ottawa: Historical Society of Ottawa.
Park, Ondine. 2016. "Private Suburban Home: The Phantasmagoric Interior and the Ghostly Individual." In *Sociology of Home: Belonging, Community, and Place in the Canadian Context*, edited by Gillian Anderson, Laura Suski, and Joseph G. Moore. Toronto: Canadian Scholars' Press.
Parks Canada. n.d. "Public Archives and National Library Building." Accessed October 15, 2024. <pc.gc.ca/apps/dfhd/page_fhbro_eng.aspx?id=11763>.
Pass, Forest. 2022. "From Modest Beginnings." Library and Archives Canada Blog, June 20. <thediscoverblog.com/tag/douglas-brymner/>.
Payne, Michael. 2023. "The Development of Ruskin Place – 'Homes for People of Good Taste and Modest Means.'" *Heritage Ottawa Newsletter*, February.
Pellerin, Brigitte. 2023. "Pellerin: Reopening Wellington Street to Vehicles Shows a Distinct Lack of Imagination." *Ottawa Citizen*, April 22. <ottawacitizen.com/opinion/pellerin-reopening-wellington-street-to-vehicles-shows-a-distinct-lack-of-imagination>.
Pettis, Jeffery S., Elinor M. Lichtenberg, Michael Andree, Jennie Stitzinger, Robyn Rose, Dennis vanEngelsdorp, and Fabio S. Nascimento. 2013. "Crop Pollination Exposes Honey Bees to Pesticides Which Alters Their Susceptibility to the Gut Pathogen Nosema Ceranae." *PLoS One* 8 (7): e70182. <doi.org/10.1371/journal.pone.0070182>.
Picton, Roger. 2010. "Selling National Urban Renewal: The National Film Board, the National Capital Commission and Post-War Planning in Ottawa, Canada." *Urban History* 37 (2): 301–21.

――――. 2015. "Rubble and Ruin: Walter Benjamin, Post-War Urban Renewal and the Residue of Everyday Life on LeBreton Flats, Ottawa, Canada (1944–1970)." *Urban History* 42 (1): 130–56.

Porter, John. 2018. *The Vertical Mosaic: An Analysis of Social Class and Power in Canada, 50th Anniversary Edition*. Toronto: University of Toronto Press.

Porter, Kate. 2021. "Tewin: The Land at the Centre of Ottawa's Reconciliation Controversy." CBC News, February 5. <bc.ca/news/canada/ottawa/tewin-parcel-details-planners-aoo-1.5901324>.

Powell, James. 2019a. "Remember This? Freiman's Becomes The Bay." *CityNews Ottawa*, November 18. <ottawa.citynews.ca/2019/11/18/remember-this-freimans-becomes-the-bay-1854496/>.

――――. 2019b. "Remember This? The Arrival of Prohibition." *CityNews Ottawa*, September 16. <ottawa.citynews.ca/2019/09/16/remember-this-the-arrival-of-prohibition-1695140/>.

――――. 2024. "Solidarity in the Chaudière District." *Historical Society of Ottawa*, October 15. <historicalsocietyottawa.ca/publications/ottawa-stories/tag/Hull>.

――――. n.d.a. "Lover's Walk." *Historical Society of Ottawa*. Accessed October 20, 2024. <historicalsocietyottawa.ca/publications/ottawa-stories/changes-in-the-city-s-landscape/lover-s-walk>.

――――. n.d.b. "Ottawa's Chinese Laundry Tax." *Historical Society of Ottawa*. Accessed October 14, 2024. <historicalsocietyottawa.ca/publications/ottawa-stories/important-services-in-ottawa/ottawa-s-chinese-laundry-tax>.

――――. n.d.c. "Strike! En Grève!." *Historical Society of Ottawa*. Accessed October 14, 2024. <historicalsocietyottawa.ca/publications/ottawa-stories/changes-in-the-city-s-landscape/strike-en-greve>.

――――. n.d.d. "The Great Epizootic." *Historical Society of Ottawa*. Accessed October 14, 2024. <historicalsocietyottawa.ca/publications/ottawa-stories/momentous-events-in-the-city-s-life/the-great-epizootic>.

POWER. 2010. "The Toolbox: What Works for Sex Workers." Prostitutes of Ottawa: Work, Educate, Resist. <static1.squarespace.com/static/6793d24198337062d472c2a1/t/680fe64c131b224e8698ff21/1745872461496/toolbox_-what-works-for-sex-workers-the-frederique-chabot.pdf>.

Pringle, Josh. 2021. "$2.9 Million Tax Break for Ottawa Porsche Dealership Receives the Green Light." *CTV News Ottawa*, May 26. <ctvnews.ca/ottawa/article/29-million-tax-break-for-ottawa-porsche-dealership-receives-the-green-light/>.

Pritchard, Trevor. 2022. "Carlington's Post-WW2 Homes Recognized for Historic Importance." CBC News, April 29. <cbc.ca/news/canada/ottawa/ottawa-carlington-post-second-world-war-two-1.6434310>.

Public Works and Government Services Canada. 2011. "Library of Parliament Interior — History of the Hill — Parliament Hill." July 6. <web.archive.org/web/20110706181633/http://www.collineduparlement-parliamenthill.gc.ca/histoire-history/bdp-lop/inbblthq-inlbrry-eng.html>.

Ramsay-Borg, Michelle. 2015. "The Château Lafayette at 166: Lowertown's Happy Place." *Lowertown Echo de La Basse-Ville* (blog), June 3. <lowertownecho.ca/2020/08/10/the-chateau-lafayette-at-166-lowertowns-happy-place/>.

Ravelli, Bruce, and Michelle Webber. 2010. *Exploring Sociology : A Canadian Perspective*. Don Mills: Pearson Canada.

Raymond, Ted. 2022. "Someone Called Police on a Woman Doing Tai Chi in an Ottawa Park." *CTV News Ottawa*, May 31. <ottawa.ctvnews.ca/someone-called-police-on-a-woman-doing-tai-chi-in-an-ottawa-park-1.5925961>.

_____. 2024. "'A Great Victory for the Industry': Taxi Drivers Celebrate Ruling That Found City of Ottawa Negligent in Allowing Uber to Operate." *CTV News Ottawa*, May 13. <ottawa.ctvnews.ca/a-great-victory-for-the-industry-taxi-drivers-celebrate-ruling-that-found-city-of-ottawa-negligent-in-allowing-uber-to-operate-1.6885044>.

Reevely, David. 2017. "Reevely: Complaints to Limit Use of Offensive Content on Ottawa's Library Computers." Ottawa Citizen, September 22. <ottawacitizen.com/news/local-news/reevely-complaints-to-limit-use-of-ottawas-library-computers>.

Regehr. 2008. "Sir Sandford Fleming." Canadian Encyclopedia, February 21. <thecanadianencyclopedia.ca/en/article/sir-sandford-fleming>.

Rickets, Shannon. 2017. "Early Apartment Buildings 1900–1918." In *From Walk-Up to High-Rise: Ottawa's Historic Apartment Buildings*, edited by Richard Belliveau, Carolyn Quinn, and Susan Ross. Ottawa: Heritage Ottawa.

Robin, Laura. 2016. "The Instant Pot, Invented in Ottawa, Is the Hottest Multi-Cooker in Kitchens." *Ottawa Citizen*, November 15. <ottawacitizen.com/life/food/the-instant-pot-invented-in-ottawa-is-the-hottest-multi-cooker-in-kitchens>.

Rockburn, Ken. 2015. *We Are as the Times Are: The Story of Café Le Hibou*. Burnstown: Burnstown Publishing House.

Rodgers, Gerry, and Janine Rodgers. 1989. *Precarious Jobs in Labour Market Regulation the Growth of Atypical Employment in Western Europe*. Geneva: International Institute for Labour Studies.

Rose, Damaris. 2015. "Gender, Sexuality, and the City." In *Canadian Cities in Transition: Perspectives for an Urban Age, 5th ed.*, edited by Pierre Filion, Marcus Moos, Tara Vinodrai, and Ryan Walker. Don Mills: Oxford University Press.

Rosenfeld, Raymond A., and Laura A. Reese. 2003. "The Anatomy of an Amalgamation: The Case of Ottawa." *State & Local Government Review* 35 (1): 57–69.

Ross, Susan. 2017. "The Windsor Arts." In *From Walk-Up to High-Rise: Ottawa's Historic Apartment Buildings*, edited by Richard Belliveau, Carolyn Quinn, and Susan Ross. Ottawa: Heritage Ottawa.

Roy, Gabrièle. 2017. "Bright Idea? Light Pollution Fears Shadow NCC Plan to Light up Capital." *Ottawa Citizen*, July 28. <ottawacitizen.com/news/local-news/bright-idea-light-pollution-fears-shadow-ncc-plan-to-light-up-capital>.

Sandy Hill History. 2021. "Strathcona Heights." January 23. <ash-acs.ca/history/strathcona-heights/>.

Satzewich, Vic. 2015. *Points of Entry: How Canada's Immigration Officers Decide Who Gets In*. Vancouver: UBC Press.

Schnurr, Joanne. 2017. "'Visitation' at Museum of History for Human Remains from 1800s." *CTV News Ottawa*, September 22. <ottawa.ctvnews.ca/visitation-at-museum-of-history-for-human-remains-from-1800-s-1.3602340>.

Schuster, Eli. 2002. "Oops — There Goes Our History: Bats, Heat and Water Are Destroying Documents in Canada's National Library." *The Report Newsmagazine* 29 (1).

Scott, Clifford. 2020. *Science in Ottawa*. Ottawa: Historical Society of Ottawa.

Scott, Nicholas A. 2016. "Cycling, Performance and the Common Good: Copenhagenizing Canada's Capital." *Canadian Journal of Urban Research* 25 (1): 22–37.

SFOPHO (Société franco-ontarienne du patrimoine et de l'histoire d'Orléans [Franco-Ontario Society of the Heritage and History of Orleans]). 2017. *A Brief History of Orléans Ontario and of Its French Toponymy*.

_____. 2023. *The History Behind the French Toponymy of Orleans, Ontario, Vol. 2*.

Shafer, Kevin, Casey Scheibling, and Melissa A. Milkie. 2020. "The Division of Domestic Labor before and during the COVID-19 Pandemic in Canada: Stagnation versus

Shifts in Fathers' Contributions." *Canadian Review of Sociology* 57 (4): 523–49. <doi.org/10.1111/cars.12315>.
Shah, Shailee. 2021. "Besserer Park Saved as TCU Abandons Plans to Pave the Sandy Hill Green Space." *The Fulcrum*, November 29. <thefulcrum.ca/news/besserer-park-saved-as-tcu-abandons-plans-to-pave-the-sandy-hill-green-space/>.
Shea, Philip. 1965. *History of Eastview*. Carleton: National Capital Commission.
Shields, Rob. 1991. *Places on the Margin: Alternatives Geographies of Modernity*. London: Routledge Chapman Hall.
———. 1994. "The Logic of the Mall." In *The Socialness of Things*, edited by Stephen Riggins. New York: Mouton de Gruyter.
———. 1996. "Mobility, Space and Power: The Ceremonial Parkway." In *Driving the Ceremonial Landscape*. Ottawa: Gallery 101.
Shragge, John, and Sharon Bagnato. 1984. "From Footpaths to Freeways." Ontario Ministry of Transportation and Communications, Historical Committee.
Silver, Jim. 2011. *Good Places to Live : Poverty and Public Housing in Canada*. Halifax: Fernwood Publishing.
Slater, Tom. 2004. "North American Gentrification? Revanchist and Emancipatory Perspectives Explored." *Environment and Planning A: Economy and Space* 36 (7): 1191–1213.
Smith, Alison. 2015. "When Homelessness was Declared a National Disaster." *Mouvement pour mettre fin a l'itenerance a Montreal* (blog), June 2. <mmfim.ca/when-homelessness-was-declared-a-national-disaster/>.
Smith, Eric. 2011. "An Urban Epicentre of Decolonization in Canada : The Indigenous-Settler Alliance to Make a Place for Peace at Asinabka." MA thesis, Carleton University, <carleton.scholaris.ca/items/f0442500-ec88-45c0-978e-19830f6560b7>.
Smith, Marie-Danielle. 2014. "She's So Heavy: Love Locks Won't Break the Corktown Bridge, Professors Say." *Ottawa Citizen*, July 15. <ottawacitizen.com/news/local-news/shes-so-heavy-love-locks-wont-break-the-corktown-bridge-professors-say>.
Smith, Neil. 2000. "Gentrification." In *The Dictionary of Human Geography, 4th ed.*, edited by R.J. Johnston, Derek Gregory, Geraldine Pratt, and Michael Watts. Malden: Blackwell Publishers.
Smythe, Robert. 2011. "King Edward Avenue Massacre." *Urbsite* (blog), June 9. <urbsite.blogspot.com/2011/06/king-edward-avenue-massacre.html>.
———. 2012. "Unforgotten Ottawa: The Carnegie Library." *Urbsite* (blog), September 25. <urbsite.blogspot.com/search?q=George+Perley>.
———. 2014. "George Bemi's Public Library: Is It Really A Brute?." *Urbsite* (blog), July 12. <urbsite.blogspot.com/2014/07/george-bemis-public-library-is-it.html>.
———. 2018. "The Preston Street Urban Renewal Project (Rochester Heights)." *Centretown BUZZ*, September 14. <centretownbuzz.ca/2018/09/the-preston-street-urban-renewal-project-rochester-heights/>.
———. 2022. "Heritage Skyline: Secrets of Dundonald Park." *Centretown BUZZ*, September 15. <centretownbuzz.ca/2022/09/heritage-skyline-secrets-of-dundonald-park/>.
Spain, Daphne. 2011. "The Chicago of Jane Addams and Ernest Burgess: Same City, Different Visions." In *The City, Revisited*, edited by Dennis Judd and Dick Simpson. Minneapolis: University of Minnesota Press.
Stacey, Jocelyn, and Nomi Claire Lazar. 2023. "Emergencies Act Inquiry Final Report Is a Reminder That We All Have a Role in Upholding the Rule of Law." *The Conversation*, February 21. <theconversation.com/emergencies-act-inquiry-final-report-is-a-reminder-that-we-all-have-a-role-in-upholding-the-rule-of-law-200230>.

Statistics Canada. 2018a. "Crude Birth Rate, Age-Specific Fertility Rates and Total Fertility Rate (Live Births)." June 27. <www150.statcan.gc.ca/t1/tbl1/en/tv.action?pid=1310041801>.

———. 2018b. "Labour Force Characteristics by Industry, Annual." June 27. <www150.statcan.gc.ca/t1/tbl1/en/tv.action?pid=1410002301>.

———. 2022. "Focus on Geography Series, 2021 Census — Ottawa (Census Division)." July 13. <www12.statcan.gc.ca/census-recensement/2021/as-sa/fogs-spg/Page.cfm?lang=E&topic=11&dguid=2021A00033506>.

———. 2024a. "Distribution of Total Income by Census Family Type and Age of Older Partner, Parent or Individual." June 27. <www150.statcan.gc.ca/t1/tbl1/en/tv.action?pid=1110001201>.

———. 2024b. "Fertility in Canada, 1921 to 2022." January 31. <www150.statcan.gc.ca/n1/pub/91f0015m/91f0015m2024001-eng.htm>.

———. 2024c. "Labour Force Characteristics by Industry, Annual." January 5. <www150.statcan.gc.ca/t1/tbl1/en/tv.action?pid=1410002301>.

———. 2024d. "Union Status by Industry." October 2. <www150.statcan.gc.ca/t1/tbl1/en/tv.action?pid=1410013201>.

Steinberg, Theodore. 2006. *American Green: The Obsessive Quest for the Perfect Lawn.* New York: W.W. Norton.

Straw, Will. 2014. "The Urban Night." In *Cartographies of Place: Navigating the Urban,* edited by Michael Darroch and Janine Marchessault. Montreal: McGill-Queen's University Press.

Straw, Will, and Jess Reia. 2021. "Nightlife in a Pandemic." In *Pandemic Societies, 1st ed.,* edited by Jean-Louis Denis, Catherine Régis, Daniel M. Weinstock, and Clara Champagne. Montreal: McGill-Queen's University Press.

Strong-Boag, Veronica. 1991. "Home Dreams: Women and the Suburban Experiment in Canada, 1945–60." *Canadian Historical Review* 72 (4): 471–504.

Sugiman, Pamela. 2012. "Work and the Economy." In *Sociology: A Canadian Perspective, 3rd ed.,* edited by Lorne Tepperman, Patrizia Albanese, and James Curtis. Don Mills: Oxford University Press.

Supreme Court of Canada. n.d. *Munro v. National Capital Commission* — SCC Cases. Accessed November 4, 2024. <decisions.scc-csc.ca/scc-csc/scc-csc/en/item/6893/index.do>.

Svirplys, Saul. 2011. "Campeau in Alta Vista." *Campeau in the Late 1950s and Early 1960s* (blog). <modernrealtor.blogspot.com/2011/09/campeau-in-late-1950s-and-early-1960s.html>.

SWC (Somerset West Community Health Centre) and CC (Centretown Community Health Centre). 2016. "Health and Housing in West-Central Ottawa: The Facts on Rooming Houses." <swchc.on.ca/_files/ugd/6c6d9d_4b8d77b2a3db400ebf99061c06b030d1.pdf>.

Taekema, Dan. 2022. "Controversial Group Creates 'Private Security Force' to Guard Former Church." CBC News, August 10. <cbc.ca/news/canada/ottawa/united-people-of-canada-st-brigids-security-force-1.6546148>.

Taylor, Jennifer. 2019. "The Persons Case Then and Now." Canadian Bar Association — *National Magazine,* October 18. <nationalmagazine.ca/en-ca/articles/law/opinion/2019/the-persons-case-then-and-now>.

Taylor, John H. 1986. *Ottawa: An Illustrated History.* Gatineau: Canadian Museum of Civilization.

Tepperman, Charles. 2009. "'Stolen from the Realm of Night': Modernity, Visual Culture, and the Reception of Cinema in Ottawa." *Canadian Journal of Film Studies* 18 (2).

Thibedeau, Hannah. 2015. "RCMP Hiring 30 Officers for New Parliament Hill Security Force." CBC News, May 14. <cbc.ca/news/politics/rcmp-hiring-30-officers-for-new-parliament-hill-security-force-1.307310>.

Thistle, Jesse. 2017. "Definition of Indigenous Homelessness in Canada." Canadian Observatory on Homelessness. <homelesshub.ca/sites/default/files/COHIndigenousHomelessnessDefinition.pdf>.

Thumbadoo, Romola Vasantha. 2018. "Ginawaydaganuc and the Circle of All Nations The Remarkable Environmental Legacy of Elder William Commanda." PhD thesis, Carleton University.

———. n.d. "Asinabka." <asinabka.com/geninfo.htm>.

Tierney, Tim. 2020. "A Broader Conversation on Homelessness." *Ottawa Citizen*, February 20. <pressreader.com/canada/ottawa-citizen/20200218/281646782156685>.

Tomiak, Julie. 2016. "Unsettling Ottawa: Settler Colonialism, Indigenous Resistance, and the Politics of Scale." *Canadian Journal of Urban Research* 25 (1): 8–22.

Trew, Johanne. 1999. ""Ottawa Valley Irish: Place, Culture and Identity." In *Ottawa: Making a Capital*, edited by Jeff Keshen and Nicole St-Onge. Ottawa: University of Ottawa Press.

Trinh, Judy. 2021. "Police Officer Who Pleaded Guilty to Assaulting Women Resigns, Gets Probation." CBC News, April 1. <cbc.ca/news/canada/ottawa/eric-post-ottawa-police-resignation-pleaded-guilty-charges-1.5973513>.

Tunbridge, John E. 1986. "Clarence Street, Ottawa: Contemporary Change in an Inner City 'Zone of Discard.'" *Urban History Review* 14 (3): 247–57. <doi.org/10.7202/1018082ar>.

Union of Canadian Transportation Employees (blog). 2019. "The 1980 CR Strike." April 18. <unioncte.ca/the-1980-cr-strike/>.

Urry, John. 2004. "The 'System' of Automobility." *Theory, Culture & Society* 21 (4/5): 25–39.

———. 2007. *Mobilities*. Cambridge, UK: Polity.

US Forest Service. 2021. "Trees Are Climate Change, Carbon Storage Heroes." November 8. <fs.usda.gov/about-agency/features/trees-are-climate-change-carbon-storage-heroes>.

Vance, Michael E. 2012. *Imperial Immigrants: Scottish Settlers of the Upper Ottawa Valley, 1815–1840*. Toronto: Dundurn Press.

Village Legacy Project. n.d. "VIDEO: Hate Crimes and the Murder Spree of 1989." Accessed April 27, 2025. <villagelegacy.ca/items/show/112?tour=4&index=8>.

Village Legacy Project. n.d. "Rialto Theatre." Accessed October 20, 2024. <villagelegacy.ca/items/show/47>.

Vincent-Domey, Odette. 1994. "Eddy, Ezra Butler." Dictionary of Canadian Biography, Vol. 13. Accessed May 14, 2025. <biographi.ca/en/bio/eddy_ezra_butler_13E.html>.

Vlasveld, Mike. 2020. "Ottawa Public Library Helping Out Where It Can during COVID-19." *CityNews Ottawa* (blog), April 25. <ottawa.citynews.ca/2020/04/24/ottawa-public-library-helping-out-where-it-can-during-covid-19-2281132/>.

Walby, Kevin, and Kelly Gorkoff. 2023. "10.2 Marx and the Basis of Critical Criminology." In *Introduction to Criminology*. Surrey: Kwantlen Polytechnic University. <kpu.pressbooks.pub/introcrim/chapter/10-2-marx-and-the-basis-of-critical-criminology/>.

Walby, Kevin, and Randy Lippert. 2012. "Spatial Regulation, Dispersal, and the Aesthetics of the City: Conservation Officer Policing of Homeless People in Ottawa, Canada." *Antipode* 44 (3): 1015–33.

Waldron, Andrew, Peter Coffman, and Harold Kalman. 2017. *Exploring the Capital: An Architectural Guide to the Ottawa Region, 1st ed*. Vancouver: Figure 1 Publishing.

Walker, Jason. 2023. "Mounties in Crisis: The Systemic Failure to Address Sexual Abuse within the RCMP." *The Conversation*, July 13. <theconversation.com/mounties-in-crisis-the-systemic-failure-to-address-sexual-abuse-within-the-rcmp-209090>.

Walks, Alan. 2015. "Growing Divisions: Inequality, Neighbourhood Poverty, and Homelessness in the Canadian City." In *Canadian Cities in Transition: Perspectives for an Urban Age, 5th Ed.*, edited by Pierre Filion, Marcus Moos, Tara Vinodrai, and Ryan Walker. Don Mills: Oxford University Press.

Walsh, John. 2001. "Modern Citizens for a Modern City? Ottawa's Great Fire of 1900." In *Ottawa: Making a Capital*, edited by Jeff Keshen and Nicole St-Onge. Ottawa: University of Ottawa Press.

Weber, Max. 2009. *From Max Weber: Essays in Sociology, 1st ed*. London: Routledge.

White, Erik. 2024. "Forest Industry and Environmentalists Disagree as Province Moves to Protect Black Ash Trees." CBC News, January 2. <cbc.ca/news/canada/sudbury/black-ash-endangered-species-ontario-1.7062354>.

White-Crummey, Arthur. 2024. "Latest Offer in Bank Street Demoviction Saga Fails to Win over Tenants." CBC News, December 11. <cbc.ca/news/canada/ottawa/latest-offer-in-bank-street-demoviction-saga-fails-to-win-over-tenants-1.7406784>.

____. 2025. "What Has Ottawa's Night Mayor Actually Done?" CBC News, March 26. <cbc.ca/news/canada/ottawa/what-has-ottawa-s-night-mayor-actually-done-1.7492564>.

Whitzman, Carolyn. 2024. *Home Truths: Fixing Canada's Housing Crisis, 1st ed*. Vancouver: UBC Press.

Williams, Nicole. 2022. "Living in Fear." CBC News, May 2. <cbc.ca/i/phoenix/player/syndicate/?mediaId=2028417091608>.

Williams, Patricia. 2017. "Zibi Redevelopment Project 'A Model of Collaboration' with First Nations." *Daily Commercial News*, September 22.

Willing, Jon. 2018. "'Goodness' Came to Capital Region from Failed Amazon HQ2 Bid, Invest Ottawa Says." *Ottawa Citizen*, January 18. <ottawacitizen.com/news/local-news/goodness-came-to-capital-region-from-failed-amazon-hq2-bid-invest-ottawa-says>.

Wolfe, Patrick. 2006. "Settler Colonialism and the Elimination of the Native." *Journal of Genocide Research* 8, no. 4: 387–409. <doi.org/10.1080/14623520601056240>.

Woods, Shirley E. 1980. *Ottawa, The Capital of Canada*. Toronto: Garden City.

Workers' History Museum. 2018a. *A Struggle to Remember: Fighting for Our Families* (film). <youtube.com/watch?v=9czpIswnj9g>.

____. 2018b. *The Wong Brothers Make Their Mark*. Capital History Comics. <workershistorymuseum.ca/the-wong-brothers-make-their-mark/>.

Wotherspoon, Terry. 2012. "Education." In *Sociology: A Canadian Perspective, 3rd ed.*, edited by Lorne Tepperman, Patrizia Albanese, and James Curtis. Don Mills: Oxford University Press.

Yasin, Amina. 2022. "Walking with My Mother." *Briarpatch*, September 12. <briarpatch-magazine.com/articles/view/walking-with-my-mother>.

Yee, Paul. 2005. *Chinatown: An Illustrated History of the Chinese Communities of Victoria, Vancouver, Calgary, Winnipeg, Toronto, Ottawa, Montréal, and Halifax*. James Lorimer & Co.

Yogaretnam, Shaamini. 2020. "Murder Accused in Chinatown Death Maintains Innocence." *Ottawa Citizen*, November 13. <ottawacitizen.com/news/local-news/murder-accused-in-chinatown-death-maintains-innocence>.

____. 2021. "Ottawa Police Cleared of Wrongdoing in Falling Death of Anthony Aust." CBC News, September 9. <cbc.ca/news/canada/ottawa/anthony-aust-no-charges-siu-police-1.6169873>.

Young, Carolyn A. 1995. *The Glory of Ottawa Canada's First Parliament Buildings.* Montreal: McGill-Queen's University Press.

Young, Janet. 2023a. "Bone Detective — The 'Iron Man' of the Barrack Hill Cemetery: A Life in Contrast." *Your Museum. Your Stories* (blog), October 6. <historymuseum.ca/blog/bone-detective-the-iron-man-of-the-barrack-hill-cemetery-a-life-in-contrast/>.

———. 2023b. "Bone Detective — The Maiden: Could She Have Been a 'Mad Hatter'?" *Your Museum. Your Stories* (blog), October 6. <historymuseum.ca/blog/bone-detective-the-maiden/>.

———. 2023c. "Bone Detective — 'The Violated': Not Buried Alone." *Your Museum. Your Stories* (blog), October 6. <historymuseum.ca/blog/bone-detective-the-violated-not-buried-alone/>.

Zhang, Michael. 2013. "The Life of John Redpath: A Neglected Legacy and Its Rediscovery through Print Materials." In *Beyond the Roddick Gates* (Redpath Museum Research Journal), 3: 25–35. Montreal: Students' Society of McGill University.

Zukin, Sharon. 1991. *Landscapes of Power: From Detroit to Disney World.* Berkeley: University of California Press.

INDEX

Abdi, Abdirahman, 140–141
Action Sandy Hill, 87
active transportation, 123, 132
   see also cycling; walking
Adams, Thomas, 106
Addams, Jane, 5–6, 8
Ādisōke, 43, 48
adolescence, *see* youth
affordable housing, 84, 86, 87, 91, 93, 99
   see also housing; public housing
agriculture, 32, 51–55, 75
   see also Central Experimental Farm
Ahearn, Thomas, 124–125, 169, 171
Albert Island, 76, 95
Algonquin, 13–15, 20, 26, 95, 120
   dispossession of, 76, 100
   see also Anishinaabe Algonquin Nation; Indigenous peoples
Algonquin College, 110–111
Algonquins of Ontario Reality Corporation (AOO), 112–113
allumettières, 57
Amazon, 58, 155, 167, 168
American Revolution, 18
Americans, 21, 51
Anchor: Alternative Neighbourhood Crisis Response, 154
Anishinaabe Algonquin Nation, 11–12, 13, 16
Anka, Paul, 176
anthropocentrism, 27, 36
anti-Black racism, 12, 26, 64, 127, 140–141
   see also race
anti-Semitism, 6,
   see also Jewish population
architecture, 7, 8
   of bureaucracy, 63
   of courts, 150
   of libraries, 41–44
   and retail, 158, 165
   and urban development, 105

arts, 58, 63, 184–185
   see also music; theatre
Asian Canadians, 4, 25, 111, 164
Asinabka, 16
"auto-burbs," 107–108, 111, 116–117, 118, 164
   see also suburbia
automobiles, 107, 111, 115, 135
   dominance of, 128
   and the environment, 133
   ideology of, 120–124, 130–132
   and public transit, 125
   and shopping, 166
   and traffic control, 171
   see also parking
Aylen, Peter, 138

baby boom, 116
Bank of Canada, 72–73
Barber, Paul, 121
Barrhaven, 109, 115, 123, 187
bars and nightclubs, 173, 176–179
"Battle of Billings Bridge," 142
Bawating Water Protectors, 16
Bell Canada, 152–153
Bell's Corners, 22
Bennett, Richard, 57, 72
Besserer, Louis-Théodore, 14, 87
big box stores, 166–167
bike lanes, 123, 133–134, 135
bilingualism, 22, 24
Billings, Braddish, 51, 75–76
Billings, Sabra and Sarah, 94
Billings Estate National Historic Site, 55, 75, 108
Bilsky, Moses, 156–157
Black community, 5, 12, 25–26, 64, 90–91, 121
   policing of, 151–152
   see also anti-Black racism

Black railway porters, 127–128
Booth, J.R., 31, 34, 127, 188
Borden, Robert, 1, 45, 62, 188
Boushey's Fruit Market, 23
Boushie, Colten, 149
branding, 44, 96, 102–103, 108, 171, 179
British Empire, 14, 28–29, 31
    see also settler colonialism
British North America, 15, 18–19
British North America Act, 43
Brookfield Asset Management, 84
Brown, George, 56
Brown, Herbert, 164
bunkhouses, 86–88, 100
bus rapid transit (BRT), 125–126, 130
By, John (Colonel), 15, 156, 190
Bytown, 4, 15, 19–20
    courts in, 149
    libraries of, 40
    policing of, 138
    transit in, 121
    work in, 51
Bytown Athenaeum, 40
Bytown Mechanics' Institute, 40–41
Bytown Museum, 144, 188, 190
ByWard Market, 10, 15, 21, 28, 53, 155–157
    competition to, 161, 168
    and homelessness, 80, 81
    surveillance of, 141–142, 153

Café Le Hibou, 177
Campbell, William Wilfrid, 63
Campeau, Robert, 7, 108
Canada, government of, 60, 70–73, 137
    and housing, 83, 98, 106–107, 118
    and immigration, 24–25, 90–91, 128, 163–164
    and Indigenous people, 15
    and policing, 143, 146–148
    and transportation, 122
    and urban planning, 89–90
    see also civil service; settler colonialism
Canada Agriculture and Food Museum, 52
Canada Mortgage and Housing Corporation (CMHC), 83, 107
Canada Revenue Agency, 73
Canadian Association of Professional Employees (CAPE), 66
Canadian Charter of Rights and Freedoms, 147
    see also human rights and freedoms
Canadian Museum of History, 13, 17, 43
Canadian Security Intelligence Service (CSIS), 145–146, 147–148, 153
Canadian Tribute to Human Rights, 16, 174
Canadian Union of Postal Workers (CUPW), 68
Canadian War Museum, 90, 146
capitalism, 4, 61, 70–73, 137, 155
    and death, 188
    and nighttime, 170
    see also consumerism; neoliberalism
Cardinal, Douglas, 17
Carleton University, 42, 61, 65–66, 146, 176, 183
Carlington, 88, 103, 107–108
Carnegie libraries, 41–42
Carney, Mark, 84
cars, see automobiles
Cartier, Georges-Étienne, 15
Cartier Square Drill Hall, 18
Catholic Church, 10, 19–20, 22, 23, 26, 64
cemeteries, 188–189
Centennial 1967, 15–16, 32, 89
Central Experimental Farm, 32–33, 52, 54, 69, 172
Centretown, 7, 26, 101, 106, 131, 137
    gentrification of, 92–93, 100
    housing in, 83, 88
Champlain, Samuel de, 13, 26, 27–28
Chapman Mills Conservation Area, 115
charity, 76, 79, 99, 161–162
Charron, Donalda, 57
Château Lafayette, 176–177, 179
Château Laurier, 23, 190
Chaudière Falls, 12, 16, 182
Chaudière Island, 76, 95
Chicago, IL, 5–7, 8
child care, 116
"Child Migrant Scheme," 20
children, see youth
Chinatown, 25, 26, 162, 163, 168
Chinese head tax, 26, 163–164
"Circle of All Nations," 15–16
Citizens for Safe Cycling, 134
City for All Women Initiative (CAWI), 126
civil service, 4, 9, 54, 58, 69–70

homosexuality in, 68–69
power of, 70–74
segregation in, 64–65
sociology of, 60–63
and suburban development, 105, 107–108, 116
and transit, 124, 125–126
unionization of, 66
class, 8, 12, 21, 35, 71
and education, 65
and housing, 82, 88, 93, 100
and labour, 50
and law, 150
and libraries, 40, 42, 44
and nightlife, 179
and policing, 141
and power, 137, 151
and retail, 167
and suburbanism, 102–103, 105, 106–108
see also working class
Cloutier, Jean, 92
Coalition Against More Security (CAMS), 142, 146, 153
Coalition Against the Proposed Prison (CAPP), 54, 151–152
Cold War, 67, 68, 146
Cole-Harris, Bertha, 78–79
colonization, 11, 19, 24, 120
see also settler colonialism
Commanda, William (Chief), 13, 16–17
Compass Group, 153
condominiums, 8, 88, 93–95, 96, 119
and gentrification, 90, 92–93, 180
see also housing
Confederation of 1867, 15, 25
Constitution Act of 1982, 43
Constitutional Act of 1791, 14
consumerism, 102–103, 117–118, 119, 121, 161, 164–165
"conspicuous consumption," 180–181
see also retail stores
Corktown, 18, 181–182
COVID-19 pandemic, 34, 47
and the civil service, 74
and entertainment, 187
and housing, 76, 78, 99
and outdoor space, 132
and shopping, 163, 168

and work, 50, 63
see also "Freedom Convoy"
creative economy, 178, 179
see also arts
crime, 137, 138, 139, 141–142, 148, 154
see also legal system; policing; prisons
criminalization, 76, 78–81, 84, 100, 174–175
Criminalization and Punishment Education Project (CPEP), 5, 151–153
criminology, 136–137, 139, 152, 153
see also sociology
Cumberland Heritage Village Museum, 14
Cummings, Charles, 75–76
Cummings Island, 75
cycling, 123, 133–134, 135

Daly Building, 7
Davis-Moore hypothesis, 49–50
Dawn (Belmore), 191
death, 187–190
de Costa, Mathieu, 26
deindustrialization, 55
Department of Indian Affairs, 15, 71
Department of National Defence (DND), 74, 90, 109
department stores, 157–159, 168
derecho 2022, 34, 111, 113
Dewar, Marion, 24
Diane Deans Greenboro Community Centre, 118
Diefenbaker, John, 83
disability, 8, 126–127, 132–133, 135, 177
diversity, 26
see also class; ethnicity; gender; race
Dominion Arboretum, 27, 32, 33, 36–37, 69
Dominion Observatory, 172
Doughty, Arthur, 40, 60, 189–90
Douglas, Tommy, 83, 188
drug abuse, 79–80, 81, 154
Dundonald Park, 1–3, 7, 9, 10, 36, 106
Dupuis, François, 14
Durkheim, Émile, 3, 4, 21
Dwell, 85–86

Eddy, E.B., 22, 29, 56, 72, 170
"edge cities," 101, 104, 109, 118
see also suburbia

education, 46, 50, 57–58, 60, 65
   and colonialism, 11–12
   and immigration, 25
   and security, 154
"emancipatory" spaces, 39, 44
Emergencies Act, 136, 137, 147–148, 153
Enclave, the Women's Monument, 174
Engels, Friedrich, 4
Enriched Bread Artists, 57
environment, 9, 34–36, 74, 189
   and agriculture, 54–55
   and cars, 122, 130, 133
   and condominiums, 94, 95–96, 100
   and forestry, 29, 30–31
   and light pollution, 171–172
   and security, 154
   and suburbs, 105–106, 108–109, 111–115, 118–119
ethnicity, 4, 8, 17, 20–21, 24–25, 157, 167
   see also race; small, ethnic, retail grocery stores (SERGs)
Ewart, David, 40, 72–73, 172, 190
extractive colonialism, 28, 30, 31, 36
   see also resource extraction; settler colonialism

Federation of Canadian Municipalities, 78
femininity, 67, 117
   see also gender; women
feminism, 59, 116
film industry, 183, 185–187
Findlay Creek, 112, 119, 123
Fleming, Sanford, 169, 188
"FLQ crisis," 147
Ford, Doug, 46
Forty-part Motet (Cardiff), 2–3
Fox, Terry, 82
Franco-Ontarians, 22–23
   see also French Canadians
"Freedom Convoy," 96, 136–137, 141–142, 145, 147–148, 149, 168
French Canadians, 19–21, 22–23, 138, 184
Fruit Machine, The (TVO), 68

Garden City movement, 8, 105–106, 108, 118
Gatineau, Quebec, 28, 35, 167
   see also Hull, Quebec
Gatineau Park, 7, 8, 51, 97

gay pride, 69
gay purge, 68
   see also homosexuality
gender, 8, 39, 47
   and cycling, 134
   and inequality, 159
   and labour, 49–50, 56, 64, 66–68
   and nighttime, 172–173, 177
   and poverty, 126
   and power, 137, 151
   and shopping, 159, 163, 167–168
   and suburbanism, 114–118, 119
   and transit, 132
   see also homosexuality; queer people; trans people; women
gender-based violence, 140, 141, 148–149, 167, 173, 188
gentrification, 76, 85, 88, 95, 100, 163
   and condominiums, 92–93
   fast, 91–92
   of nightlife, 177–181
   slow, 90
   see also housing
Gen Z, 58
Glebe, the, 22, 78, 105, 106, 162
Gloucester, 94, 107, 110
golf, 114, 115
Gotta Go! campaign, 132–133
Goulbourn Museum, 15
Goulbourn Ward, 51, 110
Gouzenko, Igor, 145–146
Gréber, Jacques, 8, 63, 89, 122–123, 128, 160, 171
Greenbelt, 8, 31, 52, 115, 131, 150, 172
Greystone Village, 95, 100
grocery stores, 162–163
   see also small, ethnic, retail grocery stores (SERGs)
Guigues, Joseph-Bruno, 19

Harper, Henry Albert, 60
Harper, Stephen, 16
Harris, Mike, 78, 109
Hazelview, 92
health care, 11, 17, 25, 188
   insurance for, 65, 73, 159
   and security, 152, 154
   work in, 57–58
   see also mental health

Healthy Transportation Coalition, 126
Heritage Ottawa, 128
Herongate, 76, 84, 88, 90–92, 93, 100
   see also Somali community
heteronormativity, 114–115, 137, 177, 179
Hinton, Joseph and Robert, 105
Hinton Animation Studios, 57
Hintonburg, 21, 105, 131, 176
Holocaust, 89
Home for Friendless Women, 78–79, 163, 174
homelessness, 46, 77–82, 84, 98–99, 100
   and criminalization, 142
   Indigenous, 76
   and violence, 173
   see also housing; poverty
"homelessness industrial complex," 79
homosexuality, 68–69, 115, 137, 146, 187
   and nightlife, 178–179
   violence against, 173, 175
   see also queer people
housing, 4, 7–8, 9, 12, 46, 100
   access to, 82, 91, 96, 154
   conditions of, 86–88
   and gentrification, 88, 90
   for immigrants, 25
   ownership of, 76, 102–103, 107, 179
   renting of, 82–85
   responsibility for, 79–80
   socially supported, 98–99
   and women, 94–95
   see also affordable housing; condominiums; homelessness; public housing
Howard, Ebenezer, 105–106
Hull, Quebec, 6, 21, 28, 63, 72, 176
   see also Gatineau, Quebec
Hull House (Chicago), 5–6
human rights and freedoms, 137, 140, 144, 147, 150, 153
Hydro Ottawa, 170–171

immigrants, 5, 12, 20, 23–24, 25, 46
   community spaces of, 162–164, 168
   and housing, 77, 85, 97
   and transit, 126
immigration, 4, 6, 12, 17–21, 23–25, 26
   and labour, 59
   policy for, 90–91, 163
   and racism, 128
   and suburbanism, 108, 110–111
Indian Act of 1876, 15, 25–26, 71
Indian residential schools, 17, 26, 96
Indigenous peoples, 13, 16–17, 25
   colonization of, 11–12, 15, 19
   cultures of, 33, 185
   and homelessness, 77–78
   and land, 76, 95
   policing of, 139, 143–144, 146, 151–152, 175
   and reconciliation, 112–113
   sovereignty of, 55
   violence against, 71, 188
individualism, 102–103, 114, 121
industrialization, 6, 28–29, 36, 155
   and the environment, 30
   and suburbanization, 103, 104
   and time, 169
inequality, 4, 30, 49–50, 148
   in employment, 79, 159
   and the state, 64, 70, 143
   see also class; disability; gender; race
infectious diseases, 4, 188–189
   see also COVID-19 pandemic
internet, 38, 44–45, 47, 126–127, 167–168, 177
Inuit, 11, 12, 17
Invest Ottawa, 167
Irish, 15, 17–19, 26, 89, 98, 138, 149
Islam, 24
Italians, 21, 89, 97, 157, 161, 163

Jafri, Amen, 63
James Street Feed Company, 92–93, 180
Janeville, 22
Japanese internment, 6
JDS Uniphase, 109
Jewish population, 21, 64, 89, 156–157, 161, 167

Kanata, 69, 108–109, 110, 118, 133, 166, 187
Keefer, Thomas, 104
Kichi Zibi Innini, 13
Kiji S/Zibi, 13
Kitigan Zibi, 15, 95
Kìwekì Point, 13, 27–28
Klippert, Everett George, 137
Konoval, Pylyp, 85

labour, 5–6, 9, 49, 51, 57–58
   and agriculture, 53
   capitalist, 155
   gender and, 67, 119, 158–159
   governing of, 72
   outsourcing of, 70
   precarious, 58–59, 167
   segregation in, 64, 163
   unionized, 55–56, 58, 66, 125
   value of, 50, 164
   see also unions
Landlord and Tenant Board, 85
land speculation, 14
   see also real estate developers
language, 8, 12, 17, 20–21, 23, 64
"La Patente," 22–23
Laurier, Wilfrid, 6, 184, 188, 190
Laurier House, 190
"lawn industrial complex," 113–115
Lebanese, 23–24, 26, 89, 176
LeBreton Flats, 8, 10, 43–44
   gentrification of, 88–89, 100, 180–181
   settlement of, 12, 105
legal system, 148–150, 153
   see also policing; prisons
leisure, 47, 88, 96, 102, 103, 117–118
Leitram Wetlands, 112
liberal democracy, 70–71, 148, 153
libraries, 38–39, 44, 45–46, 47–48
Library and Archives Canada, 40, 43–44, 46, 60
Library of Parliament, 39–40, 45, 46
light rail transit (LRT), 125, 126, 129–130, 133, 135
Lim, Sujin, 96
Lindenlea, 7, 106–107, 116
Little Italy, 97
Living Room (Urban Keios), 96
"living wage," 73, 79
Loeb, Bertram, 162
Log Driver's Waltz (NFB), 30
Lombroso, Cesare, 136–137
Lowertown, 21, 26, 83, 97–98, 157
   see also ByWard Market
lumber industry, 14, 15, 27, 28–29, 120, 189
   culture of, 30
   and the environment, 31, 36
   and manufacturing, 55
   work in, 49, 51

Macdonald, John A., 15, 43, 56, 71, 82, 149
Mackenzie King, William Lyon, 5–6, 8, 57, 122, 181, 189–190
malls, 159, 164–166, 168, 191
   pedestrian, 8, 160, 164, 183
Maman (Bourgeois), 10
"man caves," 117–118, 119
Manor Park, 7, 107
manufacturing, 55–57
   see also industrialization
Marx, Karl, 5
masculinity, 30, 116–117
   see also gender; men; patriarchy
matchmaking, 56–57
McGee, Thomas D'Arcy, 144, 149
McKay, Thomas, 40, 50–51, 104
McKenney, Catherine, 104, 135
McMillan, Archibald, 20–21
mechanics' institutes, 40–41
media, 79, 102–103, 108, 126
men, 25–26, 30, 67, 114–115, 172–173
   and cycling, 134
   and gender-based violence, 174
   immigration of, 156
   labour of, 57, 64
   and shopping, 159, 162
   social clubs for, 22, 40, 173
   and walking, 131, 172
   see also gender; homosexuality; "man caves"
mental health, 79, 86, 152–153, 154
Metcalfe Fair, 54
military, 15, 61, 62, 68, 147, 188
millennials, 58
Mill Street Brew Pub, 90, 181
Minto Properties, 92, 95
misogyny, 140–141, 143, 158
Montferrand, Joseph ("Big Joe Mufferaw"), 30, 138
monuments, 13, 17, 25, 60, 82, 174, 188
multiculturalism, 12, 24
Museum of Nature, 33, 101, 113, 170, 171–172, 190
music, 179, 183, 184, 187

National Arts Centre, 42, 184–185
National Capital and Planning Committee, 89, 98
National Capital Commission (NCC), 6, 20, 52, 90, 134

and fun!, 177, 180
and gentrification, 181
and homelessness, 81, 100
and romance, 182
National Film Board (NFB), 30, 60
National Gallery of Canada (NGC), 2–3, 10, 33
nationalism, 30, 36
National Research Council of Canada (NRC), 69
National War Memorial, 136, 188
Negro Citizenship Association, 127
neoliberalism, 46, 96, 125
  see also capitalism
Nepean, 110
Nepean Point, 13, 27–28
nepotism, 67
New Edinburgh, 34, 50, 104, 105
New Orpington Lodge for British Home Children, 20
"nocturnalization," 169, 170
"non-places," 166–167
Norman Paterson School of International Affairs, 66
Nortel, 109
Notre Dame Basilica, 10, 19
Nunavut Sivuniksavut College, 17

Oblates, 19, 76, 78, 95–96, 100
O'Brien, Larry, 81
O'Connell, Dorothy, 96–97
OC Transpo, 125–126, 130
  see also transit
O'Donoghue, Daniel, 56
Official Languages Act 1967, 23
Olmstead, Frederick, 7, 104
Ontario, 14, 22, 28, 56
  agriculture in, 54
  environment of, 31
  highway construction in, 122
  homelessness in, 78, 80
  and housing, 84, 91, 98
  library funding from, 46
  liquor laws of, 176
  and municipal amalgamation, 109–110
  Pesticides Act of, 114
  police in, 140
  transit in, 125, 126, 132
Ontario Disability Support Program, 84

Options Bytown, 99
Orange Order, 21–22
Order of Jacques Cartier, 22–23
Orléans, 14, 35, 118, 171, 182
  development of, 54, 111, 166
Osgoode Chambers, 85–86
Ottawa, City of, 6, 11, 13
  and civic investment, 92, 167
  and housing, 87, 90, 97–99
  libraries of, 40–43, 47
  and nightlife, 169, 179–180
  policing of, 138, 141
  public washrooms in, 132–133
  and regional amalgamation, 101, 104, 109–110, 118
  and transportation, 58, 123–127, 134, 135
  see also National Capital Commission (NCC); Regional Municipality of Ottawa-Carleton
Ottawa Car Company, 124
Ottawa-Carleton Detention Centre (OCDC), 151–153
Ottawa City Passenger Railway, 124
Ottawa Coalition to End Violence Against Women, 174
Ottawa Community Housing (OCH), 98–99, 100
Ottawa Community Land Trust (OCLT), 99
Ottawa Council of Women, 41
Ottawa Electric Light Company, 171
Ottawa Electric Railway (OER), 105, 124–125
Ottawa Housing Commission, 106
Ottawa Labour Council, 164
Ottawa Land Association (OLA), 83–84, 105, 186
Ottawa Literary and Scientific Society, 41
Ottawa Little Theatre, 184
Ottawa Music Strategy (OMS), 179
Ottawa Panhandlers' Union, 81
Ottawa Police Service (OPS), 136, 138, 140–141, 148, 153
  and homophobia, 173
  and sex work, 174–175
  and violence, 176
  see also policing
Ottawa Public Library (OPL), 42–45, 46–47, 48

"Ottawa Public Surveillance Project," 141–142
Ottawa River, 1, 12–14, 43, 121
   and the lumbering industry, 27–29, 30–31, 120
Ottawa Tenants' Council, 96–97
Ottawa Trades Council, 56
Ottawa Transportation Commission, 125
Ottawa Typological Union, 56
Ottawa Winter Carnival, 171, 185
Our Lady of the Sacred Heart Convent, 2
Our Shepherds (Berubé), 70

Pakinawatik (Algonquin Chief), 13
Paperland (NFB-CBC), 60, 62–63
Papineau, Joseph, 20
Para Transpo, 126–127
parking, 107, 118, 122, 125, 128, 130, 134–135
   see also automobiles
Parliamentary Protective Service, 167
Parliament buildings, 10, 45, 55–56, 144–145, 170, 171
Parliament Hill, 16–17, 133, 171
Pasapkwediwanong Sibi, 15
   see also Rideau River
patriarchy, 56, 94, 117, 172
   and crime, 137, 148
   and labour, 67, 119, 159
   violence of, 175
pay equity, 4, 79
Pearson, Lester B. "Mike," 65–66
Perley House for the Incurables, 41
"Persons case," 150
pesticides, 114
Petite Nation seigneury, 19–20
Petrie, Archibald, 14
Petrie Island, 14, 78
Phoenix pay system, 70
Pikwakanagan First Nation, 15, 95
Pinesi, Pierre-Louis Constant (Chief), 14
Pinhey, Hamnett, 51
police villages, 101, 103, 104, 118
policing, 1–2, 4, 47, 131, 153–154, 167
   "broken windows" theory of, 139–140
   by citizens, 142–143
   and colonialism, 11, 71
   and the courts, 148
   federal, 146–148

   and homelessness, 80–82
   and incarceration, 151
   moralizing agenda of, 174
   politicization of, 136–137
   and power, 61, 73–74
   violence of, 38, 141, 143–144, 176
   see also legal system; Ottawa Police Service (OPS); Royal Canadian Mounted Police (RCMP)
Polish, 77
Pompadour, 50
Pootoogook, Annie, 17
pornography, 45, 68
Porter, John, 61, 64, 69, 74
poverty, 77, 79–80, 117, 173–174, 187
   criminalization of, 139–140, 142, 151, 153–154
   and gender, 126
   see also homelessness
power centres, 166–167
   see also retail stores
POWER (Prostitutes of Ottawa, Work, Educate, Resist), 175
Preston, Isabella, 32–33
prisons, 151–153, 154
private property, 102–103, 121
private sphere, 3–4, 62, 116, 117–118, 188–189
Professional Institute of the Public Service of Canada (PIPSC), 66
prohibition, 176
Project 4000, 24–25
protest, 2, 3, 132
   for Indigenous rights, 16–17, 95, 113, 143–144, 149
   policing of, 136, 148
   and urban causes, 34, 38, 54, 122, 165
   see also "Freedom Convoy"
public housing, 8, 76, 77, 82, 89, 94, 96–99
   divestment from, 100
   and security, 154
public-private partnerships, 130, 151
Public Service Alliance of Canada (PSAC), 66, 67–68
public sphere, 3–4, 62, 116–117, 173, 188–189

Quebec, 14, 24, 181
Queensway, 8, 122–123

queer people, 173–174, 178–179
  see also gender; homosexuality

race, 8, 25, 53, 159
  and housing, 95
  and labour, 49–50, 64, 163
  and policing, 139–141, 143, 153–154
  and power, 137, 151–152, 173–174
  and retail, 167–168
  and suburbanism, 108, 110–111
  and transportation, 126
racism, 4, 12, 64, 128
railways, 28, 64, 71, 127–128, 169
real estate developers, 85–86, 91–92, 94–96, 100
  and retail space, 165, 167
  and suburbanization, 107–108, 112–113
real estate investment trusts (REITS), 84, 87, 166
Rebellions of 1837, 21
Redpath, John, 50–51
refugees, 24–25, 90–91
  see also immigrants
Regional Municipality of Ottawa-Carleton, 109–110, 125
religion, 8, 12, 19–22, 26, 64, 99
Renfrew County, 19, 77, 120
reserve system, 15, 78
resource extraction, 14, 28, 36, 51, 58, 120
  see also lumber industry
retail stores, 155, 157, 160, 162, 167–168
  see also consumerism
Rideau Canal, 15, 50–51, 77, 122, 172, 181–182
Rideau Centre, 159, 165–166, 168, 187
Rideau Chapel, 2–3
Rideau Hall, 27, 50, 97, 104
Rideau River, 15, 19, 22, 75, 111, 120, 139
Rideau Transit Group (RGT), 129–130
Riel, Louis, 71
RioCan, 165
roads and highways, 120, 122–124
Robinson, Peter, 18
Rochester Heights, 97
Rockcliffe Park, 42, 104, 105, 110, 147
rooming houses, 8, 84–86, 87–88, 94, 100
  see also housing
Royal Canadian Mint, 72

Royal Canadian Mounted Police (RCMP), 68, 74, 136, 138, 143–144, 153, 188
  Security Service of, 146, 147
Royal Commission on the Status of Women, 67
Royal Proclamation of 1763, 14
rural nostalgia, 53, 54
Ruskin Place, 100, 107
Russell, Peter, 50

Saikali, Halim "Al," 23–24
Salvation Army, 80, 99, 161
Sandy Hill, 14, 83, 84, 86–87, 98, 100, 123
Saunders, Charles, 52
Saunders, William, 32, 52
Sawmill Creek, 110, 111–112, 115
science and technology, 58, 69, 109, 190
Science and Technology Museum, 57, 133–134
Scots, 18–19, 21
Scott, Duncan Campbell, 63, 71
settler colonialism, 8, 11–13, 15, 23–24, 61, 71, 73
  gentrification as, 92, 93
  and land, 76, 78m
  and law, 148
  and roads, 120
  see also extractive colonialism
Seven Fires Prophecy Belt, 13
Sexual Assault Network, 174
sex work, 140, 150, 174–175
Shapiro, Louis, 157
Shiners' War, The, 138
Shopify, 58
Simmel, Georg, 4
Sisters of Charity, 2, 20
slavery, 50–51, 59
slums, 89, 91
small, ethnic, retail grocery stores (SERGs), 162, 164, 168
Smart Living, 85–86
social clubs, 22, 40, 173
"social contract," 137, 140–141, 145, 147–148
socialization, 8, 38–39, 42, 95, 102
social services, 46–47, 78, 80, 92
social stratification, *see* inequality
sociology, 3–7, 8–9, 17, 26
  of brunch, 180–181

of the civil service, 60–62
of death, 187–188
of disability, 126
of homelessness, 78–79
of nighttime, 169, 173–174
of religion, 21
of suburbs, 102–103
of transportation, 120–122, 130
see also criminology
Somali Centre for Family Services, 91
Somali community, 90–91, 141
Soper, Warren, 88, 124, 171
SOS Vanier, 80
Southway Inn, 17
Sparks Street Mall, 8, 160, 164, 183
spectacle, 39, 44, 47, 48
Spence, Theresa (Chief), 16
spiritualism, 190
Stewart, William and Catherine, 101
Stewarton, 101, 104
Stittsville, 53, 110, 111, 115, 119, 133
"Stoney Monday," 21, 156
St. Patrick's College, 65
streetcars, 124–125, 128, 160
  see also transit
streetcar suburbs, 101, 105, 118
St. Vincent de Paul, 161
suburbanism, 102, 104, 109, 110, 115, 118–119, 179
suburbia, 8, 9, 101–103
  and agriculture, 54
  escape to, 98
  expansion of, 104–109
  and gender, 116–118
  heteronormativity of, 114–115
  movie theatres of, 187
  and nature, 111–114
  politics of, 110
  retail spaces of, 160, 191
  and transportation, 123, 126
  see also "auto-burbs"
Sullivan, Francis C., 7
Supreme Court of Canada, 1, 8, 137, 140, 149–150
  see also legal system
surveillance, 1–2, 39, 47, 141–142, 146
  in bars, 177
  of homeless people, 80–82
  of Indigenous people, 71

of queer people, 68, 178
  see also policing
Sutcliffe, Mark, 138
Syndicat Catholique des Allumettières de Hull, 57
Syria, 12, 23, 25

Taggart, 112–113
Take Back the Night, 174
Talbot, Richard, 18, 26
taxation, 70, 72–73, 92, 104, 109–110, 122, 135
TCU, 87
Teron, Bill, 108–109
terra nullius, 11–12, 92
Tessouat (Algonquin Chief), 13
Tewin, 112–113
theatre, 183–187, 191
The United People of Canada (TUPC), 142–143
"third places," 9, 38, 155, 158, 165, 177, 179
Timbercreek, 91–92, 139
timber industry, *see* lumber industry
Todd, Frederick, 1, 7, 34, 106
Toronto Disaster Relief Committee, 78
tourism, 10, 57, 143, 170
  and agriculture, 53
  and architecture, 44
  and branding, 179
  and gentrification, 90, 177, 179, 181
Trade Union Act of 1872, 56
trains, *see* railways
TransGlobe, 91
transit
  active, 93, 123–124, 130, 131–134
  inter-city, 127–129
  private, 121–123
  public, 4–5, 105, 110, 117, 120, 124–127, 129–130, 135
trans people, 173–174, 175
  see also gender
trees, 1–2, 9, 27, 37, 51, 189, 191
  for the city, 4, 34–36, 113, 160, 171
  and empire, 28–29, 31
  and nation, 32–33
  see also lumber industry
Trudeau, Justin, 136, 147
Trudeau, Pierre, 96–97, 137, 147

Truth and Reconciliation Commission of
   Canada (TRC), 26, 71
Tungasuvvingat Inuit, 17
24 Sussex Drive, 97

unemployment, 49, 67–68, 77, 78, 138
unhoused people, *see* homelessness
Union ouvrière féminine de Hull, 57
unions, 9, 49, 56–57, 58–59, 60
   and the civil service, 63, 66–68
   and homosexuality, 69
United Empire Loyalists, 15, 18, 21
United Nations (UN), 77
University of Chicago, 5–6
University of Ottawa, 65, 85, 86–87, 176
Upper Canada, 18–19, 50
Uppertown, 21, 160
urbanization, 6, 30, 76, 169
urban planning, 5, 7–8, 89–90, 160
   and gender, 116
   and transportation, 122–123, 128
   and trees, 34–35
urban sociology, 4–7

vagrancy, 80, 131, 137, 154
Vanier, 17, 23, 80, 106, 110, 173
Vanier, Georges-Philias, 23
Victoria Island, 6, 16
Vietnam War, 24
violence, 4, 9
   bureaucratic, 70
   colonial, 11–12, 16, 26, 71, 95
   and housing, 80, 86
   and police, 38, 140–141, 143–144, 154, 175
   and power, 61
   and public transit, 126
   vulnerability to, 173–174

Wabano Centre for Aboriginal Health, 17
walking, 38, 121, 131–132, 164, 170, 172
Walmart, 166, 167
wampum belts, 13
War Measures Act, 147
War of 1812, 14–15, 18, 20, 28
Wartime Housing Limited, 83
waterfalls, 1, 28, 170, 182–183
Watson, Jim, 92, 129–130, 167
Weber, Max, 61–62, 64, 69

welfare state, 61, 65, 67–68, 73, 74, 108
   see also social services
White, Vern, 174
white supremacy, 137, 149
   see also racism
Whitton, Charlotte, 90, 97, 122, 123
Wilde, Oscar, 30
Wilno, Ontario, 77
Winterlude, 171, 185
women
   in the civil service, 66–68
   and cycling, 133–134
   and homelessness, 78–79
   and housing, 88, 94–95
   and labour, 6, 56–57
   and law, 150
   and nighttime, 170, 172
   and police, 140, 141, 154
   in public, 131, 173–174
   and shopping, 158–159, 168
   in suburbia, 115–118, 119
   and transportation, 126, 132
   violence against, 175, 188
   see also gender-based violence; misogyny
working class, 40, 122, 170
   gentrification of, 178, 180–181
   and housing, 88, 90, 91, 106–107
   policing of, 139
   socialization of, 42
Wright, Frank Lloyd, 7
Wright, Philemon, 14, 20–21, 26, 51–52

Young Women's Christian Temperance
   Union, 78–79
youth, 38–39, 126, 132, 164, 176–177, 186

Zibi developments, 95, 100